William Shakespeare's

# Teaching Students Hamlet!

*A Teacher's Guide to Shakespeare's Play*

*Includes Lesson Plans, Discussion Questions, Study Guide, Biography, and Modern Retelling*

BookCaps™ Study Guides

www.bookcaps.com

Cover Image © auremar - Fotolia.com

© 2013. All Rights Reserved.

## Table of Contents

**LESSON PLANS** ............................................................................................................. 5

   INTRODUCTION ................................................................................................................. 6
   LESSON PLAN FORMAT ..................................................................................................... 7
      *Writer's Journal* ........................................................................................................ 7
      *Standards* ................................................................................................................. 7
      *Sample Rubrics* ..................................................................................................... 13
      *Sample Schedule* ................................................................................................... 13
   DAY ONE: SHAKESPEARE BIOGRAPHY & HISTORICAL CONTEXT ...................................... 15
      *Objective* ................................................................................................................ 16
      *Discussion Questions/Writing Journal Responses* ............................................... 16
      *Homework Assignments* ....................................................................................... 17
   DAY 2: NARRATIVE, STRUCTURE, AND POINT OF VIEW ..................................................... 18
      *Objective* ................................................................................................................ 19
      *Discussion Questions/Writing Journal Responses* ............................................... 19
      *Homework Assignments* ....................................................................................... 20
   DAY 3: CHARACTERS AND CHARACTER DEVELOPMENT ................................................... 21
      *Objective* ................................................................................................................ 22
      *Discussion Questions/Writing Journal Responses* ............................................... 22
      *Homework Assignments* ....................................................................................... 22
   DAY 4: THEMES/SYMBOLS/FIGURATIVE LANGUAGE .......................................................... 24
      *Objective* ................................................................................................................ 25
      *Discussion Questions/Writing Journal Responses* ............................................... 25
      *Homework Assignments* ....................................................................................... 26
   DAY 5: WHAT MAKES IT A GREAT BOOK? ......................................................................... 27
      *Objective* ................................................................................................................ 28
      *Discussion Questions/Writing Journal Responses* ............................................... 28
      *Homework Assignments* ....................................................................................... 28
   LESSON RESOURCES ..................................................................................................... 30

**DISCUSSION QUESTIONS** ........................................................................................ 31

   ACT ONE ....................................................................................................................... 32
   ACT TWO ....................................................................................................................... 34
   ACT THREE .................................................................................................................... 35
   ACT FOUR ...................................................................................................................... 36
   ACT FIVE ........................................................................................................................ 37
   OVERALL DISCUSSION QUESTIONS ................................................................................ 38

**STUDY GUIDE** ............................................................................................................. 39

   HISTORICAL CONTEXT .................................................................................................... 40
   PLOT OVERVIEW ............................................................................................................ 41
      *Short Synopsis* ...................................................................................................... 41
      *Detailed Synopsis* ................................................................................................. 41
   THEMES/MOTIFS ............................................................................................................ 48
      *The Ghost* .............................................................................................................. 48
      *Poison* ................................................................................................................... 48
      *Forgiveness* ........................................................................................................... 48

- *Indecision* .................................................................................................. 48
- *Misunderstanding* ....................................................................................... 49
- *Political Plots & Intrigue* ............................................................................. 49
- *Madness* ..................................................................................................... 49
- *Incest* .......................................................................................................... 50
- *Decay* .......................................................................................................... 50
- *Suicide* ........................................................................................................ 50

CHARACTER SUMMARIES ............................................................................... 52
- *Hamlet (Ham-let)* ........................................................................................ 52
- *Claudius (Clow-dee-us)* ............................................................................. 52
- *Gertrude (Ger-trude)* ................................................................................... 52
- *The Ghost* .................................................................................................... 52
- *Horatio (Her-rach-eo)* ................................................................................ 53
- *Laertes (Lay-er-teez)* .................................................................................. 53
- *Ophelia (O-phee-lee-a)* ............................................................................... 53
- *Rosencrantz & Guildenstern (Rose-en-crants & Guild-en-stern)* ............. 53
- *Polonius (Po-low-nee-us)* ........................................................................... 53
- *Osric (Oz-rick)* ............................................................................................ 54
- *Young Fortinbras (Fort-in-braz)* ................................................................. 54
- *Marcellus (Mar-sell-us)* .............................................................................. 54
- *Reynaldo (Ray-nall-do)* .............................................................................. 54
- *Gravediggers (also known as the Clowns)* ................................................. 54
- *Barnardo (Bar-nar-do)* ................................................................................ 55

SCENE SUMMARIES ......................................................................................... 56
- *Act 1* ........................................................................................................... 57
- *Act 2* ........................................................................................................... 66
- *Act 3* ........................................................................................................... 72
- *Act 4* ........................................................................................................... 80
- *Act 5* ........................................................................................................... 89

# THE LIFE AND TIMES OF WILLIAM SHAKESPEARE .................................... 95

THE TIMES SHAKESPEARE LIVED IN ............................................................... 96
SHAKEPEARE'S FAMILY ..................................................................................... 98
SHAKESPEARE'S CHILDHOOD AND EDUCATION ............................................ 100
SHAKEPEARE'S ADULTHOOD ........................................................................... 102

# MODERN VERSION OF THE PLAY ................................................................. 106

CHARACTERS ................................................................................................. 107
ACT I ............................................................................................................. 108
- *Scene I* ........................................................................................................ 109
- *Scene II* ...................................................................................................... 122
- *Scene III* ..................................................................................................... 139
- *Scene IV* ..................................................................................................... 146
- *SCENE V* .................................................................................................... 153

ACT II ............................................................................................................ 167
- *Scene I* ........................................................................................................ 168
- *Scene II* ...................................................................................................... 177

ACT III ........................................................................................................... 216
- *Scene I* ........................................................................................................ 217

| | |
|---|---|
| *Scene II* | *228* |
| *Scene III.* | *256* |
| *Scene IV* | *261* |
| Act IV | 275 |
| *Scene I* | *276* |
| *Scene II* | *279* |
| *Scene III* | *282* |
| *Scene IV* | *288* |
| *Scene V* | *292* |
| *Scene VI* | *307* |
| *Scene VII* | *309* |
| Act V | 320 |
| *Scene I* | *321* |
| *Scene II* | *343* |
| **ABOUT BOOKCAPS** | **372** |

**Lesson Plans**

# Introduction

The full name of this Shakespearean play is "The Tragedy of Hamlet, Prince of Denmark". This is a dark story about revenge and how it can become all consuming. Students will learn many lessons throughout reading of this play. "Hamlet" is loosely based on the history of Denmark, and is suspected to have been written at the end of the $16^{th}$ century or the beginning of the $17^{th}$ century. As with many of this other works, Shakespeare was highly influenced by the world around him.

"Hamlet" is performed regularly on stage, and 4 mainstream movies from 1946 to 2000, with actors ranging from Lawrence Olivier to Mel Gibson to Julia Stiles starring in these productions. It is a play known by many, which shows just how far Shakespeare's influenced has reached over the centuries.

# Lesson Plan Format

Shakespeare as a man, poet, and writer is significant. He was highly influenced by what was happening around him in Elizabethan England. During each session, students will read portions of the play, look at historical context for what was written, delve into the various controversies that surround William Shakespeare and how these relate to his writings and the world today.

Students should have a copy of "Hamlet" to read and work with. If they do not, the following online resources can be used to read the text. Also, encompassed here are books and online resources the teacher can use in presenting the lessons:

**Books:**

Branagh, Kenneth, and William Shakespeare. *Hamlet*. New York: W.W. Norton &, 1996. Print.

Muir, Kenneth. *Shakespeare: Hamlet*. Woodbury, NY: Barron's Educational Series, 1963. Print.

Shakespeare, William, and Harold Jenkins. *Hamlet*. London: Methuen, 1982. Print.

**Websites:**

"Hamlet: Entire Play." *Hamlet: Entire Play*. MIT n.d. Web. 28 Sept. 2012. <http://shakespeare.mit.edu/hamlet/full.html>.

"Hamlet." *By William Shakespeare. Search EText, Read Online, Study, Discuss*. On-Line Literature, n.d. Web. 28 Sept. 2012. <http://www.online-literature.com/shakespeare/hamlet/>.

"Video." *PBS*. PBS, n.d. Web. 28 Sept. 2012. <http://www.pbs.org/wnet/gperf/episodes/hamlet/watch-the-film/980/>.

## Writer's Journal

Writers have been using journals to keep track of daily activities, their thoughts, their inspirations, and their life questions for as long as there has been the written word. Journals can be used for free-writing or to facilitate classroom discussion. They can be a way for students to discover what they know and don't know about a subject. Journals are also perfect for students who may be too shy to speak their thoughts and opinions aloud.

These journals will be used to answer specific writing prompts, complete class and homework assignments, including drawings and writings, and also for a way to communicate with their teacher any questions that may arise as they work through the lessons.

## Standards

## Common Core State Standards for ELA
*From NCTE (National Council of Teachers of English)*

| Common Core Standards – Literature Craft and Structure | Grade 9-12 |
|---|---|
| Area 4 | **Grade 9-10:** Determine the meaning of words and phrases as they are used in the text, including figurative and connotative meanings; analyze the cumulative impact of specific word choices on meaning and tone (e.g., how the language evokes a sense of time and place; how it sets a formal or informal tone).<br>**Grade 11-12:** Determine the meaning of words and phrases as they are used in the text, including figurative and connotative meanings; analyze the impact of specific word choices on meaning and tone, including words with multiple meanings or language that is particularly fresh, engaging, or beautiful. (Include Shakespeare as well as other authors.) |
| Area 5 | **Grade 9-10:** Analyze how an author's choices concerning how to structure a text, order events within it (e.g., parallel plots), and manipulate time (e.g., pacing, flashbacks) create such effects as mystery, tension, or surprise.<br>**Grade 11-12:** Analyze how an author's choices concerning how to structure specific parts of a text (e.g., the choice of where to begin or end a story, the choice to provide a comedic or tragic resolution) contribute to its overall structure and meaning as well as its aesthetic impact. |

| Common Core Standards - Literature Key Ideas and Details | Grades 9-12 |
| --- | --- |
| Area 1 | **Grade 9-10:** Cite strong and thorough textual evidence to support analysis of what the text says explicitly as well as inferences drawn from the text.<br>**Grade 11-12:** Cite strong and thorough textual evidence to support analysis of what the text says explicitly as well as inferences drawn from the text, including determining where the text leaves matters uncertain |
| Area 2 | **Grade 9-10:** Determine a theme or central idea of a text and analyze in detail its development over the course of the text, including how it emerges and is shaped and refined by specific details; provide an objective summary of the text.<br>**Grade 11-12:** Determine two or more themes or central ideas of a text and analyze their development over the course of the text, including how they interact and build on one another to produce a complex account; provide an objective summary of the text. |
| Area 3 | **Grade 9-10:** Analyze how complex characters (e.g., those with multiple or conflicting motivations) develop over the course of a text, interact with other characters, and advance the plot or develop the theme.<br>**Grade 11-12:** Analyze the impact of the author's choices regarding how to develop and relate elements of a story or drama (e.g., where a story is set, how the action is ordered, how the characters are introduced and developed). |

| Common Core Standards – Literature Integration of Knowledge and Ideas | Grade: 9-12 |
|---|---|
| Area 9 | **Grade 9-10:** Analyze how an author draws on and transforms source material in a specific work (e.g., how Shakespeare treats a theme or topic from Ovid or the Bible or how a later author draws on a play by Shakespeare). |

| Common Core Standards – Writing Text Type and Purposes | Grade 9-12 |
|---|---|
| Area 1 | **Grade 9-12:** Write arguments to support claims in an analysis of substantive topics or texts, using valid reasoning and relevant and sufficient evidence. |
| Area 2 | **Grade 9-12:** Write informative/explanatory texts to examine and convey complex ideas, concepts, and information clearly and accurately through the effective selection, organization, and analysis of content. |
| Area 3 | **Grade 9-12:** Write narratives to develop real or imagined experiences or events using effective technique, well-chosen details, and well-structured event sequences. |

| Common Core Standards – Writing Production and Distribution of Writing | Grade 9-12 |
|---|---|
| Area 4 | **Grade 9-12:** Produce clear and coherent writing in which the development, organization, and style are appropriate to task, purpose, and audience. (Grade-specific expectations for writing types are defined in standards 1–3 above.) |
| Area 5 | **Grade 9-12:** Develop and strengthen writing as needed by planning, revising, editing, rewriting, or trying a new approach, focusing on addressing what is most significant for a specific purpose and audience. |
| Area 6 | **Grade 9-12:** Use technology, including the Internet, to produce, publish, and update individual or shared writing products, taking advantage of technology's capacity to link to other information and to display information flexibly and dynamically. |

| Common Core Standards – Writing Research to Build and present knowledge | Grade 9-12 |
|---|---|
| Area 7 | **Grade 9-12:** Conduct short as well as more sustained research projects to answer a question (including a self-generated question) or solve a problem; narrow or broaden the inquiry when appropriate; synthesize multiple sources on the subject, demonstrating understanding of the subject under investigation. |
| Area 8 | **Grade 9-12:** Gather relevant information from multiple authoritative print and digital sources, using advanced searches effectively; assess the usefulness of each source in answering the research question; integrate information into the text selectively to maintain the flow of ideas, avoiding plagiarism and following a standard format for citation. |
| Area 9 | **Grade 9-12:** Draw evidence from literary or informational texts to support analysis, reflection, and research. |

| Common Core Standards – Writing Range of Writing | Grade 9-12 |
|---|---|
| Area 10 | **Grade 9-12:** Write routinely over extended time frames (time for research, reflection, and revision) and shorter time frames (a single sitting or a day or two) for a range of tasks, purposes, and audiences. |

| Common Core Standards – Language<br>Conventions of Standard English | Grade 9-12 |
|---|---|
| Area 1 | **Grade 9-10:** Demonstrate command of the conventions of standard English grammar and usage when writing or speaking.<br>a. Use parallel structure.<br>b. Use various types of phrases (noun, verb, adjectival, adverbial, participial, prepositional, absolute) and clauses (independent, dependent; noun, relative, adverbial) to convey specific meanings and add variety and interest to writing or presentations.<br>**Grade 11-12:** Demonstrate command of the conventions of standard English grammar and usage when writing or speaking.<br>a. Apply the understanding that usage is a matter of convention, can change over time, and is sometimes contested.<br>b. Resolve issues of complex or contested usage, consulting references (e.g., *Merriam-Webster's Dictionary of English Usage, Garner's Modern American Usage*) as needed. |
| Area 2 | **Grade 9-12:** Demonstrate command of the conventions of standard English capitalization, punctuation, and spelling when writing |


| Common Core Standards – Language<br>Knowledge of Language | Grade 9-12 |
|---|---|
| Area 3 | **Grade 9-12:** Apply knowledge of language to understand how language functions in different contexts, to make effective choices for meaning or style, and to comprehend more fully when reading or listening. |


| Common Core Standards – Language<br>Vocabulary Acquisition and Use | Grade 9-12 |
|---|---|
| Area 4 | **Grade 9-12:** Determine or clarify the meaning of unknown and multiple-meaning words and phrases based, choosing flexibly from a range of strategies. |
| Area 5 | **Grade 9-12:** Demonstrate understanding of figurative language, word relationships, and nuances in word meanings. |

Retrieved from: http://www.ncte.org/standards
Grade 9-12 Common Core Standards – ELA:
http://www.corestandards.org/assets/CCSSI_ELA%20Standards.pdf

*Use your state and district standards to align these common core standards with your lesson plans.*

## Sample Rubrics

General Rubrics:
- http://rubistar.4teachers.org/
- http://www.rcampus.com/indexrubric.cfm
- http://www.teach-nology.com/web_tools/rubrics/

Writing Rubrics
- http://www.rubrics4teachers.com/writing.php
- http://www.teach-nology.com/web_tools/rubrics/writing/

Graphic Organizers
- http://www.eduplace.com/graphicorganizer/
- http://www.educationoasis.com/curriculum/graphic_organizers.htm
- http://www.teachervision.fen.com/graphic-organizers/printable/6293.html

Resources Needed
- Dictionary
- Thesaurus
- Internet Access
- Writing Journal
- Pens/Pencils
- PosterBoard
- Markers/Crayons/Colored Pencils
- Glue/Adhesive

## Sample Schedule

**Day/Session 1**

Biography/Historical Context

**Day/Session 2**

Narrative/Structure/POV of "Hamlet"

**Day/Session 3**

Characters and Character Development

**Day/Session 4**

Themes/Symbols/Figurative Language

**Day/Session 5**

What Makes it a Great Book?

**Day One: Shakespeare Biography & Historical Context**

# Objective

Students will gain a better understanding of "Hamlet" if they understand the life of William Shakespeare and the era he grew up in. They will be able to see and understand how history affected Shakespeare's writing and the controversy surrounding his life and works. Students will be able to demonstrate their knowledge and understanding of Elizabethan England as well as how Shakespeare's influence still reaches us today.

For today students should read Act I of "Hamlet".

## Discussion Questions/Writing Journal Responses

1. (Prewrite) What do you know about "Hamlet"? When you hear the name William Shakespeare, what comes to mind? For this assignment just write everything you know (or think you know) about Shakespeare and "Hamlet". Also, write down any questions you may have.

2. Thinking about what you've learned about William Shakespeare: his upbringing, his writings, his education, etc., what do you think happened during those ten "lost" years?

3. In the Elizabethan era, plays were not considered good literature or even praiseworthy reading material. Based on what you've learned about history during this time, why do you think that is?

4. Starting with Shakespeare's birth what where the greatest events of his life, and how do you think they influenced his writings?

5. *The Globe*. What is the significance of it? When did it come into play? How does it compare to theatres today? Include an illustration with your response, making sure it is labeled properly.

6. Given the discussion on blank verse and iambic pentameter, find examples of this in "Hamlet". How did Shakespeare's writing style change written language as it was known during Elizabethan England? Give some examples for comparison.

7. When was "Hamlet" first written; when and where was it first performed; and who were the performers?

8. What was Shakespeare's influence in writing this play? Remember, everything Shakespeare did has a purpose, what was the point of this?

9. Take the main characters you've met so far in the play and write down what you think about them. Do you like them? What part do you believe they will play in the remainder of the story? Give examples of what you think – use quotes from the play.

10. Some say that Shakespeare wasn't certainly Shakespeare. Some way he stole all these writings and then published them under his name. Others believe it was multiple people working together and using this assumed name. Still others believe it was a nobleman who didn't want his friends and family to know he was writing such crass material. What do you think and why? Find proof to back up your thoughts.

# Homework Assignments

<u>Links</u>

- Globe Theatre History
  http://www.william-shakespeare.info/william-shakespeare-globe-theatre.htm
- BBC Video History of the Globe
  http://www.bbc.co.uk/learningzone/clips/shakespeare-and-the-globe-theatre/3342.html
- Globe Theatre Pictures
- Elizabethan England
  http://www.bardweb.net/england.html

1. **Foreshadowing Essay**: You've read Act I of the play. The tragedy of 'Hamlet" begins right away, but there is foreshadowing of what is to come. In an essay (2-3 pages) define foreshadowing and find the instances of foreshadowing. What does this tell us about each character so far in the play? Give examples to back up your thoughts.

2. **Design Time**: Design your own Globe Theatre! You can use whatever materials you would like to create your 3D replica of Shakespeare's Globe Theatre. Each section must be labeled correctly. Along with your replica, please provide a description of each section: names, what they were used for, who used them, and any other facts you may have found compelling (will be 1-2 pages in length).

3. **Biography**: Get to know Queen Elizabeth – the woman the Elizabethan Age was named after. Write a 3-4 page biography on the woman who influenced a nation. This will NOT just be a recap of her life – how did her decisions affect England during her reign and for years after? Make sure to give your insights and back up what you state. Use MLA formatting throughout.

4. **Timeline**: Create a timeline of historically significant events during Elizabethan England, carefully adding in Shakespeare's own timeline. Make sure you complete it in two different colors so that overlaps and patterns can emerge. Once you've completed it, look for patterns and write a 1-2 page essay on what you see – how did they affect one another?

5. **Gaming**: Take the facts you have learned about Shakespeare and Elizabethan England and create a board game. You must have at least 20 questions about each (so 40 total) – more is acceptable, but not less. Your game must have a clear beginning, purpose, path (how it's played/directions) and a clear way to win/end. You can create something straightforward like SORRY© or something as complex as Monopoly or Trivial Pursuit. You will need pictures, poster board (or cardboard), markers, glue, crayons, etc. Don't forget to write out the directions.

6. **Art Fair:** This was a marvellous time of writing, painting, and history. Find pictures of the art that speaks to you. Create a poster and/or collage of what you like. You must have at least 10 images. For each image, you will write 1-2 paragraphs (4-6 sentences each paragraph) about why you chose that piece.

**Day 2: Narrative, Structure, and Point of View**

# Objective

In today's lesson/session students will learn about narratives, how they are structured, point of view, and how each relates to "Hamlet". Each plays a strong role in how Shakespeare shares the point of his play. Journals will be used to facilitate class discussion; homework will further critical thinking skills and application skills, as well as helping students learn to see Shakespeare's relevance today.

According to the Merriam Webster Dictionary, a **narrative** is a "story, or a representation in art of an event or story". **Structure** is "the action of building or something that is arranged in a definite pattern of organization". Lastly, **point of view** is "the position from which something is considered or evaluated".

Students are expected to read Act II of the play for this section.

# Discussion Questions/Writing Journal Responses

1. What is the difference between reading this play and reading other works you've come across? Think of at least 3 things and describe them. Use your notes and books if need be. Also, if you have any questions about these differences, write them down, as well.

2. Thinking about narratives and how they tell a story, but that they can also represent something else in order to tell about an event, what do you believe is the purpose behind Shakespeare's "Hamlet"? Use information you've learned about Shakespeare, Elizabethan England, and what you have read thus far.

3. The literal meaning behind structure is building. Structure for literary works also refers to how it was built and the purpose of putting the written word together the way the author did. It implies a deliberate set up of each word and line in the play. What is your opinion about this? Did Shakespeare write deliberately?

4. Whose point of view is "Hamlet" written? Why is this relevant? What would it be like if someone else "told" the story?

5. It's time to look at the remaining characters. At this point, you've "met" all the main characters in the play. What do you think about those you've just met? Have any of your opinions of other characters changed? Don't forget to explain your answers and give examples.

6. In Act II, there are two more scenes with foreshadowing. Find them and describe them. What do you think they are foreshadowing?

7. So far in the play there have been many coincidences: think about the ghost and his role and some of the minor characters. What are 2 of these coincidences and how are they affecting the play to this point?

# Homework Assignments

<u>Links</u>
- Shakespeare and Narrative – to offer example
  http://www.ashgate.com/pdf/samplepages/narrating_the_visual_in_shakespeare_intro.pdf
- Play Structure – Example from Hamlet
  http://www.folger.edu/documents/lesson3-handout1.pdf
- Point of View Breakdown
  http://staff.fcps.net/tcarr/shortstory/pointofview.htm
- Elizabethan Clothing
  http://www.elizabethan-era.org.uk/elizabethan-clothing.htm
- Elizabethan Masks
  http://www.elizabethan-era.org.uk/elizabethan-masques.htm

1. **Family Tree:** Using a poster (or your computer), create a family tree for Hamlet. Make sure each person is labeled and shows their relationship to others. Include servants (of importance), as well.

2. **Funeral**: We hear about some people being in mourning. What would funeral/mourning clothes look like during the time in which "Hamlet" was written and performed. Design clothes for the main characters who should be in mourning.

3. **Mini-Autobiography**: Think about your life for a moment. Now, think about the life of Hamlet. Are there any similarities? I'm sure there are differences. Write a compare and contrast essay (2 pages) looking at your life and comparing it with each of theirs.

4. **Interview**: Choose Hamlet, Claudius, or Gertrude and interview them. Think of at least 10 open-ended questions (no simple yes or no answers) that you would like to ask them. Write what you think their response would be based on what you've read in Act I and Act II.

5. **In Your Own Words:** Rewrite Act II Scene 2 into whatever time period you choose. You can use accents, dialect, choose an era (20s, 50s, western, etc.) – the trick is to stay consistent and have fun with it.

**Day 3: Characters and Character Development**

# Objective

Without the characters, there would be no play. How do the characters change throughout the play? Do they change? These are the types of discussions to have with students during this lesson/session. Students will learn how character development moves a story along; how characters interact with each other affect the story; and how these character relationships parallel what students are living today (how they can be translated to today's world).

Students are expected to read through Act III of the play.

# Discussion Questions/Writing Journal Responses

1. Based on what we know about Hamlet so far, is he losing his mind? What makes you think yes, or no? Give examples.

2. Write a letter from Hamlet to his father. What would he say and/or ask? Use it as a way to help Hamlet deal with his grief. Swap letters with someone else in the class and answer their letter.

3. Claudius is the play's villain. What has he done that is so reprehensible? What would you do in this situation? Do you believe Hamlet is doing the right thing?

4. A lot of emphasis is given to Hamlet throughout the play as it is his father who is being avenged, but what about Gertrude? Do you think she is innocent or guilty? What could she have done differently up until this point in the play?

5. Ophelia: in some places, she seems weak, and, in others, she appears strong. She tries to be loyal to her father and to Hamlet. She begins to go mad after what happens? How does this affect other aspects of the play?

6. Are Polonius' intentions pure? Why does he do what he does, and what are some of the consequences of his actions?

7. The Ghost seems to be the root of Hamlet's problems. When does the Ghost appear and who does he appear to first? Do you believe Hamlet would be seeking revenge if the Ghost hadn't appeared?

# Homework Assignments

<u>Links</u>
- Video on Elizabethan Street Fighting
  http://www.youtube.com/watch?v=dvoNQgy2yEQ&feature=channel_page&noredirect=1
- Shakespeare Character List
  http://www.shakespeare-online.com/plays/characters/charactermain.html
- 10 Best Shakespearean Characters
  http://www.guardian.co.uk/culture/gallery/2012/mar/25/ten-best-shakespeare-characters-pictures#/?picture=387763692&index=0

- Hamlet Characters
  http://www.auburn.edu/~tuckebr/Site/Analysis.html

1. **Editorial**: Start by reading your local and national newspapers for a few days. What types of topics do they discuss in their editorials? Your job is to write an editorial on he following characters: Hamlet, Gertrude, Horatio, Claudius, and Ophelia. Each editorial will be about 1 page in length.

2. **Timeline**: Start a timeline of events up until this point. You will finish it at the end of Act V. Take the greatest events: meetings, parties, love proclamations, etc. and place create a timeline. On the back of your poster, write a short summary (2-3 sentences) of why each event is noteworthy.

3. **Memoir**: Choose Hamlet or Gertrude and write a short memoir, making sure to refer to the other main characters and how they make you (Hamlet or Gertrude) feel. Speak from their point of view and in the way they would talk about their friends and enemies.

4. **Blame Game:** Many times people blame others for what happens to them. Look at what you know up until this point. The Ghost blames Claudius and who else? Write a 1-2 page essay on who you think is to blame and why.

5. **Compare/Contrast**: Think about what you know about the families thus far. Create a Venn diagram detailing the similarities and differences. Keep it so you can add to it through the rest of the reading of the play.

6. **Costumes**: Knowing what you know about each character and Elizabethan England, design costumes for Hamlet, the Ghost, Gertrude, Claudius, Ophelia, and Laertes. How would you update them for today? Make sure you label your drawings.

**Day 4: Themes/Symbols/Figurative Language**

# Objective

In this lesson/session students will review the themes, symbols, and figurative language happening throughout the play. Each of these plays a significant role in moving the play forward, character development, and overall understanding of the play. Shakespeare is brilliant at weaving themes and symbols into his works in a way that appeals to the masses and transcends time, making him relevant even today.

**Symbols** are, "something used for or regarded as representing something else; a material object representing something, often something immaterial; emblem, token, or sign," per www.dictionary.com.

**Themes**, according to www.dictionary.com, are a unifying or dominant idea, motif, etc.

**Figurative Language** is "language that contains or uses figures of speech, especially metaphors" and similes. This definition can also be found at www.dictionary.com.

Students should read through Act IV for today's lesson.

# Discussion Questions/Writing Journal Responses

1. There are two greatest symbols used in the play; what are they? Write 1-2 paragraphs (4-7 sentences each) about what the symbols mean and how they are used in "Hamlet". Can these symbols be found in literature today? Give examples.

2. There are four main themes to "Hamlet". What are at least two of them? Give examples of each theme from the play, and also give examples from contemporary literature of each theme, as well.

3. Metaphors, similes, hyperbole, alliteration and others can be found within the works of William Shakespeare. Define each of the following, find an example from the play, and then create your own example:

    a. Metaphor
    b. Simile
    c. Hyperbole
    d. Alliteration

4. Another type of figurative language used quite often in "Hamlet" is the apostrophe. What is an apostrophe (as far as plays are concerned)? How does it help or hinder the speech of the characters? What do you think would happen to the play if they were taken out? Be specific with your answer and explain examples you use.

5. Another important aspect of any play is who is speaking and to whom. A character could be speaking to another character, themselves, or directly to the audience. Depending on who is being spoken to determine what other characters "know" about what is happening in the play.

These are called soliloquies, monologues, and asides. Define them, give an example of each, and all write the significance of it for the overall direction of the play.

# Homework Assignments

<u>Links</u>

- Figurative Language
  http://languagearts.mrdonn.org/figurative.html
- Quizlet – Interactive Practice
  http://quizlet.com/10010267/hamlet-11-figurative-language-flash-cards/
- "Hamlet" Themes
  http://www.litcharts.com/lit/hamlet/themes
- Shakespeare Themes
  http://shakespeare-navigators.com/hamlet/Revenge.html

1. **Collage**: Create a collage of modern-day symbols found in "Hamlet". Accompany it with a 1 page explanation of why you chose the pictures you chose.

2. **Making Connections**: Symbols are found in all parts of our life, not just the literature we read for school. Where else are symbols located (think of arrows and stop signs)? Why do you think we have universal symbols for various things? You will have to conduct some research to back up what you think.

3. **Bulletin Board (Poster):** Take each type of figurative language and create a picture board of them. Place the type (personification) at the top and below it a line or two from the play; below that a modern day version, and then either find a picture (or draw it) of a representation of each.

4. **Jeopardy**: Working with a partner, design a Jeopardy style game encompassing all you've learned about "Hamlet," William Shakespeare, and Elizabethan England. You should have categories, double jeopardy, flash cards with questions, and don't forget to assign point values to the questions.

5. **Research Paper:** Choose a theme from the play to expand upon, a historical figure from Elizabethan England, or William Shakespeare to write research and write a paper about. Your paper will be 4-5 pages in length and follow MLA formatting guidelines.

6. **Scrapbook**: Create a scrapbook from Ophelia or Gertrude's perspective; something she can show her family friends. Make sure have at least 5 pages.

7. **Social Media:** Design a social media page (FB, Twitter, Google+, etc.) for Hamlet, Horatio, Claudius, Ophelia, Gertrude, Laertes, and Fortinbras. How do you think social media would have changed their relationships or even the outcome of the story?

**Day 5:  What Makes it a Great Book?**

# Objective

What makes "Hamlet" a terrific play? Could it be the timeless theme? Students will spend this lesson/session reviewing the play and deciding whether or not they do think it's a fantastic play and making connections to their world today to back up their thoughts and ideas.

Students should complete reading through Act V for this lesson. They should also review the earlier acts in order to make connections.

## Discussion Questions/Writing Journal Responses

1. Think back (or look back) to your first journal entry. Were all your questions answered about Shakespeare and about "Hamlet"? If not, what questions do you still have? What have you learned that you didn't know before?

2. Now that you've read the entire play, is it easier to see the foreshadowing? Go back and make a list of any you may have missed.

3. Why does Claudius hate Hamlet, senior so much? Does he get what he wants? What are the consequences of his actions?

4. Who is your favorite character and why? What would happen to the story if they were not in the play (or if they died (or died earlier)? Could the play work without them? How?

5. We only catch glimpses of the parents in the play. Why do you think this is? With what little we do know, we've learned from others. Do you believe we have an accurate picture? What are your thoughts on the parents and their role?

## Homework Assignments

Link
- Podcast on Arms
  http://www.folger.edu/documents/Armor_podcast.mp3
- Persuasive Essay Graphic Organizer
  http://steckvaughnadult.hmhco.com/HA/correlations/pdf/l/LEh5_graphicorg.pdf
- Interactive Persuasive Guide
  http://www.readwritethink.org/files/resources/interactives/persuasion_map/

1. **Modernize**: Choose your favorite scene from the play and rewrite it for today. Don't forget stage directions; costuming; and relationships. Go back and review some of the videos in the lesson for help.

2. **Persuasion**: Write a persuasive essay on why you think "Hamlet" was a terrific read (or not so great). Why others should read it (or why not)? Use text to back up your opinion and don't forget to include a rebuttal of the opposition's argument, as well.

3. **Retraction**: Pretend Shakespeare's readers demanded he rewrite the ending of the play because they didn't want to see so much death. Rewrite the ending so that Hamlet lives. Is it possible to only rewrite the ending?

4. **Nightly News**: With a small group prepare and deliver interviews with Fortinbras, Horatio, and the Ghost. Create a nightly news bulletin or be the media at the "scene". Do you think there would have been more punishment doled out if there was a media presence like there is today?

5. **Time Lines**: Complete the timeline you began in Lesson 3. Is the time period realistic based on what you have?

6. **Replica**: In the first lesson, you designed the Globe Theatre. Here, you will create a replica (shadow boxes, for example) of one scene from each Act in "Hamlet".

7. **Perform**: Choose either one monologue or one soliloquy and prepare to perform/recite it for the class. You must also describe the significance of the piece you chose and what the meaning of it is. This is a memorization piece, and you will not use notes (other than for meaning).

8. **Comic**: Recreate "Hamlet" as a graphic novel or comic. You can either use typical Shakespearean characters and dialogue or you can modernize it. Make sure you are consistent throughout.

9. **Choose Your Own:** Choose your own project to complete. It must show your understanding of the entire play, and it must be approved by me before you begin.

10. **Playbill**: Do some research on what a playbill is and what they looked like during Elizabethan England. Design one for "Hamlet".

# Lesson Resources

Branagh, Kenneth, and William Shakespeare. *Hamlet*. New York: W.W. Norton &, 1996. Print.

*Dictionary.com*. Dictionary.com, n.d. Web. 28 Sept. 2012. <http://dictionary.reference.com/>.

"Hamlet." *By William Shakespeare. Search EText, Read Online, Study, Discuss.* On-Line Literature, n.d. Web. 28 Sept. 2012. <http://www.online-literature.com/shakespeare/hamlet/>.

"Hamlet: Entire Play." *Hamlet: Entire Play*. MIT n.d. Web. 28 Sept. 2012. <http://shakespeare.mit.edu/hamlet/full.html>.

*Merriam-Webster's Collegiate Dictionary*. Springfield, MA: Merriam-Webster, 2001. Print.

Muir, Kenneth. *Shakespeare: Hamlet*. Woodbury, NY: Barron's Educational Series, 1963. Print.

Shakespeare, William, and Harold Jenkins. *Hamlet*. London: Methuen, 1982. Print.

"Video." *PBS*. PBS, n.d. Web. 28 Sept. 2012. <http://www.pbs.org/wnet/gperf/episodes/hamlet/watch-the-film/980/>.

# Discussion Questions

# ACT ONE

Scene 1:

1) Describe the mood in this scene and explain the methods Shakespeare uses in the setting to help establish this mood.

2) Why does Horatio provide a history lesson on the conflict with Fortinbras? How could this be seen as a parallel with the new King (Claudius)?

Scene 2:

3) This scene opens with Claudius addressing his court. Examine his speech. How does he handle the difficult nature of his situation?

4) Contrast the ways Claudius and Gertrude talk with Hamlet.

5) In his first soliloquy, what does Hamlet reveal as his feelings towards his mother and Claudius? Identify at least two main points in his opinion.

6) What are Hamlet's suspicions regarding the appearance of his father's ghost?

Scene 3:

7) Outline the advice that Laertes gives Ophelia regarding Hamlet.

8) How does Polonius respond to the advice Laertes has given Ophelia and what request does he make of his daughter?

Scene 4:

9) What details does Hamlet provide that illustrate Claudius as a shameful example as a ruler?

10) Why are Horatio and Marcellus so concerned with Hamlet talking to the ghost? What are their fears?

Scene 5:

11) List details that suggest that Hamlet's father's spirit is suffering in purgatory.

12) Paraphrase the important details the ghost relays to Hamlet. What is Hamlet "charged" to do?

13) What details are provided in this scene that suggest Hamlet will not be swift in his revenge?

# ACT TWO

Scene 1:

14) What does Polonius want Reynaldo to do when he gets to France? What does this reveal about Polonius's character?

15) Why does Hamlet's appearance to Ophelia frighten her so much? What are Polonius's suspicions about Hamlet?

Scene 2:

16) Why have the King and Queen invited Rosencrantz and Guildenstern to Elsinore?

17) How does Shakespeare make a mockery of Polonius in this scene?

18) In what ways does Hamlet reveal his "antic disposition" in this scene?

19) What is Hamlet's attitude toward Rosencrantz's and Guildenstern's visit?

20) Why does the player's speech have such an effect on Hamlet? How does he connect it to his plight?

21) Why does Hamlet feel it is necessary to test Claudius?

# ACT THREE

Scene 1:

22) Closely examine Hamlet's most famous soliloquy. Summarize the arguments he is contemplating in his speech.

23) How can the "To be, or not to be" soliloquy be seen as an examination of his role in revenge?

24) How does Hamlet respond to Ophelia when she goes to return some of his gifts to him? How does Hamlet treat her in this scene?

Scene 3:

25) What frame of mind is Claudius in as this scene opens?

26) What truth does Claudius reveal of his crimes? What was his motivation behind them?

27) At the close of this scene Hamlet plans to kill Claudius. What convinces him to hold off killing him?

Scene 4:

28) Why does King Hamlet's ghost appear? What other interesting circumstances about the ghost's appearance are revealed in this scene, in contrast to the last time he appeared?

# ACT FOUR

Scene 3:

29) What plan does Claudius set in motion regarding the fate of Hamlet? What does this reveal about Claudius's guilt?

Scene 4:

30) Why is Hamlet's guilt, regarding the delay in avenging his father's death, exacerbated by what Fortinbras's men are preparing to do?

Scene 7:

31) What reasons does Claudius offer for not directly dealing with Hamlet?

# ACT FIVE

Scene 1:

32) Why does this Act begin with two clowns trading jokes? Do their jokes make any sense in the context of the play?

33) Examine the existential ideas that Hamlet proposes inspired by Yorick's skull.

34) How can one interpret Hamlet's actions based on the conclusion of this scene? What may it reveal about a) his state of mind and b) his feelings for Ophelia?

35) Critics have noted that there is a distinct change in Hamlet's sense of purpose. Quote lines from this scene to defend this idea.

Scene 2:

36) Hamlet's "fall of a sparrow" speech has two clear, distinct allusions to scripture. Which passages are referred to in this speech, and how does Shakespeare use them?

37) Why would Fortinbras want the funeral rites for Hamlet to be that for a soldier?

## Overall Discussion Questions

38) Outline the events that led Hamlet further and further into isolation.

39) Modern psychologists could diagnose Hamlet as suffering from depression. Defend this diagnosis with evidence from the play.

40) What is the function of the Polonius-Ophelia-Laertes family in this play? What parallels exist between their situation and that of the ruling family?

41) What is the function of the Fortinbras-Norway conflict in the play, especially in terms of King Hamlet's presence in Denmark?

42) Like many Shakespearean plays, the theme of appearance vs. reality is rampant in *Hamlet*. Discuss this thematic development in the play, noting the primary figures that illustrate this paradigm.

43) Why is the murder of Polonius so important in the play, or what does the death of this figure represent?

44) Who are Hamlet's foils, and in what ways do their characters shed light on his?

45) Examine the use of the decaying imagery in the play. What does the pattern suggest about the state of Denmark, and Hamlet's role?

46) Critics suggest that Hamlet's internal struggle (and subsequent delay) has to do with maintaining moral integrity. Defend this idea.

47) Which parts of the play are 'unnecessary' in terms of plot and character development? Argue that which could be removed and still maintain the integrity of the play.

48) Critics argue that Hamlet's weakness has to do with his procrastination and over-thinking. How could these be viewed as his strengths?

49) The moment that can be labeled the climax of the play isn't as clear one would think. Choose one moment and defend why this can be seen as the climax.

50) Ophelia and Gertrude are considered very weak characters. Defend this idea.

**Study Guide**

# Historical Context

William Shakespeare, playwright extraordinaire, lived in 16th to 17th Century England. He wrote a considerable number of plays, including the still popular Macbeth, A Midsummer Night's Dream, and Romeo & Juliet. Many of his plays were written as part of the Lord Chamberlain's Men—later known as the King's Men—who were a company of players, or actors. Although Shakespeare is synonymous with the Globe Theatre, a great number of his plays were performed at Blackfriars Theatre and at court for royalty and their guests. He was also a seasoned poet and is still celebrated for his 154 sonnets, including the popular Sonnet 18. The beginning lines are possibly the most quoted out of all the sonnets: "Shall I compare thee to a Summer's day? Thou art more lovely and more temperate." I bet you've heard those lines before!

The 16th and early 17th Centuries in England were periods of considerable wealth and strength. Shakespeare lived through the Spanish war, saw the end of Elizabeth the Virgin Queen's reign, and heralded in the reunification of the English and Scottish thrones under one monarch, King James VI. However, despite the Royal family's immense wealth and rich noblemen in the upper classes, the poor were extremely poor. Famine, poor hygiene and the lack of wages created an environment full of disease, crime and pestilence. If you were poor during this time, you had exceedingly little to look forward to! Some would visit the theatre as a means to escape their lives if they could afford it, but they would only be able to afford standing room. Imagine standing up through an hour long play! Other entertainment available to the poor included watching executions, tormenting those placed in stocks and attending witch trials. A pretty grim past-time, but there was little else to do!

Hamlet is one of Shakespeare's most loved, most studied and most often performed plays. Many actors strive to play the lead role of Hamlet on stage as it is considered one of the most challenging and rewarding roles to play. It is also Shakespeare's longest play!

Some theorists believe that the story of Hamlet was based on the legend of Amleth, a fictional figure in Scandinavian romance. Most of the written work about Amleth was written by Saxo Grammaticus, in the Gesta Danorum, in the 13th Century. No evidence exists to suggest that Saxo's work was his own or was collected through other oral and written sources. Another source of Shakespeare's may have been a since-lost play called Ur-Hamlet, which no one is certainly sure who wrote. Many suggest either Thomas Kyd or Shakespeare himself wrote the play, but there is evidence to suggest that Shakespeare's company, the Chamberlain's Men, performed this play which may have led to his interest in the legend.

There are also some who suggest the grief and tragedy of the play was fuelled by the loss of Shakespeare's young son, Hamnet, who died at age 11. While the legend of Hamlet was the most obvious source for the play, many theorists believe that this event prompted Shakespeare to write Hamlet.

# Plot Overview

## Short Synopsis

Hamlet, the Prince of Denmark, is visited by his late father's Ghost who tells him he was murdered. The murderer, Hamlet's Uncle Claudius, who is now the King of Denmark and married to his mother, Gertrude, had poisoned Hamlet's father while he slept. Hamlet is ordered to take revenge for his murder, but his indecision, madness and his Uncle's political plots keep Hamlet from acting on his impulse for vengeance until it threatens the entire royal family and leads to a bloody end.

## Detailed Synopsis

At Elsinore Castle in Denmark two sentinel Guards, Barnardo and Francisco, are frightened. Barnardo tells Francisco to go to bed as it is almost midnight. He swaps with Horatio and Marcellus. The three men talk about the Ghost two of them have seen walking the halls for a few nights. Horatio is there to verify what they have seen is real. The Ghost appears to them. The men ask Horatio if he thinks the Ghost looks like the dead King of Denmark. He does. Horatio asks the Ghost questions, but it does not answer and leaves. The men believe this is a bad omen for the state of their country and for the future. Marcellus asks why everyone seems to be on edge and if it is because the young Fortinbras has come to challenge the King of Denmark for the territory the dead King Hamlet took from him. The Ghost re-enters but once again says nothing to Horatio. It seems like it might speak, but the rooster crows to signal the coming dawn and startles it. They decide to find the younger Hamlet to tell him what they've seen.

Claudius, Gertrude, Hamlet, Polonius, Polonius' son, Laertes, and daughter, Ophelia, and many Lords are gathered in the throne room. Claudius is sad that his brother is dead, but feels the best way to mourn is to carry on with life. He is happy that he has married Gertrude, his late brother's wife. Claudius calls Voltemand and Cornelius, two ambassadors, and tells them to take a letter to Fortinbras' Uncle, the King of Norway, to request he interfere with Fortinbras' plans to attack Denmark. They leave to take the letters to Norway.

Laertes asks for Claudius' permission to go back to France. He has Polonius' permission as well, but only because he has asked so many times. Laertes is allowed to go.

Hamlet is sorry he has so little family to show him kindness now, especially after his mother's marriage to his Uncle. Claudius wants to know why Hamlet is so depressed. Hamlet assures him he is happy. Gertrude echoes Claudius' worries for Hamlet. Hamlet admits he is upset about his father's death, but that doesn't seem to have stopped his own mother from remarrying so quickly. Claudius complements him on his grief, but points out that everyone has lost a father at some point. Hamlet agrees to stay at Elsinore Castle and not go back to school. Claudius thinks this is evidence of Hamlet's love for him. Everyone but Hamlet leaves the room.

Hamlet wishes there were no laws against suicide. He can't believe that his father has only been dead for two months, and his mother is remarried already. King Hamlet was so good to Gertrude, but scarcely a month had gone by before she agreed to marry his brother. Hamlet doesn't think he can talk about it with anyone though. He should keep quiet.

Horatio, Marcellus and Barnardo enter and tell Hamlet about the Ghost of his father. Hamlet doubts that they could see the Ghost's face if it was armoured from head to toe, but Horatio assures him it was the late King. Hamlet will stand guard with them that night to see if the Ghost comes back. He makes the other men promise not to tell anyone else what they have seen.

Laertes and Ophelia talk about Hamlet's flirtatious behaviour. Laertes doesn't think Hamlet loves Ophelia, and she is to be careful with herself. Hamlet might love her now, but he is young and part of the royal family. His decisions are not his own to make. Polonius enters. He gives Laertes some advice: he is to be careful, make the best judgements, spend all he can on clothes but not on rich or gaudy ones, and not to lend money to anyone as this can lead to loss of friendship. Laertes says goodbye and then leaves. Polonius adds to Laertes' advice about Hamlet to Ophelia. He orders her to spend less time with him and make herself harder to get to. Ophelia thinks he has made true vows to her, but Polonius disagrees. Ophelia will do as her father tells her.

On the gun terrace of Elsinore Castle, Horatio, Hamlet and Marcellus wait for the Ghost to appear. It does. Hamlet asks the Ghost to reveal why he has returned and what they can do to help him. The Ghost waves to Hamlet. He wants Hamlet to follow him. The other men don't want him to go, but Hamlet thinks this is fate. He leaves with the Ghost. Marcellus and Horatio decide to follow in case the Ghost makes Hamlet do something awful.

Hamlet and the Ghost talk. The Ghost reveals how he was murdered—Uncle Claudius poured poison into his ear while he slept. Hamlet must take revenge for his murder, but he must not hurt Gertrude. He must leave Gertrude to God's wrath. The morning approaches and the Ghost has to leave. Hamlet vows to take revenge in his father's name.

Marcellus and Horatio enter and ask Hamlet if he is alright. Hamlet can't tell them everything, but makes them vow not to say anything about what they have seen. They can't even hint that they know what's wrong with Hamlet.

Polonius and his servant, Reynaldo, discuss Laertes. Polonius wants Reynaldo to go to France and find out who Laertes spends time with and what he does while he is there. Reynaldo is not to rely solely on gossip, however. He is also to go and see Laertes for himself. Reynaldo leaves. Ophelia enters, frightened by Hamlet's behaviour. He came into her room with his clothes half on and stared at her for a long time. Polonius thinks Hamlet has gone mad with love for her, and they need to tell the King. He wishes he had better judgement than to force Ophelia to refuse him, as Hamlet was obviously not just flirting with her.

Claudius, Gertrude, and servants enter the court room with two of Hamlet's old friends, Rosencrantz and Guildenstern. They have been called to Elsinore to help Hamlet out of his depression and find out why he is so upset. Gertrude thanks them for their help, and sends them off with a servant to find Hamlet.

Polonius announces the arrival of Ambassadors from Norway and that he may know the reason for Hamlet's madness. The Ambassadors announce that the King of Norway has ordered Fortinbras to stop what he was doing. He immediately called off his army, and was rewarded with another army to lead into Poland. The King of Norway has asked for Claudius' permission for the army to march across Denmark and assures them of Denmark's safety. Claudius likes this news.

Polonius reveals that Ophelia was given a love letter from Hamlet, and has been courted by him. Polonius, doing his fatherly duty, warned Ophelia against Hamlet, and she refused him and sent his letters back. Claudius wonders if this is the reason Hamlet is depressed. Polonius suggests that they should "accidentally" have Hamlet and Ophelia meet to see how Hamlet reacts.

Hamlet enters, reading a book. Polonius tells Gertrude and Claudius to go away so he can talk to Hamlet alone. Hamlet claims not to recognize Polonius, who he calls a fishmonger. If Polonius has a daughter, he should not let her walk around by herself just in case she becomes pregnant. Polonius takes this mention of his daughter as a sign that Hamlet is still in love with her. He leaves Hamlet so he can go and arrange a meeting between him and Ophelia.

Rosencrantz and Guildenstern arrive. After exchanging lewd jokes about their fortunes, Hamlet presses them to tell him why they are there and if Claudius has summoned them. He reminds them of their love and friendship for one another. Guildenstern admits they were sent for. Hamlet knows that they are here to try and cheer him up. Rosencrantz reveals that a company of actors are on their way to entertain Hamlet. They debate about the state of the local theatre: Hamlet is amazed to hear that child actors are the current fashion in theatre, but then Denmark as a whole is in such a bad shape that it is hardly surprising.

Trumpets sound and Polonius enters. Hamlet, in a series of asides to Guildenstern and Rosencrantz, teases Polonius for the way he talks and acts. Polonius announces the arrival of the actors. Hamlet welcomes them all and marvels at how some of them have grown beards. The First Player asks Hamlet what he would like to hear. Hamlet and the Player recite a part from a play detailing Priam's murder. Hamlet stops him after a while—he will hear the rest later. Hamlet orders Polonius to see to the actors' needs as a bad reputation will hurt the royal family. They should be treated well. Just before they leave, Hamlet asks the First Player if he could learn a new speech for the play tomorrow. Hamlet will write it. The First Player will do so, and then follows the actors and Polonius out.

Hamlet sends Rosencrantz and Guildenstern out. Hamlet wonders how monstrous it could be for an actor to be able to conjure tears over something pretend while he still can't take revenge for his father's murder. He wonders if the Ghost was a devil trying to tempt him and decides he needs more evidence before he takes his revenge. He will watch for Claudius' reaction to the play closely to see if he appears guilty for the King's murder.

Claudius, Gertrude, Polonius, Ophelia, Rosencrantz and Guildenstern gather. Claudius doesn't understand why Hamlet is so upset and mad. Neither Rosencrantz or Guildenstern have been able to get Hamlet to admit what is wrong with him. They have invited a group of actors to put on a play. Hamlet has specifically requested the King and Queen attend the play. Claudius is happy for this and sends the two friends to Hamlet to get him more excited about the play.

Claudius tells Gertrude she needs to leave too as he and Polonius have arranged for Hamlet and Ophelia to bump into one another by "accident". Claudius and Polonius will hide and watch Hamlet's reaction to see if it is his love for Ophelia that has sent him into madness. Gertrude hopes the plan works and then leaves. Polonius orders Ophelia to read from a prayer book so that she looks lonely. They hear Hamlet coming and hide from view.

Hamlet wonders if it would be better to be alive or dead, and if putting up with all the suffering you experience while alive is worth it. He wonders if death is just like going to sleep for a long time. He sees Ophelia and asks her to remember him while she prays. Ophelia has things to hand back to him now that Hamlet has rejected her. Hamlet used to love her, and then changes his mind and insists he never loved her. He orders her to get herself to a convent so she will not give birth to anymore sinners. It might have been best if Hamlet had never been born at all either, as he is only filled with the need for vengeance. Hamlet wonders where Polonius is. Hamlet tells her to get herself to a convent. If she marries, even if she keeps her reputation as an innocent, she will still end up with a bad reputation in the end. Hamlet leaves her. Ophelia is sad that Hamlet has changed so much. She used to admire him. Claudius doesn't think Hamlet was ever in love with Ophelia. Claudius doesn't even think Hamlet sounds that mad and suspects he might be up to something. He will send Hamlet to England to get them to repay their debts to Denmark. Polonius still believes that Hamlet is mad because of unrequited love and requests Gertrude talk to him while Polonius listens in. Claudius agrees.

Hamlet and the actors enter. He tells them to perform the speech he has just taught them. The actors leave to get ready. Polonius, Guildenstern and Rosencrantz enter. Hamlet asks them if the King and Queen are attending. They are. Hamlet tells Polonius and the others to go help the actors prepare. Horatio enters. Hamlet begs him to watch for Claudius' reactions to the play to see if the Ghost was right or if he was a devil trying to tempt Hamlet. Horatio will do this.

Trumpets play and the audience, including Claudius and Gertrude, enter. Claudius asks him how he is, and Hamlet deflects, answering the question with nonsense. Hamlet and Polonius talk about a role Polonius once performed—that of Julius Caesar who was killed by Brutus. Hamlet sits beside Ophelia as it is an attractive place to sit. They talk about his happier mood. Hamlet shouldn't see why he wouldn't be happy, with his father dead and his mother remarried so soon. He has not forgotten his father but will shed his mourning clothes soon enough.

The play begins. The Player-King tells the Player-Queen that she will have to remarry soon as he thinks he will die. The Player-Queen would never remarry as it would be as if she had killed her own husband. If she does end up remarrying, she hopes the Earth will refuse her food. The Player-King asks her to leave so he can sleep. She does.

Hamlet asks if Gertrude is enjoying the play. Gertrude thinks the Player-Queen is over-acting. Claudius asks if anything offensive is in the play. Hamlet tells them to not care too much: after all, they have nothing to be guilty about. Lucianus, the Player-King's nephew, appears on stage. He pours poison into the Player-King's ears. Hamlet tells the audience that the nephew will win the Player-Queen's heart soon. Claudius stands up and orders for light. He needs to get away. Everyone leaves except for Hamlet and Horatio.

They discuss that the Ghost was right all along. Rosencrantz and Guildenstern enter: they are worried about Hamlet. Hamlet teases them—they are trying to play him like they might play an instrument. They tell him Gertrude wants to see him. Polonius also enters and asks Hamlet to go see his mother. He knows that they are trying to trick him, but he will go. They leave Hamlet alone for a moment. Hamlet will not harm Gertrude, but that won't stop him from attacking her with words.

Claudius, Rosencrantz and Guildenstern talk about Hamlet. Claudius doesn't like the way he is acting. He will send the two men with Hamlet to England. They will take care of him. They leave Claudius alone. Polonius enters to report that Hamlet will visit Gertrude soon. While they do, Polonius will hide behind the tapestry in her bedroom so he can listen in. He will report to Claudius what has been said after the meeting. Polonius leaves.

Claudius is guilty for the crimes he has committed, but at times doesn't feel his guilt. He tries to pray for forgiveness, but finds he can't put the emotion he needs to into the prayers. At the same time, Hamlet enters and sees Claudius alone and unprotected. He considers taking his revenge then and there, but Claudius would go straight to Heaven as he has prayed for forgiveness. He should kill Claudius while he is committing a sin, so he faces the same fate as his late father. Hamlet leaves.

Polonius tells Gertrude what she should and shouldn't say to Hamlet when he comes: she needs to let him know his behaviour has upset the King. She will do as she is asked. Polonius hides behind the tapestry. Hamlet enters—he knows exactly why Gertrude has called for him. She tells him he has insulted his father, but Hamlet throws the insults back at her: she has done the same. He wishes Gertrude were not his mother. She worries he might kill her and cries out for help, but Hamlet only wants to show her what she has truly become. Polonius echoes her cries for help. Hamlet stabs his sword through the tapestry, hoping that Claudius is behind it. He kills Polonius.

Gertrude doesn't know what she has done to be talked to this way. Hamlet is amazed she doesn't: her marriage is a sin. Even the Heavens are angry at her. Hamlet wonders why she married a villain after loving such a kind and gentlemanly man as his father. The Ghost enters, and Hamlet asks it what it wants. Gertrude can't see it and is upset that Hamlet is crazy enough to be talking to the thin air. The Ghost leaves. Gertrude calls him mad. Hamlet isn't mad—he can repeat every word he just said. Hamlet orders her to live a virtuous life and not to sleep with his Uncle again. He also begs her not to let Claudius persuade her Hamlet is mad when he is not. He reminds her that he is to go to England with the two friends he trusts least, wishes Gertrude a good night and drags Polonius off.

Claudius, Gertrude, Rosencrantz and Guildenstern talk. Gertrude ask Hamlet's two friends to leave so she can talk in private with her husband. Gertrude tells him about Polonius' murder. He will ship Hamlet off to England under the cover of night, and he will have to try and explain the murder to the public as an accident. Rosencrantz and Guildenstern re-enter. Claudius orders them to help find Polonius' body and bring it to the chapel.

Rosencrantz and Guildenstern ask Hamlet where the body is. Hamlet answers in nonsense. He calls them fools. Hamlet orders them to take him to the King right away.

Claudius enters with servants. He tells them he has sent more men to find Polonius' body. He can't lock Hamlet up because the public adore him, even if he has murdered someone. Rosencrantz enters—they can't find out where the body is, but they have brought Hamlet to him. Claudius orders Hamlet to be brought in. Claudius asks where Polonius' body is. Hamlet tells him he is being eaten by worms, and then reveals there will be a smell in the upstairs main hall in around a month. Claudius sends servants to check there. Claudius tells Hamlet that he must send him away to England for his own protection. Hamlet says goodbye and leaves.

Claudius tells Rosencrantz and Guildenstern to follow Hamlet and make sure he gets on the ship. Everyone but Claudius leaves. He admits he hopes that the King of England does as he has been asked and executes Hamlet as soon as he arrives in England.

At the Danish border, Fortinbras and a Captain enter with an army. Fortinbras tells the Captain to send the King his greetings and ask for permission to cross Denmark. Everyone except the Captain leaves. Hamlet, Rosencrantz and Guildenstern enter. Hamlet asks the Captain where the army is going to. He reveals they are off to Poland to fight for a small bit of territory no one actually wants. Hamlet thinks this is the main problem with war: small arguments can lead to larger ones until many people die. The Captain leaves. Rosencrantz asks Hamlet to come with him. He will in a moment. Everyone leaves Hamlet alone. Hamlet wonders what kind of man he is: he wants to take his revenge, but is still too afraid to do so, and in the meantime an entire army marches to fight for something they don't honestly care for. If he cannot pull himself together to take his revenge, his thoughts are for nothing.

At Elsinore Castle, Horatio, Gertrude and a Gentleman enter. Gertrude refuses to talk to Ophelia. The Gentleman reports that Ophelia truly needs to talk to Gertrude. She beats her chest, won't stop talking about her dead father and is constantly upset. Horatio thinks it would be a good idea to talk to her if she is that upset. Gertrude allows her to enter. She feels extremely guilty. Ophelia enters and sings about a dead love in a grave. Claudius enters. He asks Ophelia how she is. Ophelia sings about a virgin sleeping with a man who then refuses to marry her. Ophelia misses her father. She will talk to her brother. She wishes them a goodnight, and then leaves. Claudius orders Horatio to keep an eye on her.

Claudius sees Ophelia's madness as just one more terrible thing that has happened. He is worried Laertes will blame Claudius for Polonius' death. A noise off stage startles Gertrude. A Messenger arrives to tell them Laertes is leading a rebellion into the castle against Claudius. They shout for Laertes to be King.

Laertes enters. He tells his followers to wait outside while he talks to Claudius. He demands for his father's body. Claudius tells him Polonius is dead. Gertrude adds that he was not murdered by Claudius. Laertes wants revenge—he doesn't care what happens to him. Claudius will prove that he is innocent.

Ophelia enters. Laertes is upset to see her so mad and wonders how it was possible. She hands out flowers: fennel and columbines to Gertrude for adultery and rue for repentance to Claudius. She sings once more and then leaves.

Laertes and Claudius share in their grief. He sends for his wisest friends to be gathered so that they can both be listened to. The wise men will decide who is correct about Polonius' murder. If Claudius is wrong and guilty he will give up everything as payment, but if he is innocent, then Laertes must be patient while Claudius organizes for revenge to be taken. Laertes agrees.

Horatio is given letters by a Sailor from Hamlet. It tells him to get the Sailors to the King as there are more letters to deliver. He reports he was attacked by pirates when they were at sea. Hamlet asks Horatio to come and meet him quickly as he has news about Rosencrantz and Guildenstern.

Claudius and Laertes talk. Now that Claudius has been proven innocent of Polonius' murder, he will soon reveal what he has planned for Hamlet. A Messenger arrives with letters from Hamlet for Claudius and Gertrude. Claudius reads the letters out-loud, which reveal Hamlet is on his way back to Elsinore to confront Claudius. Laertes is pleased he will be able to get his revenge. Claudius has plans for Hamlet's death, and no one—not even Gertrude—will know it was a murder. Laertes wants to take part, which Claudius thinks is a good idea as his good qualities don't arouse envy in the general public like Hamlet's do. They will be far more forgiving if the murder is found out. Laertes wonders what those good qualities are. Claudius reveals Hamlet was extremely envious of Laertes' fencing skills and the compliments he had been given, and talked of nothing but having a match with him for long time. They will have a fencing match and the tip of one sword will be dipped in poison and sharpened. No medicine can save someone infected with this poison. They will also pour poison into a cup of wine to give to Hamlet as a back-up plan.

Gertrude enters and announces that Ophelia has drowned in a brook. She fell in accidentally and didn't know where she was. Her water logged clothes dragged her down to the bottom. Laertes leaves. They follow him to try and calm him down.

Two Gravediggers talk about Ophelia's death as they dig a grave. They don't believe for one minute that Ophelia didn't kill herself, but they guess that a rich girl would be given religious rites even if she did kill herself. Hamlet and Horatio enter. Hamlet asks him whose grave he is digging, but the Gravedigger answers in nonsense. The Gravedigger knocks skulls around while he sings and digs. He shows Hamlet a skull that has been there for twenty-three years—the skull of Yorick, the King's jester. Hamlet knew Yorick. He wonders where the man's jokes are now.

Claudius, Gertrude, Laertes, a Priest and a coffin enter. Hamlet tells Horatio to be quiet while they find out who they are burying. Laertes asks the Priest which rites he will give Ophelia—he can only give her so many religious rites as he suspects that the girl killed herself. If it wasn't for the King's interference, Ophelia would have been buried far outside the church graveyard. It would be insulting to the other bodies to have more rites performed. Hamlet is shocked to hear that Ophelia has died.

Gertrude scatters flowers across the grave. She is sad that Ophelia and Hamlet never married. Laertes jumps into the grave and demands they bury him with her. Hamlet jumps into the grave, too, and fights with Laertes. Claudius orders them to be pulled apart. No love could have matched Hamlet's. He doesn't know why Laertes treats him this way as he has always loved Laertes. They all leave.

Hamlet and Horatio enter. Hamlet tells him that he read letters from Claudius on the ship asking the King of England to execute Hamlet on the spot. He rewrote the letters, used his father's old signet ring to form a seal and replaced the old letters with the new. Rosencrantz and Guildenstern are now headed for their deaths at the hands of the King of England. Hamlet thinks they deserved it. Hamlet is upset at the bad-blood between him and Laertes, but is resolved to kill Claudius as soon as he gets the chance.

Osric, a courtier, enters. Hamlet doesn't like this man and teases him. Osric tells them that Claudius has placed a large bet on Hamlet winning the fencing match. Osric complements Laertes' fencing abilities, and Hamlet agrees with him. He sends Osric to tell the King he will fight right away. A Lord announces that Gertrude wants to talk to Hamlet before he begins.

Horatio thinks Hamlet will lose the bet, but Hamlet has been practising. Hamlet doubts the match a little, but he will put his life in fate's hands. What will happen, will happen.

Claudius, Gertrude, Laertes and Osric enter with servants carrying trumpets, drums, swords, a table and some wine. Hamlet and Laertes shake hands. Hamlet apologizes for what he has done, but points out that it was his madness that killed Polonius, not Hamlet himself. Laertes understands, but he can't forgive him so easily. Hamlet assures Laertes he will win. They pick their swords. Claudius announces that if Hamlet makes the first or second hit on Laertes that Claudius will place a pearl into a cup of wine, which is then Hamlet's to drink.

Trumpets play the fencing match begins. Hamlet makes the first hit. Osric calls it in Hamlet's favour. Claudius places the pearl into the cup and tries to hand it to Hamlet, but he will not drink it just yet. They continue fencing. Hamlet hits Laertes again. Claudius thinks Hamlet might win the game, but Gertrude thinks he is out of breath. She tries to hand him the goblet, and then tries to drink it herself. Claudius tries to stop her, but it is too late. Nothing can stop her from dying now. Laertes wounds Hamlet with the poison tipped sword. In a scuffle, they end up with each others' swords and Hamlet wounds Laertes. Claudius orders them to be separated and Gertrude collapses. Laertes is upset that he has been caught by his own trap. Gertrude realizes she has been poisoned by the wine and then dies.

Hamlet orders the door locked as he wants to know who planned this. Laertes reveals that they are both going to die, as well. They have half an hour to live, and the King is to blame. Hamlet wounds Claudius and then forces him to drink from the poisoned goblet to follow Gertrude to death. Claudius dies.

Laertes thinks Claudius got what he deserved. He begs for Hamlet's forgiveness and then dies. Hamlet gives him this forgiveness and wishes that he could tell everyone what genuinely happened. He asks Horatio to tell everyone, but Horatio doesn't want to live. He tries to drink the rest of the poisoned wine, but Hamlet stops him. If he truly loved Hamlet, he would not drink the wine and would fix Hamlet's reputation for him. He will tell the truth about the events.

Military marching can be heard from off stage, and Hamlet wonders where these noises are coming from. Osric reports that young Fortinbras is returning after his victory in Poland. Hamlet hopes that Fortinbras will end up on the Danish throne. Hamlet dies. Horatio wishes him a long sleep.

Fortinbras enters and is amazed at what he sees. Horatio asks him to erect a stage for the bodies to be placed on, and for everyone to be told the truth. An Ambassador announces that Rosencrantz and Guildenstern are dead. Fortinbras has some claim to the Danish throne and will carry it out. He orders Hamlet's body to be carried out like a soldier onto the stage and thinks he would have made a fine King. The rest of the bodies are carried out and cannons fire.

# Themes/Motifs

## The Ghost

The Ghost is a fairly loaded character in terms of meaning. In Hamlet, the Ghost can represent sin which stays behind when unforgiven, the remnants that are left of a person who has died, and the need for vengeance. The Ghost can also represent guilt. Claudius is guilty because he murdered his own brother, and Hamlet is guilty because he has let Claudius get away with this.

## Poison

There are many poisonous and poisoned items in Hamlet: the poisoned chalice, the poison tipped swords and the poison in King Hamlet's ear which led to his death. There are many interpretations for what the poison stands for exactly, but critics have agreed that the poison represents the poisonous nature of family. It is this which sends Hamlet mad with grief and confusion and sets this narrative rolling. It destroys each person and relationship except for the honest and loyal one Hamlet has with Horatio.

## Forgiveness

Forgiveness is something many characters struggle with in Hamlet. Hamlet cannot forgive Claudius and Gertrude for what they have done, and this ostracizes him from his family. Claudius begs God for forgiveness but finds he can't feel enough remorse to pray properly. At this moment, Hamlet will not kill Claudius, even though he is unarmed because he would go straight to Heaven.

This contrasts what Hamlet discovers about his father: the late King could not pray to resolve his sins before he died because he was poisoned. He now lives in a hellish environment, imprisoned during the day and forced to march through the night.

At the end of the play, Hamlet and Laertes forgive one another for the deaths they have caused and for killing one another so that they can go to Heaven. Many characters who oversee the funerals of others, such as Ophelia's and Polonius', will put pressure on the Priest to give the dead as many final rites as they can to ensure the soul goes to Heaven.

## Indecision

Hamlet can't decide if he is or isn't in love with Ophelia, so much so that it throws her off completely. One minute he tells her he doesn't want to be with her, and the next lies in her lap. He finally admits his love for her, but it's too late because she's already dead. This is a lesson to Hamlet, who extends the olive-branch to Laertes and asks him for forgiveness for what he has done.

Hamlet also can't decide when or even if he will take revenge for his father's death. He suspects the Ghost might be trying to trick him, so he needs more evidence, but even when he does have the evidence he needs, he does not kill Claudius. By the end of the play, he has debated whether or not impulsive action, like Fortinbras' army takes, might reduce the suffering self-doubt brings on, and also concludes that God and divine intervention will lead his way and create his journey for him. Hamlet will stop questioning his decisions, act on impulse and let whatever comes his way to dictate the direction his life goes in. He ignores his misgivings and doubts over the fencing match against Laertes but pushes those doubts away in favour of acting. Unfortunately, this leads to his death, suggesting that perhaps those who act on impulse only need to be tempered by some reason and thought.

## Misunderstanding

Claudius, Gertrude and Polonius think Hamlet might have turned mad because of his love for Ophelia, which Hamlet disproves. Earlier, Polonius believes Hamlet is only lusting after his daughter and couldn't possibly be in love with her. No one understands Hamlet's perspective which prompts Gertrude and Claudius calling for Rosencrantz and Guildenstern. Hamlet can't understand Gertrude's love for Claudius because his father has only just died.

Much of the confusion between Hamlet and other characters is his inability to communicate how he feels and why he feels that way to other people. Of course, he can't tell everyone about Claudius' involvement in the murder of the King, but so much of what we discover about Hamlet's mental health is revealed in asides to the audience. We understand him, but everyone else struggles to do so.

## Political Plots & Intrigue

There are many political plots in Hamlet that lead to characters' ends or beginnings. Claudius wins the Danish throne and Gertrude as a wife after he poisons the King. Young Fortinbras wins the Danish throne after everyone else in line to the throne is killed. Although he doesn't involve himself directly in the political plot, it is Claudius' plots that lead to this ending. His attempt to send letters with Hamlet when he goes to England to have him executed backfire when Hamlet reads and replaces those letters. Claudius' plot to poison Hamlet during a fencing match against Laertes backfires when Gertrude drinks the poisoned wine and both Laertes and Claudius are also killed by the poison tipped swords. And finally, Polonius' plot to figure out if the reason for Hamlet's madness is his love for Ophelia and his death while hiding in Gertrude's room sends Ophelia herself into madness and then death.

## Madness

Ophelia's madness is brought on by male interference. Polonius and Laertes advise her how to act around Hamlet and tell her to draw away from him. To refuse him. Polonius then forces her to help uncover the reason for Hamlet's insanity by tempting him with Ophelia's interest once more. Hamlet's refusal of her and her loss of her father compound, take her innocence from her and send her into a quiet melancholy.

Hamlet's madness is caused by his indecision. It is also a complete fabrication as he pretends to be mad to avoid suspicion, but like so many people who pretend, they eventually start to take on characteristics without realising it. His constant struggle between taking revenge and doubting the time, place, conditions of this revenge and the nature of death itself leave him without the ability to deal with anything else in his life. He even turns a play meant to cheer him up into a re-enactment of his father's death. Sometimes Hamlet will appear much more aware of himself, especially around Horatio who knows everything of the plots, but he will still slip into the occasional mania. Compared to Laertes who does not want proof of Hamlet's guilt before he takes his revenge, Hamlet can seem to many like a weak and confused character. Hamlet and Ophelia's madness, however, does give them a clearer view of Gertrude and Claudius' guilt, suggesting that terrible actions can only be understood by someone out of the ordinary.

## Incest

Gertrude and Claudius are in the thick of an incestuous relationship that Hamlet does not approve of. No one else in the play reveals any disgust for the quick remarriage of Gertrude to her late husband's brother, which suggests that it was in bad taste to question the royal family or that it happened more often than it does now. However, Hamlet's obsession with Gertrude's sex life can also be due to an Oedipal desire to love his mother sexually now that his father is dead. Claudius stands in the way of that. Hamlet begs her not to let Claudius sleep with her and to keep her sheets clean. That this plea comes while Hamlet is in Gertrude's bedroom, suggesting a further intimacy in their relationship, which we have not seen prior to this scene, is no accident, but what this intimacy suggests is up for debate.

Laertes also warns Ophelia away from Hamlet in a possible attempt to clear the way to keep Ophelia for himself. He jumps into her grave to embrace her again as a lover might. In fact, Hamlet copies him and expresses his anger over Laertes' passion, so much so that he felt he had to outdo him.

## Decay

Many things are decaying or diseased in <u>Hamlet</u>. After the discovery of the late King's Ghost, Marcellus announces that there is something rotten in Denmark, and there is. Much like a piece of fruit, the nation is rotting from the inside out. Claudius, the head and centre of Denmark, has only been able to take the throne because he murdered his own brother. From Hamlet's perspective, his marriage to Gertrude can be seen as the decay of the institution of marriage and family.

Hamlet's obsession with death can also be seen as an obsession with the physical body of death. As he holds Yorik's skull in Act Five, he wonders where Yorik's laughter has gone to. When questioned by Claudius where Polonius' body is, Hamlet jokes that he is going to be eaten by worms. Hamlet also considers that a King's body is just the same as a beggars—and why wouldn't a King's body end up in a beggar's stomach. Death renders them all the same, no matter their position in life or the condition of their soul, and the decay of the body makes this especially obvious to Hamlet.

## Suicide

Hamlet's consideration of suicide likens death to a long sleep. He seems weary as he contemplates the possibility of taking his own life and wonders what might happen to his soul if he did so. He thinks that if there was not a religious stigma over suicide and the fear of the unknown that many more people would kill themselves.

His contemplation links him to Ophelia, who perhaps commits suicide. We do not see her drown in the brook, and many have questioned Gertrude's story. We are told that she is dragged down to the bottom of the brook by her water logged clothes and that her death was accidental, but this could be because Gertrude wants to save her soul. The story itself might be a fabrication, and is called into question in Act Five by the Gravedigger and Priest, who are convinced that she had taken her own life.

# Character Summaries

## Hamlet (Ham-let)

When we meet the young Prince Hamlet he has just lost his father, the King of Denmark. His mother has also married his Uncle Claudius, which makes things worse, and his depression more acute. Hamlet hates his Uncle and despises his mother Gertrude for marrying another man so quickly after his father's death. When the Ghost of his father reveals what he feared and suspected most—that his father was murdered by Claudius—Hamlet becomes incensed with the need for vengeance but becomes waylaid by his own self-doubt. He contradicts himself often, and this contradiction usually lies between his need and desire for violent revenge and his more philosophical nature. His behaviour follows suit: Hamlet can be impulsive, especially in his murder of Polonius, but hesitant for much of the rest of time.

## Claudius (Clow-dee-us)

Claudius is the newly crowned King of Denmark and Hamlet's Uncle. He is also Hamlet's Stepfather after his marriage to Gertrude, the late King's wife. Claudius is an ambitious man. He killed his own brother to take the Danish throne and won over his wife with gifts to gain a Queen. Claudius will do anything to get ahead and to keep his spoils. When both young Fortinbras and Hamlet threaten to undo some of Claudius' peace he solves the problem quite quickly through political cunning and manipulation. He sends Hamlet to England on the pretence of a diplomatic mission, but sends letters with him asking the English King to execute Hamlet. He doesn't do this because he doesn't want to kill Hamlet himself, but because he doesn't want the Danish people to rebel. They love Hamlet too much to see him killed.

## Gertrude (Ger-trude)

Gertrude is the Queen of Denmark and Claudius' wife. She has little to no guilt towards her quick marriage to her late husband's brother. In fact, she seems overjoyed by it. While she has no main influence on the plot, Gertrude is in many of the scenes hoping for a cure for Hamlet's depression, and then his madness. She shows sympathy towards the mad Ophelia and regrets that she will never see Ophelia and Hamlet married. There have been many debates regarding how much Gertrude knew of her late husband's murder, and whether or not she was complicit. Some see her the way that Hamlet describes her. They believe she must be guilty of something because of the lack of remorse she shows marrying her husband's brother. Others have argued that Gertrude is an honest and loving woman who is only doing what she thinks is right for the country. She looks out for everyone's welfare and is a loving and forgiving mother to Hamlet, even though he insults and pushes her away for most of the play. Many negative things about Gertrude are spoken by Hamlet, who is angry with her. His insults, therefore, cannot be entirely trusted as they come from a place of extreme emotion.

## The Ghost

The Ghost of Hamlet's late father appears to guards at Elsinore Castle. He does not speak until Hamlet arrives, and then reveals Claudius' involvement in his murder. He begs Hamlet to take revenge on his behalf, particularly as he is damned for sins he had no time to beg forgiveness for. Hamlet blames his indecision to take revenge for his father's death on his doubts about the Ghost. Although it looks and acts like his late father, he believes it could be a devil or demon trying to trick him.

## Horatio (Her-rach-eo)

Horatio is Hamlet's closest friend and ally. Hamlet trusts Horatio above all over characters in the play, revealing and sharing news of plots and schemes he has discovered. Horatio remains loyal enough to Hamlet to stay alive at the end of the play, despite his desire to kill himself. Despite his sorrow over Hamlet's death, he stays behind to set the facts straight, tell Hamlet's story and clear his name.

## Laertes (Lay-er-teez)

Laertes is Ophelia's brother and Polonius' son. He is a good fencer and is well liked by those that know him. Laertes is fiercely loyal to his family, protects his sister Ophelia by giving her sound advice and is dutiful to his father, Polonius. Hamlet is seriously jealous of his abilities and of the number of compliments he receives from other people.

## Ophelia (O-phee-lee-a)

Ophelia is Laertes' sister and Polonius' daughter. She is an innocent girl who believes Hamlet is in love with her, but follows her father's orders dutifully when he decides Hamlet must be leading her on. Towards the end of the play, Ophelia becomes mad under the stress of her father's murder and Hamlet's refusal of her. Later she falls into a brook, does not know that she is in danger and is pulled underwater by her heavy clothing. She drowns and her death spurs debates of religious rites and suicide, and reignites Hamlet's love for her.

## Rosencrantz & Guildenstern (Rose-en-crants & Guild-en-stern)

Rosencrantz and Guildenstern have been friends with Hamlet for a long time. They grew up together and seem to have a strong bond. They are summoned to Elsinore to help Gertrude and Claudius discover the reason for Hamlet's madness so that they can help him. However, as the play progresses, these two supposed friends start to connive and scheme with Claudius behind Hamlet's back and their loyalty shifts. They even agree to take Hamlet to England where he will be executed by the King.

## Polonius (Po-low-nee-us)

Polonius is a lord and adviser to Claudius. He has two children, Laertes and Ophelia, and he looks out for their welfare. This is a man full of good intentions who rarely goes about his plans without the use of trickery. Polonius gives speeches that are long winded and idiotic, and is often teased for it by Hamlet. Polonius is also often confused about character's motivations. He can't understand Hamlet's madness, despite his unfounded claim that he does, thinks that Claudius is an excellent man and suspects his son, Laertes, of poor behaviour in France. So much so that he sends a servant to spy on him and question his acquaintances!

## Osric (Oz-rick)

Osric is a courtier who is summoned by Claudius to send a message to Hamlet about the fencing duel. We learn through Hamlet that Osric owns a fantastic deal of land and has tried to make himself look and sound like an upper class man by talking pretentiously. He does talk in a confusing manner, and Hamlet often has to ask him what he is talking about. Hamlet thinks Osric is a foul man, but we do not learn much more about him to agree or disagree with Hamlet.

## Young Fortinbras (*Fort-in-braz*)

Fortinbras is the young prince of Norway and named after his late father, the King of Norway. Fortinbras wants revenge for his father's death who was killed by Hamlet's father during a war which also lost Norway a lot of territory. He begins the play gathering an army together, which is disbanded when his Uncle finds out about it. Hamlet later admires Young Fortinbras and his army for having the tenacity to fight for land in Poland, even though it means nothing to them. Fortinbras ends the play with a claim to the Danish throne and looks set to become the next King of Denmark.

## Marcellus (Mar-sell-us)

Marcellus is a Sentinel guard at Elsinore Castle and loyal to Hamlet. He is one of the first men to see the Ghost of the dead King marching. He vows to keep the Ghost a secret and tries to keep Hamlet from venturing off with the Ghost by himself. He follows Hamlet with Horatio to make sure that the Ghost has not harmed him.

## Reynaldo (Ray-nall-do)

Reynaldo is Polonius' servant. He is asked to spy on Laertes and ask his friends and acquaintances leading questions to trick them into telling him what Laertes has actually been up to. Polonius suspects he has been gambling and behaving badly. Reynaldo is worried that these questions might harm Laertes' reputation, especially if people think he is accusing him of this kind of behaviour. That Reynaldo would feel comfortable enough to question Polonius suggests that he has been with the family for a long time and that he has their best interests at heart. He is most loyal to Polonius, however, and leaves for France to do as he is asked.

## Gravediggers (also known as the Clowns)

The two Gravediggers meet in the churchyard. The Gravedigger and the Other discuss Ophelia's recent death and whether or not she should be given religious rites after killing herself. They conclude the only reason she would have been given these rights is due to her status as a rich woman, pinpointing a class divide. Neither seems particularly affected by death, and the Gravedigger sings as he digs and tosses skulls of the dead around. They are realists, rather than characters of extreme emotion.

## Barnardo (Bar-nar-do)

Barnardo is another Sentinel in the King's guard and a loyal friend to Hamlet. He and Marcellus have witnessed the Ghost of the late King Hamlet marching. He is the first to see the Ghost resembles the late King and begs Horatio to speak to it. Beyond this not much more is known about his character.

**Scene Summaries**

# Act 1

## Act One Scene One

In the royal castle in Elsinore, Denmark, two sentinels appear on the gun terrace. These are Barnardo and Francisco. They are frightened by one another and demand to know who stands there. Once they have realized who the other is, Barnardo tells Francisco he should go to bed as it is almost midnight. He is there to take over from Francisco. Francisco is relieved to be going as it is cold, but at least it has been a quiet night. Barnardo tells Francisco if he sees Horatio and Marcellus on his way to bed to tell them to hurry as they are meant to be on watch duty with him. The two guards appear and startle the others. After verifying that they are friends, Francisco leaves to go to bed.

Barnardo, Horatio and Marcellus ask one another if they have seen "the thing" yet tonight. They haven't. Horatio thinks it is nothing but their imagination playing tricks on them, and that the spirit will not appear to them, which is why Marcellus has asked him to stay up with them so he can see it with his own eyes. Horatio doesn't believe it will appear to them. Barnardo tells him to sit down so he can tell them a bit about what they have seen. He begins by telling them that last night when the bell struck one, a spirit appeared to them, but Marcellus tells him to be quiet. The Ghost has entered! Barnardo and Marcellus ask Horatio if he thinks that the Ghost looks like the dead King of Denmark. He agrees and starts to question the Ghost under encouragements from the other men. He asks the Ghost what he is and why he stalks the hallways like the King once did. But the Ghost starts to move away and leaves.

Horatio is stunned and has gone white as a sheet. He didn't think that this was possible. They agree that the Ghost looks exactly like the King of Denmark, and wears the armor he wore when he fought the King of Norway. Marcellus has seen the Ghost twice now at the same time of the night. Horatio thinks this means something awful will happen to them and the country because of this terrifying vision. Marcellus asks Horatio why the nightly watching of guards has been so strict lately, and why they seem to be readying for a war by building many bronze cannons. Marcellus wonders what is about to happen. Horatio can only relay rumours he has heard. As Marcellus already knows the late King of Denmark was an enemy to Fortinbras, the King of Norway, who challenged him to a battle. Hamlet, the King's son, killed Fortinbras, and his lands were left to the conqueror, Denmark. However, the King of Norway had a son, also called Fortinbras, who has collected followers willing to fight for food who are going to help him take back the territories his father once ruled over. He thinks that this is the reason why they are on guard and why Denmark is in chaos. Barnardo agrees—it could even explain why the dead King's Ghost has been roaming the halls as he created the wars.

Horatio thinks the Ghost is something to worry about and likens it to the fall of Rome. Just before Julius Caesar was killed by his most trusted men, corpses rose from their graves and ran through Rome squeaking and talking nonsense. Shooting stars, bloodied dew, warning signs from the Sun and a total eclipse from the Moon were other things observed during this time, as well. Considering they have had similar visions, Horatio thinks that Heaven and Earth are trying to warn us what is about to happen.

The Ghost re-enters. Horatio tells it to stay still—he wants to talk to it. He tells the Ghost to speak if it can make sounds. He wants to know if there is anything he can do for the Ghost to give it peace, or if the Ghost knows what is going to happen to Denmark. If he does, then maybe they can avoid it! If he doesn't know any of this, then Horatio wonders if he knows about some buried treasure which is keeping him from being at peace. A rooster crows, signalling the coming of dawn. Horatio tells Marcellus to stop the spirit from leaving. Marcellus asks if he should strike it with his spear. Horatio agrees if it doesn't stand still for long enough. The Ghost leaves.

Marcellus thinks they were wrong to threaten the Ghost as it looks like the King. He doesn't think he would have been able to hurt it anyway because spirits aren't solid. Barnardo thinks the Ghost was about to speak when the rooster interrupted. Horatio agrees—he has heard that the rooster wakes the God of Day up who then warns all spirits to hide. They've just seen that in action. Marcellus agrees that the Ghost faded when the rooster crowed. He adds that he has heard that the rooster crows all night around Christmas so that no spirits rise up and the fairies and witches have no power over man. This proves how holy the night is around this time. Horatio sort of believes that theory. He tells them to look to the horizon as the sun is rising. They decide to find young Hamlet to tell him what they have seen. It is their duty. Marcellus knows where to find him. They all leave.

## Act One Scene Two

At the royal castle in Elsinore Claudius, the King of Denmark, Queen Gertrude his wife, Hamlet, Polonius and his son, Laertes, and daughter, Ophelia, and many Lords gather. They all attend to Claudius, the King. He wants life to go on, despite how sad he still feels that his brother—the older Hamlet—has died. Claudius believes that mourning while taking care of oneself is the best and proper way to do it, so he has married his former sister-in-law. The marriage was both joyous and sad, but they went along with it because their advisers suggested it. He now wants to talk about business: Young Fortinbras has underestimated Denmark's armies and has mistakenly assumed that everyone would still be mourning the death of the late King. Fortinbras has been repeatedly demanding that Claudius surrender all of his late father's territories back to him.

Voltemand and Cornelius, two ambassadors for Norway, enter. Claudius tells them that he has written to Fortinbras' Uncle who is the present King of Norway. The Uncle does not know what Fortinbras has been planning because he is old and bedridden. Claudius has told the Uncle to stop Fortinbras. Cornelius and Voltemand's job is to deliver the letter to the Uncle. He tells the two to leave quickly. They pledge they will do their duty to Claudius and then leave.

Claudius turns to Laertes and asks what news he has and what favour he needs. He tells him not to hesitate as both Laertes and his father are as closely related as the head and heart, and hand and mouth are. Laertes asks for permission to return to France. He came to Denmark for Claudius' coronation but now his duty is done he wishes to return. Claudius asks Polonius, Laertes' father, if he has given his permission. Polonius admits that he has only agreed because Laertes has asked him so many times. He begs Claudius to let him go. Claudius agrees—Laertes can leave when he like and spend his time how he wants to.

Claudius then turns to Hamlet. Hamlet, speaking in an aside, mutters that he has more family now than any real kindness or feeling from them after his mother's marriage to his uncle. Claudius doesn't understand why Hamlet is still depressed. Hamlet disagrees—he is happy. Gertrude joins in and asks Hamlet to stop wearing dark clothing and to look with a friendly eye on Claudius. He can't spend his entire life thinking about his father. Death happens all the time. Hamlet agrees that death is common. Gertrude wonders why it seems so hard for him this time. Hamlet disagrees with her use of the word "seems". It *is* hard for him. His dark clothes, crying, or any other grief he shows can accurately represent how grieved he is to have lost his father. He agrees that it might "seem" that way to some people, especially if a person is faking their grief but Hamlet is not faking it—he is actually not even showing the full extent of his grief. Claudius compliments Hamlet for his commendable attitude towards mourning his father, but reminds him that all fathers have lost their own fathers, and those sons have mourned for a certain amount of time. Mourning beyond that period is stubborn and unmanly. Everyone knows that they will eventually die, so why take it to heart? It is against heaven and nature to continue to be absurd and mourn the death of a father as all fathers must eventually die. Claudius asks Hamlet to now think of him as his new father as everyone knows that Hamlet is the closest man to the throne. Claudius loves Hamlet like he would love any son. He doesn't want Hamlet to go back to school in Wittenberg and wants him to stay as the top member of the court and as his son. Gertrude repeats Claudius prayers and wants him to stay. Hamlet will obey her as much as he can. Claudius commends him on his answer as it shows how much Hamlet loves them. Claudius is now happy enough to drink, and every toast he makes will be heard and echoed by the heavens. Everyone but Hamlet leaves.

Hamlet wishes he could kill himself and that there wasn't a law against it. Life is weary and stale for him: he thinks of it like an unweeded garden gone to seed. His father has been dead for not even two months and was an excellent King—much better than his Uncle, Claudius is. And he was loving to Hamlet's mother, who kept the wind from blowing too hard on her face. She always wanted to be with him. However, within a month of his father's death, before she had even worn in the shoes she wore to his funeral, she was set to marry his brother and

Hamlet's Uncle. He calls women frail and weak for it. She was so quick to jump into bed with him! Hamlet concludes that he must keep his heart silent because he can't talk about it.

Horatio, Marcellus and Barnardo enter. They greet Hamlet. Horatio calls himself Hamlet's poor servant, but Hamlet will have none of that. He only wants to be Horatio's friend. He wonders what Horatio is doing so far from Wittenberg, and then notices Marcellus and greets him too. Horatio tells Hamlet he felt like skipping school. Hamlet doesn't believe him: he would never skip school. He asks again what Horatio is doing in Elsinore and promises to teach him how to drink heavily before he leaves. Horatio admits he came to see Hamlet's father's funeral. Hamlet thinks Horatio is making fun of him—he came to see his mother's wedding instead. Horatio agrees that it followed quickly behind. Hamlet jokes it was to keep things cheap: leftovers from the funeral furnished the wedding tables with a feast. He would rather have met his enemies in Heaven than see that day. He thinks he sees his father. Horatio asks where, and Hamlet replies in his imagination. Horatio admits he saw the good King once. Hamlet will never meet another man like him again.

Horatio reveals he saw the King last night. Hamlet asks for excitedly asks for clarification. Horatio tells him to calm down while he tells his tale about the vision he saw with the other men. Hamlet begs him to tell all. Horatio reveals that for two nights Marcellus and Barnardo encountered a figure like Hamlet's father march slowly and stately past them. He did this three times while the two men stood shaking and unable to say anything. They then told Horatio who agreed to stand guard and see for himself. On this night, the spirit appeared. Horatio knew what Hamlet's father looked like, and the Ghost looked like him as much as his two hands look alike. Hamlet asks where it happened. Marcellus tells him it happened on the platform where they stand guard. Hamlet asks if they spoke to the Ghost. Horatio did, but it didn't answer back. He thought the Ghost was about to speak, but the rooster crowed, and the sounds made it disappear from sight. Hamlet thinks this is all strange. Horatio swears it is true; he just thought Hamlet should know about it. Hamlet agrees, but it still troubles him. He asks if they stand on guard that night too. Marcellus and Barnardo are. Hamlet asks if the Ghost was armed from head to toe. The two men confirm it was. Hamlet wonders if they couldn't see the Ghost's face then. Horatio could—the visor on the helmet was up. Hamlet asks how he looked—if he frowned or was pale or stared. Horatio tells him that he looked more sorrowful than angry, was pale and stared at them quite a bit. Hamlet wishes he was there and asks if the Ghost stayed long. Horatio thinks it would have taken someone counting slowly to a hundred to pass the time the Ghost was present. Marcellus and Barnardo disagrees—it was longer. Horatio disagrees. Hamlet asks if the Ghost's beard was gray. Horatio tells him it was like it was in real life: black mixed with silver hairs. Hamlet will stand guard tonight to see if the Ghost will come. If it does look like his father, he will speak to it. He asks them all to keep it a secret if they have been doing so and to not talk about what might happen that night either. He makes plans to meet them later. Horatio, Marcellus and Barnardo pledge their duty to Hamlet. He gives them his love. Everyone but Hamlet leaves. Hamlet thinks there is something wrong for his father to appear as a Ghost. He tells himself to remain calm until night. He concludes that bad deeds will rise and be revealed even though people try to hide them from other people's eyes. He leaves.

*Act One Scene Three*

Within the castle, Laertes and his sister, Ophelia, enter. Laertes tells her his belongings are already on the ship and tells her to write to him as long as winds are blowing. Ophelia asks if he would doubt her writing to him. Laertes ignores her question and tells her not to worry about Hamlet's flirting with her. He thinks it is just a temporary infatuation Hamlet has with her and won't last more than a minute. Ophelia asks him if he's sure. Laertes tells her that as a man gets bigger and grows up, his mind and soul also grow bigger. Hamlet might love her now, but she needs to be careful. He is a member of the royal family and, therefore, has no control over his own future. He can't make choices for himself as the entire country depends on him. He has to meet the general needs of the nation. So if Hamlet tells her that he loves her, she should remember that what the state of Denmark says has more power over him. She needs to be chaste and not give into him. She will be safe if she fears him as young people usually lose their self control. Ophelia promises to remember his wisdom and advice. She adds that he should practice what he preaches and be as virtuous as he expects her to be. Laertes agrees.

Polonius enters. Laertes wants to leave, but sees his father approaching. He is overjoyed to have his blessing to leave not just once, but twice. Polonius is amazed that Laertes hasn't left yet as the ship is ready to go. He gives Laertes some advice: he is to think before he speaks and to not act too quickly on his thoughts, to be friendly to people but not vulgar about it and to hold onto his friends once he's tested who are his real ones. He is also to avoid getting into a fight too quickly, but to fight bravely once he's in one, to listen to everyone's opinion but only follow the best judgement, to spend all he can on clothes but not buy rich or gaudy clothes. Clothes make the man, after all, especially in France. He is not to borrow or lend money to anyone as this can lead to a loss of money and friendship. And he is to be true to himself. He blesses Laertes once more and hopes his blessing will help him. Laertes says goodbye to Polonius and Ophelia and then leaves.

Polonius asks Ophelia what advice Laertes has given her. Ophelia tells him it was something about Hamlet. Polonius is pleased that he did as he has heard Hamlet has spent a lot of time alone with Ophelia lately. He doesn't think Ophelia is conducting herself properly around him. He asks for the truth over what is happening between them. Ophelia tells her father that Hamlet has been affectionate towards her lately. Polonius chastises her for sounding like an innocent girl who doesn't understand the nature of her circumstances. He asks her if she believes in Hamlet's affections. Ophelia doesn't know what to think. Polonius will tell her: she is a baby for thinking that his affections mean anything at all, and she should have more respect for herself. He wants to make sure she doesn't turn him into a foolish looking man.

Ophelia defends Hamlet. She believes he has been honourable towards her. Polonius thinks it is a passing infatuation. Ophelia tells him Hamlet has made holy vows to her, but Polonius counters: any man can make oaths and vows when he is filled with lust. The fire of his passion will be out soon enough, even before he is finished making his promises. She is not to think of this as true love. Ophelia is to spend less time with him and make herself a harder conquest. Hamlet is still young and can still have the freedom to play around, so she is not to believe in his vows. Ophelia must do as her father says. Ophelia agrees, and they both leave.

## Act One Scene Four

On the gun terrace of Elsinore Castle, Hamlet, Horatio and Marcellus enter. Hamlet comments that it is cold and then asks what time it is. Horatio tells him it is just before twelve. Marcellus thinks it is after twelve as he heard the clock strike. Horatio didn't hear it. He tells the two that this is when the Ghost is likely to appear. Trumpets suddenly sound offstage and two cannons are fired. Horatio asks Hamlet what that means. Hamlet tells them that the King is up and drinking. As he drinks his wine, the musicians play to celebrate him finishing another cup. Horatio wonders if that is a tradition. Hamlet reveals it is, but it isn't one that he appreciates. Even though it is a custom and tradition, it gives them a bad name among other nations for their loud parties. They are called drunks and are insulted. And the drinking does lessen their achievements, even if they are great ones. Hamlet compares this situation to that of a person born with a birth defect which they can't help because it is in their nature, or to a habit that changes them. Men who carry only one defect can have all their talents and virtues seen as nothing. In fact, they can also be seen as evil to other people which totally ruins their reputations even if they have done nothing wrong.

The Ghost returns. Horatio tells them to look. Hamlet calls on angels to defend them. He wants to talk to the Ghost whether or not it is a good or bad spirit. He decides to call it Hamlet, King, Father and royal Dane to try and get it to talk to him. He asks the Ghost not to drive him mad with ignorance, but to answer his question: why has he returned after they have so quietly buried him? What has made him put his armor on again and come back to stare at the moon, make the night terrifying and scare humans. He asks what they should do to help him. The Ghost waves to Hamlet to come with him. Horatio thinks the Ghost wants to tell Hamlet something alone. Marcellus thinks the Ghost is quite polite, but doesn't want Hamlet to go. Horatio agrees, but Hamlet wants to follow it if the Ghost will not speak. He wonders what the danger is when he doesn't value his life one bit. The Ghost cannot harm his soul as it is just as immortal as the Ghost itself. The Ghost waves again. Horatio worries that the Ghost will tempt Hamlet to jump into the sea or will take on a horrible form that will drive him into madness. Hamlet is resigned to go. Marcellus and Horatio try to hold Hamlet back, but Hamlet tells them to let go of him. Hamlet thinks that this is fate. He draws his sword and threatens to make a Ghost out of anyone who tries to stop him from going. The Ghost and Hamlet leave.

Horatio thinks his imagination has driven him into desperation. Marcellus suggests they should follow him and not obey his orders to leave them alone. Horatio wonders what will happen now. Marcellus suggests that it means something is rotten in Denmark. Horatio wants to let God take care of it if that is true. Marcellus disagrees—they should follow Hamlet. They leave.

## Act One Scene Five

Hamlet and the Ghost enter. Hamlet asks where they are going. He tells it to speak or he won't go any further. The Ghost tells him to listen. Hamlet will. The Ghost has to return to purgatory soon, but doesn't want Hamlet's pity. He needs him to listen carefully. Hamlet must also be ready for revenge too. The Ghost reveals that he is the ghost of his father and is doomed to walk the night for a certain amount of time. During the day, he is confined in fire until the crimes he committed in life are purged and his penance is complete. He could tell Hamlet things that would freeze his soul if he were not bound to secrecy about his imprisonment. Mortals like Hamlet are not allowed to hear it. He tells Hamlet to listen if he ever loved his father. The Ghost wants Hamlet to take revenge for his murder. Hamlet is shocked: murder? The Ghost reveals that this murder in particular was strange and horrid. Hamlet wants him to hurry up and tell him about it so he can take revenge quickly. The Ghost is glad Hamlet is eager and not as lazy as a fat weed rooted itself on the shores of Lethe. Although everyone was told that a snake bit the King when he was sleeping in the orchard, it is a lie. The real snake that killed him is now wearing the crown. Hamlet knew it. His Uncle murdered his father!

The Ghost goes on: his wife, the Queen Gertrude, allowed herself to be seduced by Claudius. She has fallen from far. She went from a legitimate marriage to the elder Hamlet who she loved dearly to becoming a wretch. She is a lustful person. The Ghost thinks he can smell the morning air and decides to be brief in telling his tale. He was sleeping in the orchard, as he always does in the afternoon. Hamlet's Uncle crept up behind him and poured a vial of hebenon—a poison—into his ear. This poison moves quickly through the veins and curdles the blood like drops of milk. And this is how his own brother took his life, his crown and his queen at once and cut him off in the middle of his sinful life. He had not chance to redeem himself or repent his sins before he died. He begs Hamlet to not let the King's bed be an incestuous one, but if he takes his revenge to not corrupt his own mind or hurt his mother. He must leave Gertrude to her own guilt and to God. Morning is approaching, so the Ghost bids Hamlet good-bye and asks him to remember his father. The Ghost leaves Hamlet alone.

Hamlet calls to Heaven and Earth and even Hell that he will remember his father, the poor Ghost, as long as he can command his own memory in his distracted head. He will wipe his memory clean of trivia and facts, or books and other memories and only remember the Ghost's commands and requests in their place. He wonders where his notebook is so that he can write down that people like his mother can smile away and still be villainous. He writes it down. It is now time to see to the vow Hamlet made his father.

Marcellus and Horatio enter. They ask Hamlet if he is alright. He replies that he is. They ask what happened, but Hamlet is worried they might talk about it. He asks them if they can keep it a secret. They can. He tells them that a villain in Denmark is still a villain. Horatio doesn't think that he would need a Ghost to tell him that. Hamlet agrees with him. He decides that it would be best if they shook hands and parted ways. He tells the two men to go and take care of their own business while Hamlet goes to pray. Horatio thinks he is talking in a crazy way. Hamlet is sorry if he has offended them. He tells them the Ghost they saw was a real one, but he can't tell them anything that happened between them. He asks his friends to do him a favour: to not tell anyone what they have seen. Horatio and Marcellus swear to it. Hamlet then asks them to swear on his sword, but they've already sworn it. The Ghost cries out from beneath the stage to swear on it. Hamlet laughs—even the man in the cellar wants them to swear. Horatio asks what they are to swear. Hamlet wants them to swear they will never mention what they've seen. The Ghost repeats it. Hamlet asks them to put their hands on the sword and swear. He keeps moving them away from the Ghost's voice to try and get them to swear on the sword. No matter how strange or oddly Hamlet acts, neither of the men are to say or gesture or intimate that something is wrong with him. They must never hint to another person that they know something more.

Hamlet tells the Ghost he can rest now. He tells the two that he loves them and their friendship. He suggests they go back to court together but to keep quiet. There is so much wrong at the moment, and Hamlet damns the fact that he has to put everything right again. They all leave.

**Act 2**

*Act Two Scene One*

Within Elsinore Castle, Polonius and his servant, Reynaldo, enter. Polonius tells Reynaldo to give Laertes money and letters. His servant agrees to do this. Polonius also asks him to see what Danish people are in Paris, who they are, what they do and who they are friends with. During this general questioning, Reynaldo may find out more about Laertes than he would by asking straight questions. If they ask, he can tell them that he sort of knows Laertes, is a friend of his father's, or something similar. Reynaldo understands. Polonius suggests he can ask if Laertes is a party animal and so on as leading questions. Reynaldo is worried that his would hurt Laertes' reputation, but Polonius thinks this will only happen if Reynaldo asks the questions in the wrong way. He is to mention his faults lightly so that he seems that he has only gone a little too far. Polonius asks if Reynaldo wants to know why he is doing this. He does. Polonius is quite proud of his plan. When Reynaldo talks to someone about Laertes' faults and sins he can watch for the reaction of the other person. If that person agrees with what Reynaldo says, then he will know Laertes is guilty of these things. Polonius loses track of where he was in the plan and asks Reynaldo what he was saying. Reynaldo reminds him. Polonius goes on: whoever Reynaldo speaks to will then be willing to say something about the things he has seen Laertes doing, like gambling or fighting or going into a brothel. Reynaldo's little lies will bring out the truth. And this is how Reynaldo will find out what Laertes is up to in Paris. Reynaldo agrees.

Polonius reminds him not to rely on gossip only, though. He is to go and see Laertes with his own eyes. Polonius hopes that Laertes is studying music. Reynaldo leaves.

Ophelia enters. She is frightened. Polonius asks her what the matter is. Ophelia tells him that while she was in her room sewing, Hamlet came in with no hat, shirt undone, dirty stockings undone and as pale as his undershirt. He came up to her. Polonius asks if he was mad for her love. Ophelia isn't sure, but it could possibly be so. Polonius asks what he said. Hamlet grabbed her hard around the wrist and then backed away at an arm's length and stared at her like an artist stares at something they are about to draw. He stayed like this for a long time. He sighed, and then finally let her go. He left the room with his eyes on her. Since then, she has felt his eyes were still on her.

Polonius decides they will tell the King about this as he is convinced Hamlet has gone mad with love. It is a violent emotion which sends people to desperate actions. Polonius wonders if Ophelia has said anything recently to hurt his feelings. Ophelia hasn't, but she has turned him away and sent his letters back as Polonius has asked her. Polonius concludes this must have sent him into his madness. He wishes he had better judgement as he thought Hamlet was just toying with her emotions. Polonius blames his old age which leads him to assume he knows more than young people do. They leave to tell the King as it could cause more trouble and grief if they keep it a secret.

## Act Two Scene Two

Trumpets play. Claudius, Gertrude—the King and Queen of Denmark—and Rosencrantz and Guildenstern enter, followed by attendants. Claudius welcomes Rosencrantz and Guildenstern to Elsinore Castle. He wishes that he has long needed to see them, but quickly sent for them when they saw Hamlet's transformation. Hamlet is so unlike what he was before, and Claudius can only conclude that it was his father's death that has made him the way he is. Since Rosencrantz and Guildenstern have grown up with Hamlet and know him well, Claudius asks them to stay for a while and spend some time with Hamlet. They should try and get Hamlet to have some fun and find out what afflicts and torments him so that they can try to fix the problem. Gertrude adds that Hamlet has talked much about the two gentlemen and that they are probably the two Hamlet loves most. If they do agree to stay for a while to help, they will have a royal thanks.

Rosencrantz points out that they could have ordered them to stay instead of asking so nicely. Guildenstern adds that they will obey though, and will provide all of their services and help that they can. Claudius and Gertrude thank them. She asks them to visit Hamlet right away and calls for servants to lead them to Hamlet. Guildenstern echoes this hope and leaves with Rosencrantz, following servants.

Polonius enters. He announces that the ambassadors are back from Norway. Claudius believes that he has brought good news. Polonius wonders if he has. He assures Claudius that he is only doing his job and duty to his King. He believes that he has discovered why Hamlet has turned mad. Claudius orders him to speak immediately. Polonius tells him he will as soon as the ambassadors have given their news. Polonius leaves to bring them in.

Claudius tells Gertrude that Polonius has discovered the reason for Hamlet's madness. Gertrude is sure it is just because of Hamlet's father's death and their quick marriage to one another.

Polonius enters with the ambassadors Voltemand and Cornelius. Claudius asks them what news they have brought from Norway. Voltemand reports that as soon as they told the King of Norway, he sent messengers out to stop his nephew's preparations for war. He had originally thought this preparation was against Poland, but discovered that it was against Denmark. He was upset that his nephew, Fortinbras, had taken advantage of his age and sickness in order to deceive him and has ordered Fortinbras' arrest. He has vowed to never threaten Denmark again. The King of Norway was made so happy by these vows that he gave young Fortinbras an annual income of three thousand crowns and a commission to lead his army into Poland. He has sent a letter asking to allow Fortinbras' troops to pass through Denmark on their way to Poland and has assured them of Claudius' safety. Voltemand hands the letter to Claudius. Claudius likes this news: he will read the letter at another time and think about how to reply to it. He thanks them for their efforts and tells them to go and rest. Voltemand and Cornelius leave to do exactly that.

Polonius is pleased that everything has turned out alright in the end. Instead of making speeches he will launch right into what he has to say. Their son is mad. He's calling it madness because what else is madness but madness? Gertrude asks him to get on with it. Polonius assures her he is: it is common knowledge that he is crazy, even if it is a shame. He decides to get right to the point instead of sound foolish. Now the next step is work out why Hamlet has turned mad. Polonius tells them he has a daughter who was given a letter by Hamlet. She has given it to Polonius out of her daughterly duty. He reads the letter to them. Hamlet addresses Ophelia as "beautified" which Polonius dismisses as a vile phrase. He goes on: Ophelia with her excellent white bosom—. Gertrude interrupts to confirm that Hamlet wrote the letter to Ophelia. Polonius asks her to be patient and to wait until he has read the entire letter to her. It is a love note full of poetry, which Hamlet claims he is poor at writing. He tells her he loves her. Polonius adds that Ophelia has told him Hamlet has been courting her.

Claudius wants to know how Ophelia reacted. Polonius wants to know what Claudius thinks of him. Claudius thinks him a faithful and honourable man. Polonius wonders what Claudius might have thought about him had he not kept quiet about Hamlet's actions prior to the letter. He thought that Hamlet was lusting after his daughter, not that he was in love with her. He wonders what the Queen would have thought of Polonius had he turned a blind eye to what was happening between Hamlet and Ophelia. He told Ophelia that Hamlet is a Prince, and that they would never be together, and then ordered her to stay away from him. She did as she was told, and immediately Hamlet fell into sadness, stopped eating and sleeping and became dizzy and weak. This led to his madness, which they are all worried about. Claudius wonders if this is the reason Hamlet is depressed. Gertrude thinks it might be. Polonius asks them if he has ever been wrong. Claudius doesn't think so. Polonius tells them to chop off his head if he is wrong. He will uncover the truth. Claudius wonders how they will do that. Polonius suggests that while Hamlet walks in the lobby for four hours, which he does often, Ophelia will approach him. Claudius and Polonius will hide and watch what happens. If Hamlet is not in love with her and this isn't the reason for his madness, then Polonius can be fired and will go to work on a farm. Claudius agrees to try.

Hamlet enters, reading a book. Gertrude tells the men gathered to look how sad Hamlet looks. Polonius tells them to both go away so that he can speak to Hamlet alone. Claudius and Gertrude leave. Polonius asks Hamlet how he is. Hamlet is fine. Polonius wonders if Hamlet knows who he is. Hamlet thinks he is a fishmonger. Polonius is not, but Hamlet wishes Polonius were as honest as a fishmonger is. Polonius wonders what he means by this. Hamlet laments that there is only one honest man in the world out of ten thousand. Polonius agrees. Hamlet asks if Polonius has a daughter. He suggests that the daughter should never walk around in public just in case she should become pregnant.

In an aside, Polonius wonders what he meant by that, but notices that Hamlet is still going on about his daughter. Polonius thinks he is crazy for mistaking him for a fishmonger and thinks he is almost as crazy for love as he was when he was younger. Polonius asks what Hamlet is reading. Hamlet replies with only: "words." Polonius asks again. Hamlet tells him he is reading lies. The writer has written that all old men have gray beards, wrinkled faces and poor intellect. Hamlet believes this, but he doesn't think that it is nice to have written it down. Polonius could grow as young as Hamlet if he could go backwards like a crab. Polonius thinks that there is some method to his madness. He asks Hamlet if he could step outside for a moment. Hamlet will into his grave. Polonius comments to himself that Hamlet's answers are full of meaning, which is often a condition mad people have and sane people have no talent for. He will leave Hamlet now so he can arrange a meeting between him and Ophelia. To Hamlet he says goodbye. Hamlet tells Polonius that he cannot take anything from him that he cares less about except for his life.

Rosencrantz and Guildenstern enter. Polonius points them in the direction of Hamlet, and then leaves. Guildenstern and Rosencrantz greet Hamlet, who asks them how they are both doing. Guildenstern is happy that they're not too happy or lucky. Hamlet jokes that they are in the middle, around a lady's waist. They exchange jokes about sexual favours and call Fortune a whore. Hamlet asks what news they have for him. Rosencrantz reports that the world has grown more honest. If that is true, Hamlet thinks that the apocalypse is coming. Their news can't be true, though. He asks them what crimes they have committed to be sent to this prison. Guildenstern doesn't know what he means by this. Hamlet calls Denmark a prison. Rosencrantz concludes that the entire world must be a prison, then, but Hamlet thinks if that is so then Denmark is the worst one. Rosencrantz disagrees. Hamlet insists that a thing can either be good or bad depending on someone's personal view of it, and so to him Denmark is a prison. Rosencrantz thinks it is his ambition that has made Denmark a prison to him, as it is too small for his goals. Hamlet could live in a nutshell and still think of himself as a King if he didn't have bad dreams. Guildenstern thinks dreams are a sign of ambition. They debate whether or not a dream is a shadow of ambition or if ambition is a shadow of dreams. Rosencrantz thinks that ambition is so light and airy that it can only be considered a shadow's shadow. If that is true then Hamlet thinks beggars are the ones with actual bodies and the monarchs and heroes are the beggar's shadows.

Hamlet wonders if they should go to court. Rosencrantz and Guildenstern will wait on him. Hamlet doesn't want that: his servants are terrible. He asks them as friends why they are at Elsinore Castle. Rosencrantz admits they are there to visit Hamlet and for no other reason. Hamlet thanks them, but wonders if they came by themselves or were sent for by someone. Guildenstern wonders what they should say in response. They can say anything they like as long as they answer Hamlet's question. He thinks they look guilty, which means that they were sent for. They are too honest to hide it from him. Rosencrantz wonders why they would call for them to come. Hamlet wants them to admit it themselves: he reminds them of their friendship and the duties of their love for one another, and whatever will make them answer honestly. Rosencrantz asks Guildenstern what he thinks they should say. To himself, Hamlet admits he has his eye on them, and then asks Guildenstern to be honest if he truly cares about Hamlet. Guildenstern admits that they were sent for.

Hamlet won't make them tell him why they were sent for in case they have to give up the secrecy they have with the King and Queen. He knows why they are here: recently he has lost all sense of joy and has stopped doing everything he used to do. The entire world feels sterile to him. The sky and sunlight are boring and diseased. He marvels at how delightful a construction man is, but can take no delight or interest in them, or women for that matter.

Hamlet asks Rosencrantz why he laughed. Rosencrantz thinks that if he has no interest in men, then he will be bored by the actors on their way to entertain Hamlet. Hamlet thinks the actor who plays the King will be the most welcomed. Hamlet will treat him like a real King. The Knights shall wave his sword, the lover rewarded for his sighs, the clown shall make people laugh, and the lady can say whatever she wants to. He asks which company of actors are on their way. The company is the one from the city. Hamlet enjoys this company a lot. Hamlet wonders why they are on the road and touring as they made so much more money in the city. Rosencrantz thinks that it is easier for them on the road now as the city has changed so much. Hamlet asks if they are as popular as they used to be in the city. They are not. Hamlet asks why this is and if they are not as talented as they were. Rosencrantz thinks that they are as wonderful as they ever have been, but they have to compete with a group of children who yell out their lines during performances and receive applause for it. The child actors are in fashion now on the stage and have scared off most of the upper class audiences. Hamlet wants to know more: he asks who takes care of them and pays them, and what will happen to the actors when they grow up. He thinks the playwrights might be hurting the child actors by encouraging them to upstage the adult actors. They will have no future in acting. Rosencrantz reveals that there has been a huge debate about this. For a long while no play was sold to a theatre without an argument between the adult actors and the childrens' playwright. Hamlet is surprised at first, but then concludes it is not so strange if they think about the state of Denmark. Many people pay up to a hundred ducats for a little portrait of Hamlet's Uncle, the King. It is unnatural.

Trumpets play offstage, announcing the arrival of the Players. Hamlet welcomes Rosencrantz and Guildenstern to Elsinore and shakes their hands. He wants to go through all of these polite customs to make sure that they don't think Hamlet is happier to see the actors. Hamlet still thinks that the King and Queen have the wrong idea, though. Hamlet is only crazy at times.

Polonius enters. He hopes that everyone is well. Hamlet quietly jokes to Guildenstern and Rosencrantz that Polonius still wears diapers. Rosencrantz agrees—many old people become children again. Hamlet thinks that Polonius has come to tell him about the actors' arrival. Polonius does, in fact, announce the actor's arrival, but Hamlet is bored by the news. Polonius insists that the actors are the best for any genre. Hamlet calls Polonius by the name Jephthah and sings about his treasured daughter. Polonius admits he has a daughter. Hamlet doesn't think that is logical. Polonius wonders what is logical then. Hamlet sings again about things happening as they would expect but has to stop because the Players have entered.

Hamlet welcomes them all. He talks to some of them personally and marvels out how this one has grown, at someone's beard, and how they look well. Hamlet requests that they give a passionate speech to start the festivities with. The First Player asks which speech Hamlet would like. Hamlet would like a speech that was never performed before, or only once if it had been because the play was not popular. The critics and Hamlet found the play to be excellent, but the rest of the populace did not. One critic wrote that there was no vulgar language for the playwright to show off with and called it an excellent play. Hamlet loved the part when Aeneas told Dido about Priam's murder. He recites the beginning to the Players. Polonius congratulates Hamlet on his excellent pronunciation. The First Player carries on with the tale of Priam's murder. Polonius thinks the speech is far too long. Hamlet asks them to continue—he thinks Polonius can only like the dancing or sleeps through the rest of it. The First Player continues, but Hamlet stops him at the "veiled" queen to question the word. Polonius likes it. The First Player goes on until Polonius stops him because of the actor's tears. Hamlet will have him recite the rest of it later.

Hamlet asks Polonius to make sure the actors are comfortable, especially as they could talk if they are mistreated. They would be better to have a bad epitaph on their graves than the insults of these men while they are still alive. Polonius will give them what they deserve. Hamlet disagrees: Polonius should treat them better than they deserve. If everyone was treated this way, then no one would ever escape a whipping. If the Players deserve less, the more Polonius' generosity will be worth. Hamlet asks the First Player if he composed an extra speech for the play tomorrow whether they could learn it. He can. Hamlet tells the Players to follow Polonius in. They leave.

Hamlet welcomes Rosencrantz and Guildenstern to Elsinore once more and then sends them away. They leave. Hamlet is finally alone. He thinks it is monstrous that an actor could work himself up to feel sorrow in a made-up situation. He shed real tears for nothing. What could Hecuba mean to him to cry that much? He wonders what the actor would do if he felt the same way Hamlet does. He would probably drown the stage with tears and appal everyone with his words. But, what does Hamlet do? Nothing but mope around. He hasn't even taken his revenge or planned for it, and can say nothing against the King who stole the crown. He wonders if he is a coward and if there is anyone out there who could push him to do his task. He has heard, however, that guilty people have been driven so mad by their guilt and affected by the sentiments of a play that they have confessed to their sins. Hamlet will have a similar murder scene to his father's played out to see what his Uncle might do or look like. If he turns pale, Hamlet will know what to do. The spirit could have been the devil in disguise tempting Hamlet and using his weaknesses against him, so Hamlet needs more evidence before he takes revenge. He leaves.

**Act 3**

## Act Three Scene One

Claudius, Gertrude, Polonius, Ophelia, Rosencrantz and Guildenstern enter. Claudius can't understand why they can't think of a reason why Hamlet acts so confused and ruins peace with madness. Rosencrantz tells them Hamlet has admitted he feels distracted but has not told him the reason for it. Guildenstern adds that Hamlet doesn't want to be questioned. He dances around the questions when they try to get him to talk. Gertrude wonders if Hamlet treated them kindly. He did, but Guildenstern thinks Hamlet had to force himself to be nice. Gertrude asks if they tried to tempt him with a fun activity. They admit they have invited a group of actors which seems to have made Hamlet happier. They have been asked to perform that night. Polonius adds that the King and Queen have also been invited by Hamlet. Claudius is happy about this. He hopes the play will do him good and sends Rosencrantz and Guildenstern to increase his interest in the play.

Claudius tells Gertrude that they have arranged for Hamlet to bump into Ophelia by "accident". He and Polonius will hide themselves and spy on them to see if it is Hamlet's love for her that makes him suffer so much. Gertrude will leave them to it. She hopes that Ophelia's beauty is the reason for Hamlet's madness, and that she will return Hamlet to himself. Gertrude leaves.

Polonius tells Ophelia to read from her prayer book so that she looks lonely. Polonius concludes that most people do this anyway to hide from their sins. In an aside, Claudius agrees with Polonius. He feels terribly guilty for the murder of the former King. Polonius hears Hamlet coming and tells the King to hide. They do.

Hamlet enters. He wonders to himself if it would be better to be alive or dead, if it is nobler to put up with all the nasty things the world throws your way or to just put them to an end by dying? Dying is like sleeping, after all, and sleep reduces the amount of heartache a person has. He wonders and worries what kind of dreams death might bring, and that this might be the reason why people tend to avoid death and continue putting up with suffering and sadness for so long. Fear of death makes people cowardly.

He sees Ophelia and asks her to remember him when she prays. Ophelia asks him how he has been. She has some things of Hamlet's to hand back to him. Hamlet didn't give her anything. Ophelia tells him off—he knows he gave her letters and trinkets to go with them. The gifts aren't so valuable to her anymore now that Hamlet has been unkind to her. Hamlet asks her if she is honest and good and beautiful. Ophelia doesn't understand the questions. Hamlet explains that if she is good, her goodness must have nothing to do with her beauty. Ophelia doesn't understand how anything beautiful could not be related to goodness. Hamlet tells her it can be: beauty can turn a girl into a whore more easily than goodness can turn a beautiful girl into a virgin. He used to love her. Ophelia agrees that he made her think she did. Hamlet insists she shouldn't have believed him. He didn't love her. Ophelia was misled, then. Hamlet tells her to go to a convent. He doesn't know why she would want to give birth to more sinners. He is a slightly good man himself, but even he is guilty of sins; it might have been better if he'd never been born at all. Hamlet calls himself arrogant, ambitious and filled with the need for vengeance. Hamlet doesn't think people like him should be on Earth.

Hamlet wonders where Polonius is. Ophelia insists he is at home. Hamlet tells her to lock him up so he can only be a fool in his own home. He tells her good-bye. Ophelia begs God to help Hamlet. Hamlet ignores her. He tells her that if she marries, he will curse her that even if she is a pure as snow, she will still have a lousy reputation. She must get herself to a convent or marry a fool as wise men will know she will cheat on them. Hamlet goes on to question a woman's need to put make-up on. They hide their face given to them by God with another face. They plead ignorance to sex and pretend to be innocent. Hamlet declares that they will have no more marriage—everyone he knows by one person will stay married, but everyone else will remain single. He tells her once more to get herself to a convent, and then leaves her alone.

Ophelia is sad that Hamlet is so changed. He used to have admirable qualities and was the one everyone admired and imitated. His madness has ruined him.

Claudius and Polonius come forward. Claudius doesn't think he was in love, and his words were not crazy, just disorganized in form. Claudius suspects that his sorrow is hatching something dangerous and so he will send Hamlet to England to get the debt back that they owe Denmark. He hopes that a different setting will clear the thoughts in his head. Polonius still believes his madness was caused by unrequited love. He suggests that Claudius can do what he wants as long as Gertrude has a moment with him to try and get him to open up. Polonius will hide and listen in. Claudius agrees: when someone is mad they must be watched closely. They all leave.

## Act Three Scene Two

Hamlet and the Players enter. Hamlet tells them to perform the speech that he has taught them. They are to not use too many hand gestures and to keep their passion moderate. He hates it when actors go over the top. The First Player promises not to do that. Hamlet goes on: the acting should not be tame either. The actors should let their good sense guide them and fit the actions to the words. They must be natural as theatre is meant to hold a mirror to reality and represent it. If they handle it badly, this could offend people in the audience who are the ones they need to keep happy. He has seen actors who are highly praised but can't act like normal people. The First Player thinks they've corrected those faults already in their company. After a few more corrections from Hamlet to make sure the important question of the play is highlighted, the Players leave to get ready.

Polonius, Guildenstern and Rosencrantz enter. Hamlet asks them if the King and Queen are attending. They are. Hamlet tells Polonius to get the actors to hurry up. He leaves to do so. He asks Rosencrantz and Guildenstern to help. They leave.

Horatio enters. Hamlet calls him the best man he has ever known, but to not think Hamlet is flattering him. Why would he flatter a poor person? He would have nothing to gain from it as Horatio is poor. He has picked Horatio for his friend because he takes everything life throws at him with acceptance and grace. Hamlet tells him there is a scene that comes close to describing his father's death. When Horatio sees it, he must watch for Claudius' reaction to see if the Ghost was right or a devil. Horatio will watch him closely.

Trumpets play. Claudius, Gertrude, Polonius, Ophelia, Rosencrantz, Guildenstern and other attending Lords enter with Guards carrying torches. Claudius asks how Hamlet is. Hamlet tells him he eats a lot of air. He is stuffed full of it. Claudius doesn't know what Hamlet is talking about—he hasn't answered the question. Hamlet doesn't think he's answered his question either. Hamlet asks Polonius if he has acted before and what role he played. Polonius played Julius Caesar who was killed by Brutus.

Gertrude asks Hamlet to sit by him, but he wants to sit by Ophelia because it's a more attractive place. Polonius asks Claudius if he saw that. Hamlet wonders if he should lie with his head in her lap. She allows him to do so. Ophelia comments that Hamlet is in a good mood that night. He wonders what else he could do but be happy. After all, his father has only been dead for two hours and his mother has remarried and is happy for it. Ophelia corrects him: it's been four months. Hamlet is surprised it has been that long. He will shed his mournful clothes soon. But, as he hasn't forgotten his father yet, he concludes that there is hope a man's memory will live on for many months.

Trumpets play and the show begins. The King and Queen enter and embrace. The King lies down on a bank of flowers and sleeps. The Queen leaves him. Another man comes in, takes his crown off and pours poison in the King's ears and leaves. The Queen returns to find the King dead. The Poisoner comes in again and woos the Queen with gifts. She accepts him after a while. The Players leave.

Ophelia asks Hamlet what the play means. He replies that they are causing mischief. The Prologue enters. Ophelia wonders if this man will tell them what the play is about. The Prologue asks the audience to be patient while they watch their tragedy and then leaves. Ophelia thinks the speech was quite short. Hamlet compares its length to a woman's love.

Actors playing the King and Queen enter. The King tells his Queen that he will have to leave her soon for death and hopes that she will find another husband. The Queen cannot remarry—she wouldn't be able to find another husband. Anyone who marries a second husband has killed off the first. Every time she would kiss her second husband, it would be like killing her first husband over again. The King thinks she will change her mind like people do over time. Promises lose their emotional power over time and people are no longer motivated to act by them. People can have their dreams, but fate decides their future and her refusal to marry again will die with her first husband. If the Queen does become a wife again, after being a widow, she hopes the earth will refuse to give her food and the heavens to go dark. She hopes she will be thick in despair and depression and have no joys. The King accepts her vow and asks the Queen to leave him alone while he sleeps. The Queen wishes him well and leaves.

Hamlet asks Gertrude if she is enjoying the play. Gertrude thinks the actor playing the Queen is overdoing it. Claudius wonders if anything offensive is in the play. Hamlet assures them that the play is a joke and not offensive at all. Claudius asks for the name of the play. Hamlet tells them it is called The Mousetrap, which is a metaphor. It is about a murder in Vienna. The Duke is called Gonzago and his wife is called Baptista. Hamlet tells them not to care too much for the play because they have free souls and no guilt. Lucianus, the King's nephew, appears on stage.

Hamlet and Ophelia tease one another. Hamlet tells the Players that they are waiting for the revenge and to get on with it. Lucianus pours poison into the Player King's ears. Hamlet tells the audience that they will see how the murderer wins Baptista's love soon. Claudius stands up. Polonius orders the play to be stopped. Claudius tells them to give him light and get him away from this space. Everyone leaves aside from Hamlet and Horatio.

Hamlet thinks he could get work as an actor in a company if he ever has bad fortune thrust on him. They joke about the level of profit Hamlet might get. Hamlet asks Horatio if he noticed the King. He bets that the Ghost was right. He wonders if Horatio watched while the actors talked about poison. Horatio watched closely.

Rosencrantz and Guildenstern enter. They want a word with Hamlet. The King is upset and in his chambers. Hamlet wonders if the King has an upset stomach from too much alcohol. The King is angry. Hamlet keeps changing the subject, and Guildenstern asks him to stick with the topic at hand. The Queen has sent for Hamlet. Rosencrantz adds that the Queen thinks Hamlet's behaviour is shocking and admiring. Hamlet is overjoyed he can still impress his mother. Gertrude wants to see Hamlet in her bedroom before he sleeps. Hamlet will obey. Rosencrantz asks Hamlet why he doesn't tell his friends what is wrong with him. Hamlet believes he has no future ahead of him. Rosencrantz doesn't understand that: Hamlet is the heir to the throne.

The Players re-enter with instruments. Hamlet takes one, and then asks why Guildenstern is standing so close to him. Guildenstern apologizes. He is worried about Hamlet which makes him forget his manners. Hamlet begs Guildenstern to play the instrument. Guildenstern has no idea how to. Hamlet tells him he only needs to play his fingers and thumb over the holes and breath into the recorder to make music. Guildenstern doesn't have the ability to play. Hamlet is amazed—he can play Hamlet but not a recorder? He seems to know exactly how to play Hamlet, but Hamlet is no fool.

Polonius enters and reiterates Gertrude's wish to see him. Hamlet points to the clouds. They discuss what animals they see in them. Hamlet knows that they are all trying to fool Hamlet. He will go to see his Mother soon, and asks them all to leave him.

Hamlet is left alone. He talks about the night: how hell escapes from graveyards, witches roam and other terrible things happen. Hamlet could do terrible things, but he has to go see his mother. He tells himself to be cruel but not unfeeling. He might speak as sharp as a dagger, but he won't use one on her. Hamlet leaves.

*Act Three Scene Three*

Claudius, Rosencrantz and Guildenstern enter. Claudius doesn't like the way Hamlet is acting. He doesn't want to allow his madness to get out of control. He is sending the two men to England with Hamlet. Guildenstern vows to take care of him. It is their duty to keep people safe from the madness of others. Rosencrantz agrees: when a King dies many other people are affected by it too. Claudius tells them to be prepared for the trip. They leave.

Polonius enters. He reports that Hamlet is going to visit Gertrude's room. He will hide behind the tapestry in the room so that he can listen in on what they say. He is sure that Gertrude will tell Hamlet off. It is good, he thinks, for someone else to be listening in as well because a mother is the most favourable to her child. He will come back to Claudius to tell him what was said before he goes to bed. Claudius thanks him and Polonius leaves.

Claudius is sorry for his crimes. His guilt is strong, but at the same time he doesn't care: this is what God's mercy is for. To provide him with forgiveness when he has sinned. He will pray, but he's not sure what to pray for. He can't ask for forgiveness for the murder as he still has the rewards from it: the crown and Gertrude. He wonders what he can do and asks the angels to help him. He kneels and begins to pray, hopeful that things will be okay.

Hamlet enters. He draws his sword. He could kill Claudius now while he prays, but then he would go off to Heaven which wouldn't be much of a revenge plot. He would be doing him a favour, especially as Claudius killed Hamlet's father before he could pray for forgiveness for his own sins. Hamlet puts away his sword. He will wait for a better time to kill Claudius: when he is committing some kind of sin. While Claudius prays, he is only keeping himself alive a little longer. Hamlet leaves.

Claudius stands up. He has tried to pray, but he can't put his thoughts into his words properly, and they will never reach Heaven. He leaves.

## Act Three Scene Four

In Gertrude's bedroom, Polonius tells her what she should say to Hamlet. She needs to let Hamlet know his pranks have caused too much trouble, and that it has upset the King. Polonius will be hidden and silent. Hamlet calls offstage for Gertrude. Gertrude assures Polonius she will do as he has asked and tells him to hide. Polonius hides behind the tapestry.

Hamlet enters. He asks why she has called for him. She tells him that he has insulted his father. Hamlet retorts: she has insulted his father. She asks if he's forgotten who she is. Hamlet has not: she is the Queen, her husband's brother's wife and Hamlet's mother, although he wishes she were not. Gertrude will call someone else in who can speak to him, then. Hamlet tells her to sit down. She is not allowed to leave until he has shown her her true reflection. Gertrude worries that he will kill her. She cries out for help. Polonius echoes the cry from behind the tapestry. Hamlet stabs his sword straight through the tapestry and kills Polonius. Gertrude asks him what he has done. Hamlet doesn't know—he wonders if it was the King. Gertrude calls the murder a senseless act. Hamlet calls what she has done an equally senseless, horrible act. Gertrude doesn't understand what he means by killing a King. Hamlet pulls back the tapestry to discover Polonius. Hamlet thought it might have been someone more important, but is still glad to see the back of Polonius.

Hamlet tells Gertrude to stop wringing her hands and sit down so that he can wring her heart too if it hasn't been hardened by her evil. Gertrude doesn't know what she's done for Hamlet to talk to her like this. Hamlet tells her that her deed has made marriage a sinful act. Even Heaven is angry for what she has done. Gertrude presses him to tell her what she has done. Hamlet tells her to look at a picture of two brothers. He points out how kind and gentlemanly one is. This was her husband, Hamlet's father. The other brother is her present husband, Claudius, who is so low. Hamlet asks her if she has eyes to not see how low she has stooped. He doesn't know why she would have married this man. Gertrude begs him to stop. He is forcing her to look into herself, and she can see black spots of sin. Hamlet agrees: she lies in her corrupted bed making love to a villain. Gertrude begs him to stop.

The Ghost enters. Hamlet addresses it and asks what it wants. Gertrude thinks Hamlet has gone totally crazy now to be talking to the air. Hamlet wonders if the Ghost has come to tell him off for not taking revenge fast enough. The Ghost orders Hamlet to talk to his mother. Hamlet asks her how she is. Gertrude doesn't reply and asks him instead why he talks to the air. She demands to know what he is looking at. Hamlet tells her to look on the Ghost. Gertrude still can't see anything. Hamlet is amazed she can't. The Ghost leaves. Gertrude thinks that the Ghost is only a figment of Hamlet's imagination and madness. Hamlet challenges her assessment. There's nothing mad about him. He will repeat every word he just said to prove he isn't crazy. He asks Gertrude not to use his madness as an excuse and to confess her sins to Heaven so she can avoid going to Hell. Gertrude is sure he has broken her heart in two. Hamlet tells her to throw away the bad part of it and to live a purer life with the other half. He tells her to go to bed, but not to his Uncle's bed. She must try to be virtuous even if she is not. Eventually saying no to sleeping with him will become a habit and she will be a better person for it. When she wants to repent he will ask for her blessing. He is sorry for killing Polonius, but Heaven and God wanted him to do it to punish him with the murder. It will only get worse from here.

Hamlet again asks Gertrude to make sure she doesn't let Claudius persuade her into his bed and ply her with kisses until she admits that Hamlet's madness is faked. Gertrude can't breathe a word of this to anyone. It has almost killed her.

Hamlet reminds her that he is off to England with two friends he trusts as much as poisonous snakes. He is pleased that Polonius, the man who prattled away in life, is now silent and still. He wishes Gertrude a good night and drags Polonius off.

# Act 4

*Act Four Scene One*

**Note: in some editions this scene is part of Act Three Scene Four, which renders Act Four Scene Seven non-existent.

Claudius, Gertrude, Rosencrantz and Guildenstern enter. Claudius wonders what Gertrude's sighs mean. He knows she knows something and asks where Hamlet is. Gertrude asks Rosencrantz and Guildenstern to leave so she can talk to Claudius privately for a while. They leave. Gertrude doesn't think Claudius will believe what has just happened. Hamlet is as mad as a storm in a rage. She tells him about Polonius' murder. Claudius is sorry. He thinks this wouldn't have happened if he had been there. Hamlet is a threat to them all and Claudius will be blamed for not restraining and controlling him when the damage is done. His love for Hamlet stops him from doing what he has to do, and now Hamlet is beyond dangerous. He asks Gertrude where he has gone. Hamlet has gone to remove Polonius' body. She sees this as evidence of his morality still shining through his madness as he cries for what he has done. Claudius vows to ship him off to England as soon as the Sun sets, especially as it will take all of his skill to explain and excuse Polonius' murder.

Rosencrantz and Guildenstern re-enter. Claudius tells them to find others to help as Hamlet has killed Polonius. They are to find Hamlet, speak nicely to him and bring the body to the chapel. They leave to do just that. Claudius asks Gertrude to come with him. They will talk to their wisest friends and tell them what they are going to do and what has been done. He hopes that they will not end up with a bad reputation. They leave.

*Act Four Scene Two*

Hamlet enters. He has hidden the body. Rosencrantz and Guildenstern enter. They ask nicely what Hamlet has done with Polonius' body. Hamlet answers in nonsense. Rosencrantz asks again so they can take it to the Chapel. Hamlet doesn't believe that he will take Rosencrantz's advice over his own. He calls Rosencrantz a sponge which soaks up the King's rewards and decisions. Hamlet doesn't understand. Hamlet is glad as clever words are never understood by fools. Rosencrantz tells Hamlet that he has to tell them where the body is and then go with them to see the King. Hamlet orders them to take him to the King right away. They all leave.

## Act Four Scene Three

Claudius enters with two or three attendants. He tells them that he has sent men to find Polonius' body. It is dangerous to have Hamlet on the loose, but they can't lock him up because he is loved by too many people. They judge on appearance rather than reason, and they'll pay attention to the punishment more than the crime itself. They have to be calm. Hamlet being sent to England must seem a deliberate plan. Rosencrantz enters and tells Claudius they can't find out where the body is. Hamlet stands outside the room under guard, waiting for Claudius' orders. Claudius orders Hamlet brought before him. Rosencrantz yells to Guildenstern to bring Hamlet in, which he does.

Claudius asks Hamlet where Polonius' body is. He is at dinner, Hamlet replies. Claudius pushes for a better answer than that. Hamlet tells him that Polonius is being eaten by worms. Such is the way of life. They fatten animals to eat, and then they fatten themselves for the worms to eat. Hamlet insists that a beggar can end up eating a King. Claudius asks Hamlet again. Hamlet tells him that Polonius is in Heaven and that Claudius should send a messenger to find out for certain. If the messenger can't find him, then Claudius can check Hell himself. If he can't find him still, then in a month they will be able to smell him in the main hall. Claudius tells his attendants to check there. Hamlet jokes that they don't need to rush out as Polonius isn't going anywhere.

Claudius tells Hamlet that he must send him away to England for his own protection. He must get ready as the ship sails the next day with the favourable wind. Hamlet is pleased to go. Hamlet says goodbye to Claudius, who he calls mother. Claudius corrects him: he is Hamlet's father. Hamlet disagrees for when he married Gertrude they became one and, so he is both father and mother. Hamlet leaves.

Claudius tells Rosencrantz and Guildenstern to follow Hamlet and make sure he gets on the ship tonight. Everyone leaves but Claudius. He hopes that the King of England will follow his orders and kill Hamlet immediately upon arrival to cure Claudius of the affliction from Hamlet. He leaves.

*Act Four Scene Four*

At the border, Fortinbras and a Captain enter with an army. Fortinbras tells the Captain to go and send the Danish King his greetings and ask for permission to cross Denmark. If they need anything else doing, they only have to ask. Everyone except the Captain leaves.

*\*\*Note: in some editions the rest of this scene is omitted.*

Hamlet, Rosencrantz and Guildenstern and others enter. Hamlet asks the Captain who the army belongs to and what they are doing there. The Captain tells Hamlet they are on their way to attack Poland. The Captain admits that they're actually fighting for a pitiful bit of land which won't increase profits for either country. Hamlet concludes that the Polish won't defend it then, but the Captain reports troops are already stationed there.

Hamlet thinks that this is the problem with war, and why nations should not have too much money and peace. An argument could start for a small reason like an abscess and then grow until it bursts and kills them with no one knowing why the man has died. He thanks the Captain for his information. The Captain leaves.

Rosencrantz asks Hamlet to come with him. He will in a moment. Everyone except for Hamlet leaves. Hamlet wants to get on with taking his revenge, but is still afraid to do so. He wonders what a man is if he just sleeps and eats. Little more than an animal. He has been given the power of thought and reason, and so he must use them. He has the means to do it, so why hasn't he acted yet? An entire army is on the march to fight for nothing while he has all of the motivation for revenge and still hasn't acted on it. If his thoughts aren't bloody and violent from now on, they will be worth nothing. He leaves.

## Act Four Scene Five

Back at Elsinore Castle, Horatio, Gertrude and a Gentleman enter. Gertrude won't speak to Ophelia. The Gentleman feels sorry for her. She genuinely wants to speak to Gertrude and talks about her father a lot. Ophelia talks nonsense and beats her chest and gets upset for small reasons. Horatio thinks it might be a good idea to speak with her because a dangerous mind can lead to horrifying and evil conclusions. Gertrude tells them to let her in. The Gentleman leaves.

Gertrude curses her guilt. It makes a person full of suspicion and gives them away even while they're trying not to. Ophelia enters. She is distracted and quite insane. Ophelia sings about a dead true love in a grave. Gertrude tries to stop her. Claudius enters. Ophelia continues with her song.

Claudius asks Ophelia how she is. Ophelia hopes God will be at his table. She tells them that they can know what they are now, but not what they will become. Claudius tells them she's talking about her dead father, Polonius. Ophelia doesn't want to talk about that and goes on singing about a virgin losing her chastity to a man who refuses to marry her after they've slept together. Ophelia hopes that everything will be fine in the end, but she can't help weeping at the thought of him lying cold and dead in the ground. She will tell her brother about this. Ophelia wishes them a goodnight and then leaves.

Claudius tells Horatio to keep an eye on her. He leaves.

Claudius sees Ophelia's madness as an outcome of the grief that has poisoned her mind. He is sorry that everything happens at once: Polonius was killed, and then Hamlet left, and there are rumours everywhere about the death. Ophelia has been robbed of her sanity, and this leaves her no better than the animals. And last but not least, Laertes has returned from France and is surrounded by people gossiping about his father's death. He will undoubtedly blame Claudius for it.

A noise sounds off stage which startles Gertrude. Claudius orders the bodyguards to the door. A Messenger enters who tells them that Laertes is leading a rebellion against Claudius. He must save himself. The crowd are shouting and calling for Laertes to be King. Gertrude is upset that they have the wrong conclusion. Another noise off stage indicates the doors of the Castle have been broken through.

Laertes and others enter. Laertes asks his followers to wait and go outside while he talks to the false King. He demands Claudius give him his father. Claudius doesn't understand why Laertes has brought a rebellion to the Castle. He doesn't worry about being hurt as God protects the King. He asks again why Laertes is so angry. Claudius tells him Polonius is dead. Gertrude adds that it was not by Claudius's hand that he is dead, but Claudius tells her he can ask what he wants to. Laertes demands to know what happened. He throws off any vows he had for the King. He doesn't care if he is damned and goes to Hell. He just wants revenge for his father's murder. Claudius wonders what is stopping him. Laertes' free will stops him. Claudius wonders if Laertes would like to know who were his father's friends and enemies, and if he would treat them the same. Laertes will only hurt his enemies. Claudius will prove that he is innocent of Polonius' death.

A voice offstage cries to "let her in". Ophelia enters carrying flowers. Laertes is upset over Ophelia's madness. He will get revenge for it. He wonders how it was possible that a young woman's mind could disappear as quickly as an old man's life. A thoughtful and fine person will send a part of themselves after the thing it loves most, which is what Ophelia has done here. Ophelia sings a song about her father's grave, and then points out which flowers are for what purpose. She has rosemary for remembering and pansies for thoughts. She hands fennel and columbines to Gertrude for her adultery and rue for repentance to Claudius. Laertes thinks she almost makes suffering beautiful. She sings once more and then leaves.

Laertes and Claudius share their grief for Ophelia's madness. Claudius sends him to fetch his wisest friends so that they can listen to both of them and decide which person is right. If Claudius is wrong, then he will give up his life, crown and everything he calls his own as payment, but if he is innocent then Laertes must be patient while Claudius assists in his revenge. Laertes agrees. His father's death, the secret funeral and no formal rites call into question the way he died. Claudius agrees with him. They leave.

*Act Four Scene Six*

Horatio and a Servant enter. The Servant tells him Sailors want to speak to them. They have letters for Horatio. The Servant leaves and Sailors enter. A Sailor hands Horatio a letter from Hamlet, which Horatio reads aloud. He must get the Sailors to the King as they have letters for him. When they were at sea, a pirate ship attacked, and they had to fight. Hamlet ended up on board the pirate ship and left the ship behind. The pirates want Hamlet to do something for them. He needs Horatio to come as quickly as he can. The Sailors will take Horatio to Hamlet, and then he has much to say about Rosencrantz and Guildenstern. They all leave.

## Act Four Scene Seven

Claudius and Laertes enter. Claudius tells him he has to acknowledge his innocence and put him in his heart as a friend as he now knows the man who killed Polonius was trying to kill Claudius himself. Laertes doesn't understand why he didn't do anything against the criminal when he was threatening Claudius's own life. Claudius couldn't for two reasons: Gertrude is devoted to him and the public loves Hamlet. Anything he would say against Hamlet would end up hurting Claudius, not Hamlet. Claudius will soon reveal what he has planned.

A Messenger arrives with letters from Hamlet for Claudius and Gertrude. The Messenger tells Claudius that Sailors delivered them. The Messenger leaves, and Claudius reads the letters aloud. Hamlet is returning to Denmark to look into Claudius' eyes and reveal why and how he has returned. Laertes and Claudius have no idea what it means, but Laertes is pleased he will be able to look Hamlet in the eyes and accuse him of Polonius' murder. Claudius has plans for Hamlet's undoing if he returns. When he dies, no one will know it was a murder, and even Gertrude will call it an accident. Laertes only wants to know the plans so that he can be the one who kills Hamlet. Claudius is okay with this as the people have been talking about a good quality of his: that his good qualities didn't arouse envy in the people like Hamlet's good qualities have done. Laertes wonders what quality that is. Claudius reports it is his little ribbon of youth. He talks about a skillful horseman from Normandy he saw who had fantastic abilities riding his horse and performing tricks. Laertes knows the horseman too. The horseman mentioned Laertes to Claudius and admired his fencing skills. Hamlet was extremely jealous of these compliments and talked of nothing at all but having a match against him.

Claudius asks if Laertes loved his father or if his grief is just a painting for his face. Laertes is shocked that he could ask such a question. Claudius has seen some people's love go out over time. He thinks that people should do what they intend to do when they think of it as intentions can be watered down by delays and time. Claudius wonders what proof will Laertes offer in actions rather than words that he is Polonius' son. Laertes will cut Hamlet's throat in Church. Claudius thinks revenge should have no limits, but asks Laertes to stay in his room. They will let Hamlet know he has returned home and let him hear compliments about Laertes' fencing skills. Hamlet won't examine the swords before they fight so Laertes can choose one with a sharp point and avenge Polonius' father. Laertes will do it and place a little poison on the point, as well. No medicine will be able to save anyone pricked with this poison. Claudius will let Laertes know which way would be the best because if people found out about it it would have been best not to try it. Claudius decides that they should get Hamlet to jump around. When he needs a drink, Claudius will have a cup ready for him in case Laertes isn't struck with the sword.

Gertrude enters. She announces that Ophelia has drowned in a brook shadowed over by a willow. Ophelia made wreaths of flowers and fell into the brook. She sang old hymns and lay there like someone who didn't quite realize the danger she was in. Her clothes, heavy with water, pulled her down to the bottom of the brook where she drowned. After Laertes has stopped crying, he will be finished acting like a woman. Laertes leaves.

Claudius thinks they should follow him to try and calm him down. They leave.

# Act 5

## *Act Five Scene One*

A Gravedigger and the Other gravedigger enter. One asks the other if they're seriously going to give Ophelia a Christian burial. They don't understand how this is possible considering that she killed herself. The Gravedigger concludes that she must have known that she was killing herself because she made the decision. The Other wants to argue that point, but the Gravedigger won't have it. The only way she couldn't have drowned herself was if the water came to her, not the other way around. The Other wonders if that is law. It is the Coroner's law. The Other thinks if the girl hadn't been rich, then she wouldn't have been given a Christian burial. The rich have much more freedom to hang themselves if they want or not.

The Gravedigger refers to Adam as a digger. He was the first person with arms. The Other is confused by this because he thought Adam didn't have any arms, and the Gravedigger is amazed he can call himself a Christian and not remember that the Bible said Adam dug in the ground. He couldn't dig in the ground without his arms.

The Gravedigger asks the Other what they could call a person who builds stronger things than other workers. The Other replies that it is the people who build the gallows to hang people as these frames live out a thousand people.

Hamlet and Horatio enter from the distance. The Gravedigger replies that the answer to his question is a gravedigger as he makes houses that will last for forever. He tells the Other to go and get some alcohol. The Gravedigger sings and digs. Hamlet wonders if the Gravedigger knows what he is doing digging a grave while singing. Horatio thinks that he must be so used to graves that he is used to it. Hamlet insults the Gravedigger for his awful singing. As the Gravedigger digs graves and toss skulls, he sings. Hamlet wonders who he could be burying. One of the possibilities is a lawyer who has lost his abilities and legal jargon now that he is dead. He wonders who killed him. He asks the Gravedigger whose grave it is. It is the Gravedigger's. Hamlet thinks it must be as he is lying in it, but is still telling a lie because he's alive and not dead yet. Hamlet pushes the question: who is it that the grave is being dug for? The Gravedigger digs it for someone who is no man, and no woman but used to be a woman. Hamlet is amazed at how precise he has to speak when in conversation with this man. He wonders how long the Gravedigger has been working. He has been working since the day the late King Hamlet defeated Fortinbras. Hamlet wonders how long ago that was. The Gravedigger is amazed he doesn't know: it was the day that young Hamlet was born—the one that turned mad and was carted off to England. The Gravedigger doesn't think it will even matter if he'll recover his sanity in England anyway because everyone in England is mad! Hamlet asks the Gravedigger how Hamlet lost his sanity. He lost it by losing his mind, the Gravedigger answers.

Hamlet asks how long it takes for a man to start rotting in his grave. If he is not rotten before he dies, then the body will last eight or nine years. A leathermaker will last longer because he is leathery from his trade. He shows Hamlet a skull that has been there for twenty three years. It was the skull of Yorick, the king's jester. Hamlet picks up the skull. He is sad because he knew the man. He used to carry Hamlet on his back. He wonders where the man's jokes are now.

Hamlet wonders if Alexander the Great looked like and smelled like Yorick when he was buried. Horatio agrees that he would have. Great men can be reduced to dust and ash. Hamlet is sad for this.

Claudius, Gertrude, Laertes and a coffin, with a Priest and attending Lords enter. Hamlet tells Horatio to be quiet. He wonders whose coffin they are following as it looks like it came from a wealthy family. He decides to stay and watch for a while. Hamlet and Horatio step aside. They notice Laertes is there.

Laertes asks the Priest what rites he will give Ophelia. He has performed as many as he has been permitted to do. If it weren't for the King, Ophelia would have been buried far outside the church graveyard in unsanctified ground. The body deserves to have stones thrown on her, but here Ophelia is dressed like a virgin while the bell tolls for her. The Priest refuses any other rites to be performed as it would be insulting to the other dead buried there. Laertes is convinced that Ophelia will be an angel in Heaven despite what the Priest says. Hamlet overhears this and is amazed that the beautiful Ophelia has died.

Gertrude scatters flowers across Ophelia's grave. She had hoped that Ophelia would be Hamlet's bride and that she would be throwing flowers on their wedding bed, not on her grave. Laertes jumps into the grave and demands that they throw dirt on him and Ophelia so he can die with her.

Hamlet steps forward and jumps into the grave. He and Laertes fight. Hamlet begs him not to fight. Claudius orders them pulled apart. Attendants help pull them apart. Hamlet will fight him until he has no strength left: he loved Ophelia and no love could have matched his. Anything dramatic that Laertes can do in mourning, Hamlet will do tenfold. His grief is far greater. Gertrude thinks him insane.

Hamlet doesn't know why Laertes treats him like he does. He always loved Laertes. He leaves. Horatio goes with him on Claudius' request. Claudius' reminds Laertes about their talk the previous night. Guards will keep watch over Hamlet. And a monument will be erected for Ophelia. In the meantime, they must proceed. They all leave.

## Act Five Scene Two

Hamlet and Horatio enter. Hamlet tells him about the conflict in his heart that wouldn't let him sleep and kept him captive. He thinks that sometimes it is crucial to act on impulse as this shows people that God and fate watch over them and guide them in the right direction even if they are messing up. Hamlet was brave enough to gather the document and letters to the King of England from Claudius and read them. They contained orders for Hamlet's immediate execution. Horatio doesn't think this could be possible. Hamlet shows Horatio a document so he can read the words for himself. Hamlet presses on with his story. He sat down and wrote a brand new letter with new instructions in neat handwriting. He used to think that neat handwriting was only for people of a lower status, but he is glad that he learned how to do it. Hamlet replaced the instructions with a plea to unite England and Denmark in friendships and then as soon as the letter had been read, the people who had delivered it should be executed immediately without time to confess their sins. Horatio wonders how an official seal was put on the letter. Hamlet had his father's signet ring in his pocket which had the Danish seal on it. He folded up the letter and put it back without anyone noticing. The following day the pirates attacked!

Horatio concludes that Rosencrantz and Guildenstern are headed to their deaths. Hamlet doesn't care—they deserved it for what they were doing. Hamlet wonders if Horatio finally sees that he has to kill Claudius for his father's death and the trap to kill Hamlet. It is now within Hamlet's moral right to kill Claudius for his actions. Hamlet is, however, upset that things are bad between him and Laertes, especially as they share similar situations. Laertes over-the-top grief annoyed Hamlet.

Osric, a courtier, enters with a hat in his hand. Hamlet asks Horatio if he knows who this man is. He doesn't. Hamlet thinks that is lucky as Osric is a unpleasant man. He owns a lot of land so is treated well despite his poor manners. Osric has a message for them from Claudius. Hamlet asks to hear it and for him to put his hat back on where it belongs. Osric doesn't want to as it is hot. They quarrel for a few moments about the temperature and whether or not Osric wants to wear his hat until Osric reveals Claudius has placed a large bet on Hamlet winning the match.

Osric complements Laertes for his outstanding abilities and gentlemanly manner. Hamlet thinks trying to list all of Laertes' good qualities would be quite difficult. Hamlet thinks that Laertes would not be able to find an equal unless he looked in the mirror at his own reflection, but he doesn't understand why Osric brought up the subject. After a while of back and forth where Osric fails to understand Hamlet, Osric points out Laertes' particular ability in fencing.

Claudius has bet six Barbary horses and has prepared six French swords and daggers for the match. The swords have excellent "carriages". Hamlet doesn't know what Osric means by this. Osric means the loops to hang swords by. Hamlet would prefer this description as carriage seems to suggest the dragging of cannons. Hamlet asks why the bet has been placed. Osric reveals that Claudius has bet that, in a dozen rounds between Hamlet and Laertes, no more than three hits will be made by Laertes.

Hamlet tells Osric to bring the swords in. He will fight if Claudius and Laertes wants him to. If the King loses his bet, Hamlet will only suffer some embarrassment. Osric leaves to tell the King.

Horatio and Hamlet don't think much of Osric's flowery and ornate way of speaking. Hamlet compares him to other successful people at this time who have collected enough ways to keep him in high esteem without any substance there.

A Lord enters. The King wants to know if Hamlet will play right away or wait. Hamlet will fight anytime. Gertrude wants to talk to Hamlet before he starts the match, however. The Lord leaves.

Horatio thinks Hamlet will lose the bet. Hamlet doesn't think so. He has been practising since Laertes went away to France. Hamlet has a slight doubt, but it doesn't matter. Horatio thinks he shouldn't play if he's not entirely comfortable with the idea. He can tell Claudius he is sick. Hamlet disagrees. Everything will work out as it is meant to. The only thing to do is to be prepared for it.

Claudius, Gertrude, Laertes, Osric and other Lords and attendants enter with trumpets, drums, swords, a table and wine. Claudius asks Hamlet to shake hands with Laertes. They do. Hamlet begs for Laertes' forgiveness as he has done him wrong. When Hamlet insulted him it was because he was mad. If Hamlet wasn't in his right mind, then it wasn't really Hamlet who was insulting him. Instead, it is his madness that is guilty and Hamlet is also a victim of it. Laertes is satisfied by the apology, but he is still unable to forgive Hamlet so quickly for what he did to Polonius and Ophelia. He will not accept any apology until he can do so without harming his name and reputation. He will, however, accept Hamlet's love. Hamlet is grateful for that.

They decide to start the match. Hamlet assures Laertes that he will win as Hamlet is so unskilled at fencing. Laertes thinks he is just making fun, but Hamlet assures him he is serious. Claudius reminds them of the bet. Hamlet thinks he's bet on the weaker man. Claudius isn't worried, but adds that this is the reason for including a handicap for Laertes. He has to outdo Hamlet by three hits to win.

They test the swords. Laertes wants a better sword as his is too heavy. Hamlet likes the one he has and wonders if they are all the same length. Osric assures them they are. Claudius orders the wine to be put on the table. If Hamlet manages to land the first or second hit, then the soldiers can give him a military salute. Claudius will then drink to Hamlet's health and throw a valuable pearl into the cup that cost more than the four last Danish King's crowns. He asks for the trumpets to play and the cannon to fire. This will signal the Heavens who will then tell the Earth that the King drinks to Hamlet's health.

Trumpets play and the fencing match begins. Hamlet makes a hit. Laertes contests it, but Osric calls it a hit in Hamlet's favour. Claudius asks for a goblet, which he places the pearl into. This is for Hamlet. He asks for the goblet to be given to Hamlet, but he won't drink from it just yet. They continue fencing. Hamlet hits Laertes again. Claudius thinks that Hamlet might win. Gertrude thinks he is fat and out of breath. She offers her handkerchief to Hamlet so he can wipe his face. She lifts the cup with the pearl to drink to Hamlet's health. Claudius tells her not to drink it, but it's too late. To himself, Claudius is upset that she has drunk from the poisoned cup. Nothing can save her now. Laertes vows to get Hamlet, but feels guilty for it. Hamlet tells Laertes to get ready for the third hit. He accuses Laertes of treating him like a child. They fence again.

Laertes wounds Hamlet. In a scuffle, they end up with each others' swords and Hamlet wounds Laertes. Claudius orders them separated. Gertrude collapses. Osric calls for help for the Queen. Horatio wonders how the fencers feel as they are both wounded. Laertes feels that he has been caught in his own trap and killed by his own treachery. He falls over. Hamlet wonders how the Queen is. Claudius tells him she fainted at the sight of the blood. Gertrude realizes she has been poisoned by the drink and dies.

Hamlet orders the door locked. He wants to know who did it. Laertes admits that he is the one, and Hamlet is to die too. Nothing can save him, and he has barely a half hour to live. The weapon that caused this is in his hand, sharp and dipped in poison. Laertes' plan has backfired, and he will die. The King is to blame. Hamlet wounds Claudius. Claudius assures everyone he has only been hurt, not killed. Hamlet forces him to drink from the poisoned goblet and follow his mother to death. Claudius dies.

Laertes thinks Claudius got what he deserved as he added the poison himself. He begs for Hamlet's forgiveness and then dies. Hamlet gives him his forgiveness. He tells everyone watching that he could tell them more about what has happened, but he has no time to. He begs Horatio to tell everyone what happened and to set the story straight in Hamlet's name. Horatio refuses: he is more Roman than Danish and will not stay. He will drink the last of the poison from the cup. Hamlet begs him to let go of the goblet. He takes it from him. If Horatio ever loved him, then he would fix Hamlet's wounded name for him and tell the truth.

Military marching can be heard off stage. Hamlet wonders where the noises are coming from. Osric returns to report that young Fortinbras is returning after his victory in Poland. Hamlet will never hear the news from England. He bets that Fortinbras will end up with the Danish throne. Hamlet would vote for him. Hamlet dies. Horatio wishes Hamlet will be sung to sleep by angels.

Fortinbras and the English Ambassador enter with a drummer and attendants. Fortinbras is amazed at what he sees. Horatio calls it a tragedy. The Ambassador is saddened because he will never be able to give them the good news that Rosencrantz and Guildenstern are dead. Who will thank the English for their actions now? Horatio admits that Claudius didn't even know about those orders so the Ambassador would not have had any thanks from him. Horatio tells them that these bodies should be displayed on a platform and let him tell the world what happened here. They will hear tales of supernatural and violent acts, accidents, murders, trickery and plots that backfired. Fortinbras will hear the story right away and invite all the noblemen to listen to it.

Fortinbras has claims to Denmark and will carry them out. Horatio has a few things to tell him about that from Hamlet, but first they will talk about other things. Fortinbras orders Hamlet to be carried like a soldier onto the stage. He thinks that he would have been a fine King. Military music and rites will speak for him. He orders the rest of the bodies to be carried out too as the court looks more like a battlefield. The soldiers should shoot outside to honour Hamlet. They leave, carrying the bodies. Cannons are fired.

# The Life and Times of William Shakespeare

# The Times Shakespeare Lived In

The Elizabethan London that William Shakespeare arrived in was much different than it is today. Significantly, the population was much smaller. Today, seven and a half million people live in the area known as Greater London. In Shakespeare's time the population was around 200,000 – this still made it an enormous metropolis for the time period and it was the leading city in Europe.

In the sixteenth century London suffered from an extremely high death rate – more people died in the city than were born. It was only the steady influx of newcomers from other English counties and immigrants from Europe that helped London's population grow. The bubonic plague was still a large factor in death counts in the city – in fact many people fled the urban area when the many epidemics rolled through. Shakespeare himself probably returned at times to Stratford when it was healthier to do so. The life expectancy in London at the time was thirty-five years; this seemingly short life expectancy would be lengthened if one survived childhood – many children did not make it to their fifth birthday.

London was a crowded and dirty place – it is not surprising that disease was rampant. The houses were built close together and the streets were very narrow – in many cases only wide enough for a single cart to navigate. There was no indoor plumbing and it would be another three hundred years before a sanitary way of disposing of sewage was built for the city of London.

Shakespeare was born into a time of religious upheaval. The Catholic Church came under pressure from the second Tudor ruler, Henry VIII, to annual his first marriage to Catherine of Aragon. Upon the death of his brother Arthur and Henry's ascendancy to the heir to the English throne, he had married his brother's widow in 1509. Over the years Catherine had given birth to only one surviving heir – a daughter Mary. Twenty-four years later, Henry asked for a divorce so he could marry the young Anne Boleyn. The Pope refused and in 1534 Henry broke from the Church, establishing the Church of England. The throne went to Henry's son Edward VI in 1547 but upon the boy's death in 1553, his half-sister Mary, daughter of Henry and Catherine, became Queen. She was a devout Catholic, and plunged the country back into a period of dissension and conflict, which included persecution and death for Protestants and the re-establishment of the Roman Catholic Church.

Queen Mary's death changed the religious *status quo* in England once again when Queen Elizabeth I came to the throne in 1558. The Catholic Church was once again banned, and the Church of England resurrected in its stead.

England also faced a turning point in its very political existence during Shakespeare's "lost years", those years before his arrival in London when his little is known about his life. In 1588, after Elizabeth I had condemned her cousin Mary, Queen of Scots, to death for conspiracy Spain decided to attack Britain in retaliation for the Roman Catholic Mary's death. The Catholic powers were increasingly fearful of the Protestant movement and with England's break from the Church of Rome now seemingly the final stroke in their relationship, it looked as though Catholicism itself was under threat. Spain rose of fleet of ships to sail upon England and it was thought to be unbeatable. However several factors led to English victory – strategic mistakes on the Spanish side and poor weather were among them. England emerged triumphant, its confidence strong, and the Church of England firmly entrenched. Queen Elizabeth I, known as "Gloriana" always serves as a backdrop to any story of Shakespeare's life. An interesting development during her reign was the acceleration of literacy in Elizabethan England – by the end of her reign, it stood at 33% (probably for males only) and was one of the highest rates in the world.

Queen Elizabeth's reign ended in 1603, when she died in her sleep at the age of sixty-nine. Her cousin's son,

James I of Scotland became England's king. He was devoutly Protestant so there was no change in the official Church, and indeed by the beginning of the 17th century, few English citizens had ever attended a Catholic mass.

James enthusiastically supported drama and in particular, Shakespeare's company. Over the next thirteen years, before William's death, the playwright's company would perform for the King one hundred and eighty seven times. It was the time of Shakepeare's greatest dramatic output.

Much information on the London theatres of the day has been gleaned from the journal and business papers of Philip Henslowe, who owned the Rose and Fortune theatres. For his papers we can extrapolate what life for actors and playwrights would have been like during Shakespeare's time. We also know something of the Fortune Theatre's building – the contract to build it has survived. These records were used to build the copy of the Globe Theatre that stands on the banks of the Thames River today. Other information has come from existing diaries and letters that survived the time – mostly from visitors to the city who found the whole experience interesting enough to record.

# Shakepeare's Family

William Shakespeare, the son of John Shakespeare and Mary, née Arden, was born in the village of Stratford-upon-Avon in the English county of Warwickshire. Stratford is northwest of London, situated somewhat south of England's center. Shakespeare was born quite possibly on 23 Apr in 1564 – his baptism in the family's parish church on April 26 suggests this. Children in that day and age were often baptized on the third day after their birth.

William was John and Mary's third known child – and the first to survive infancy. His two older sisters, Joan and Margaret, both died before he was born. Of the five younger children (Gilbert, a second Joan, Anne, Richard, and Edmund) Anne died at the age of eight but William's other siblings lived into adulthood. Only the second Joan was to reach what we would consider a good old age – she died in 1646 at the age of seventy-seven.

William's background on his paternal side was, like most of the English of his day, humble. Earlier relatives were not gentry in the least but simple tenant farmers who worked in the parish of nearby Arden. The meaning of the name Shakespeare has long been shrouded in mystery – the rarity of the surname indicates that it probably originated with one man several hundred years before William's birth. Evidence shows that the first Shakespeare was born somewhere north of Warwickshire. By 1389 an Adam Shakespeare was a tenant farmer at Baddesley Clinton in Warwickshire – unfortunately early parish records were not compelled to be kept until not long before William's time so it is not known for sure if he was a direct ancestor. In 1596 William's father John applied for a family coat of arms, citing that his grandfather had been granted land in northern Warwickshire for service under Henry VII in the War of the Roses. Historians believe this was probably a valid claim, but no records have come to light that prove it.

William was the grandson of Richard Shakespeare, a tenant farmer at Snitterfield in Arden who was not a wealthy man but did leave a will in which he named John Shakespeare as administrator, which would indicate he was the eldest surviving son. By the time of Richard's death in 1560, John had been living at nearby Stratford-upon-Avon since 1550. Records show that John had his first house in Henley Street in Stratford by 1552 and had acquired the house next door and one in Greenhill Street by 1556. John's trade was that of a glove-maker and he also worked as a wool dealer and an animal skin-cutter. He may have also worked as a butcher - it would seem that he was a man who was not afraid of work and had some ambition to better himself.

Around 1557 John Shakespeare married Mary Arden, the daughter of the owner of the Snitterfield estate where his father Richard Shakespeare farmed. Mary was the youngest of the eight daughters of Robert Arden – apparently Robert had a hand in marrying his daughters off and John must have seemed a likely prospect at the time – certainly on the social scale the Ardens would have been higher than the Shakespeares.

On his mother's side at least, William's roots in the area were deep. Just to the north of the River Avon is the village of Arden, from which Mary's family undoubtedly took their name. Surnames were beginning to be "set" about four hundred years before William's birth; it is probable that that branch of the family had been in the area for at least that long.

William's grandfather Robert Arden was a man of some means, at least locally. He owned several estates, including the one where Richard Shakespeare was a tenant farmer. The Ardens were Roman Catholic – England at the time was seesawing between the old Catholic Church and Protestantism. Although the marriage is not found in a surviving record, it is likely that it took place at Aston Cantlow where Mary's father had been buried in 1556 and the ceremony would have been a Catholic one, as Mary Tudor, who had brought Catholicism back to

England as the official church, was on the throne. Not long before William's birth in 1564 Elizabeth I became Queen of England and the country made the final break with Roman Catholicism, and the local parish church became part of the new Church of England.

# Shakespeare's Childhood and Education

William Shakespeare's accepted birth date of April 23, 1564 has long been open to dispute, but the month and year are probably correct. There are two reasons April 23rd is the sentimental favorite: it is St. George's Day in England (George is the country's patron saint) and Shakespeare died on the same date fifty-two years later. Baby William was baptized on the 26th of April in the parish church of Stratford-upon-Avon and as infants in Tudor times were traditionally baptized on the third day following their birth, historians have happily settled on the 23rd as his date of birth.

William was the third of eight known children born to John Shakespeare and Mary (Arden) Shakespeare, and the first to survive infancy. In fact young William's first year was overshadowed by the spectre of the Black Death, now known more prosaically as the bubonic plague. About 10% of the residents of Stratford died that year and the Shakespeares' must have felt relief their young family's survival. The plague was to continue to be a problem for England's citizens during the Elizabethan era. William was to lose his younger sister, eight-year-old Anne, to the disease. Quite possibly his older sister Margaret, a one-year-old baby, died of the Black Death as well, as it swept through the area in 1563. The survival of William, as the first born son, and after the deaths of older sisters Joan and Margaret, no doubt gave him a special place in the Shakespeare family.

William's childhood home, in Henley Street, Stratford, is still standing and is a typical Tudor structure with decorative half timber and small windows. In Shakespeare's time the house would have had a thatched roof. Henley Street led out of town and William apparently spent much time as a boy wandering and playing the countryside near at hand. He undoubtedly spoke the local dialect and though his own speech was probably more refined due to his education - and undoubtedly influenced by his mother, who came from a higher social stratum than the Shakespeares – William retained a good "ear" for dialectic speech which is evident in his plays and apparently retained his Warwickshire accent until his death.

William's life as a youngster was rural. His father was a craftsman and a tradesman – a glover and maker of leather goods – and records show that neighbors included a tailor and a haberdasher. But also nearby was a blacksmith – who's trade in those times would have been mostly horses – and shepherds lived nearby. As William rambled around the countryside he would have come into contact with the rural inhabitants of various occupations and he would have been well versed in the area's flora and fauna. It is very likely that he knew all the local fairy stories and tales of ghosts, witches, and hobgoblins, which England's rural denizens of the era were particularly fond of these stories. William's later writings show that he was well acquainted with the terms and practices of the rural pursuits of hunting and fishing – like most of his male contemporaries of the time, the young William probably spent many a happy hour engaged in these activities.

As the son of an alderman, William was entitled to a free education. His father John had become an alderman when William was just a baby – John was appointed to replace another alderman who got himself into trouble with the town council. By 1568 he was elected as an alderman and three years later was chief alderman and deputy to the local bailiff (the town's top magistrate). John was involved in local politics for many years, and although his fortunes and position faltered in later years, his son William was guaranteed the best education Stratford could offer.

William's learning took place at King's New School – which is still operating as a boy's school today. The school was originally granted a charter in 1553 by the learned young King Edward VI – a number of schools were erected in his name. It is thought the school was the last of the King Edward Schools as the adolescent Edward died only nine days after its charter was granted. It was familiarly known as the King's New School, and sometimes shortened even more to New School. Today it is known as King Edward VI School (or K.E.S.) and while no records exist from Shakespeare's time, it is generally accepted that William was a pupil and would have begun his education there around 1570 about the time he turned six years old.

The average school day for the middle class boys of Stratford was not an easy one. Students arrived early in the morning, not long after dawn, and remained in school until 5 PM. Breaks were given for meals. The boys also attended school on Saturdays. Church attendance was part of the school day, and much time was given over to the learning of the classical languages and translating classical texts. The Roman poet Ovid made a strong impression on young William. Classical mythology is evident in William's later works and no doubt their influence can be traced back to those formative days in Stratford's New School.

William probably left school around the age of fifteen. What he did then has not been documented but in the normal course of things, he would have worked for his father, at least for a time. He may have also been a school master – his facility with words and his sharp intellect would have made him a good candidate – but perhaps it was simply not his avocation and as time would prove, writing was. Within a few years, though, William was married. Marriage at eighteen in those days was relatively rare – physical maturation coming later to the young of that era compared to today. William, however, had been courting an older woman, and as nature took its course, Anne Hathaway became pregnant. Pregnant brides were common among the rural population – in fact many believed that fertility should be proven before heading for the altar! William Shakespeare and Anne Hathaway were married by license and as William was under twenty-one, he had to obtain his father's consent to marry. The actual parish where their wedding ceremony took place is not known, though it may have been in Shottery, Anne's home parish.

# Shakepeare's Adulthood

By the time William Shakespeare was twenty-one years old, he had become the father of three children. His wife Anne gave birth to daughter Susanna in May 1583 and to twins Judith and Hamnet early in 1785. William does appear in an existing legal record for Stratford concerning property owned by his parents in 1786. Unfortunately very little else is on record for the years before he appears in London.

William most likely remained in Stratford for the first few years of his marriage and his knowledge of leather indicates that he probably worked with his glove-making father after he left school. The story that he had been a school master or tutor has long been conjectured. A story of William teaching in a more the Catholic-friendly county of Lancashire has been bandied about. None of the stories have any real evidence to back them up, however.

William and Anne lived in the house on Henley Street with his parents. It is hard to conceive that he would have deserted his wife and children when the latter were so young – William came from a comfortable solidly middle class family and he would have likely been taught to fulfill his responsibilities. Shakespeare may have spent his working career in London, and hints of philandering came forth, but he always remained faithful to Stratford and returned often and in middle age, he returned for good. How happy or unhappy he and Anne were together is simply not known. The fact that no children were born to Anne after the twins arrived may speak volumes – but it may also simply be that the birth of twins rendered her unable to have more children. That William did send home much of his acquired wealth in London does at least indicate that he had not entirely deserted his family responsibilities – but whether it was done out of love or duty, we do not have any way of knowing. The years between 1585 and 1592 are considered Shakespeare's "lost years". Simply put, there is no hard evidence of what William was doing during those years.

We also know little about William's wife Anne – she was one of seven children of Richard Hathaway, a yeoman farmer. She was left a small sum of money in his will when he died the year before her marriage and she was to come into this inheritance upon her marriage. The house she grew up in, known as Anne Hathaway's Cottage, is now open to the public, but is more than a mere cottage, having twelve rooms. It is about a mile from the center of Stratford. Anne's gravestone is still in existence as well, and from it her approximate date of birth is calculated – it records that she died in 1623, aged sixty-seven. No verified portraits of her exist and there is no known written description of what she looked like. Some Shakespearean experts believe that Sonnet 145 was written for Anne – the sonnet only really makes sense when the reader understands the wordplay with "hate" and "away" – close enough to mimic her surname, Hathaway.

What were William's influences before he arrived in London to make his way in the world of drama? Certainly he had enjoyed a classical education as a lad and some historians that theorized that he was somehow exposed to more in his late teens and twenties – even if only as a schoolmaster. As for the world of the stage, despite Shakespeare living in a somewhat isolated and rural area, it was quite common for bands of actors to be traveling the countryside plying their trade. These plague haunted years drove many people out of London and into the healthier countryside and actors had to make a living too. They were not above staging performances wherever they could gather enough people to pay the entrance fee. Actors were usually required to have a patron and many wore a badge that identified him as such – this kept the local authorities from looking upon actors as a liability to their parishes. The companies were often sponsored by men of means and even by the nobility. The first acting company created in the reign of Queen Elizabeth I (who came to the throne in 1558) was Lord Leicester's Men in 1574 – the Earls of Sussex and Oxford also had companies by 1582. There was rivalry between the companies and apparently, the Lord Mayor of London disliked the acting groups intensely. Unfortunately, few records for the acting companies have survived.

At least one acting company, The Queen's Men, put in more than one appearance at Stratford in 1589 – and if William was still living there, he very well could have attended their performances. Again, precisely why Shakespeare went to London is not known – but he may have simply been seduced by the theatre life and combined with his love of words it would have seemed the perfect home for him. Again, conjecture comes into deciding Shakespeare's life (one theory has it that William had clung to the old Catholic ways and went to northern England where there was more toleration) but his reasons for going to London remain a mystery. Fortunately for the literary world, he *was* drawn to the theatre and left a stunning literary legacy.

What did William do once he reached London? Again, we don't know for sure, as there are few employment records that have survived from centuries past. Shakespeare did appear in the London in the late 1580's and if he was immediately attracted to the theatre, he would have headed to Southwark, on the south side of the Thames, where many of the restrictions of the city of London did not apply. The entertainment industry of its day was free to do as they wanted there. A tradition has survived down through the centuries that William first got a job holding horses outside the theatre and then moved up to be a prompter's assistant. It is known that within a few years William was "becoming Shakespeare" and was writing.

With so many blanks to fill in his life and so very little solid evidence of Shakespeare's very existence at this point, how is it known that he was writing by 1592? It is thanks to one Robert Greene, another London writer. Greene published an attack on William, accusing him of plagiarism and calling him an "upstart crow". Greene parodied some lines from the history play *Henry VI Part III* and intimated that Shakespeare was stealing from his competition. Greene died soon after this, but the publisher of the attack apologized in print – which indicates that William, still a young man at twenty-eight, had enough of a reputation or at least enough gall, to demand a retraction.

If *Henry VI Part III* had already been written by 1592, there is a good chance that Parts I and II had already been penned as well. This accomplishment would have been remarkable for such a young man, and one who had not attended university as well. His lack of higher education seemed to be an issue with some of his contemporary writers – snobbism not being exclusive to the modern world. Fellow writers, who looked at Shakespeare critically and no doubt enviously, included Christopher Marlowe and Thomas Nashe.

*Henry VI Part III* was not William's first play. *The Two Gentlemen of Verona* was written sometime between 1588 and 1590. Although it is difficult to determine exactly when many of his early plays were written, it is thought that *A Comedy of Errors* might have been his first comedic play and could have been written as early as 1591. In 1594, Shakespeare created Titus Andronicus, his first attempt at tragedy.

There is nothing in the scant surviving records to suggest that William worked for a theatrical company during his early years in London. It is very likely he worked as a freelance writer, as many of contemporaries of the time did. Looking again at his private life, it is possible that during his early years he was returning home to Stratford at regular intervals.

It is thought that during his early years, he worked with other writers to produce collaborative works. *Sir Thomas More*, a historical play about the martyred Thomas More who was executed by Henry VIII, was co-written with Anthony Munday and Henry Chettle, the latter being the very publisher who retracted Robert Greene's accusation of plagiarism in 1592. Experts believe this was written during Shakespeare's early period.

It is known that it didn't take long for William's work to attract the interest of several different theatrical companies. *Titus Andronicus* was first performed by Sussex's Men. Pembroke's Men also performed several of William's plays and at least two known performance venues are on record – The Inns of Court and the Bankside Rose playhouse. Some Shakespearean historians believe that William had joined the Queen's Men on tour before he arrived in London – some of his later plays are similar to plays they performed in the mid 1580's.

The theatres of London were not a stable entity in the 1590's. Once again, the pall of the plague hung over the city in the summer of 1592. The Puritans, a Protestant faction that had gained some power in the Elizabethan era, despised what they saw as the licentiousness of theatre life and pressured the city to shut down acting venues in London and Southwark. They blamed the theatres for spreading the Plague. The theatres remained closed for two years.

Whether William remained in London for the duration of the Plague years is unknown, but it is known that he turned to writing poetry. In 1593 the rather racy poem *Venus and Adonis* appeared and was dedicated to Henry Wriothesley, the Earl of Southampton. The Earl was a patron of the arts – he supported several poets and often attended the theatre. Shakespeare may have looked upon him as opportunity knocking; after all, having a patron was easier that freelancing. It has been conjectured that Shakespeare's poems were written to Wriothesley as expressions of love and passion; many have conjectured that Shakespeare had homosexual or bisexual leanings. This could be or it might just be that Shakespeare saw an opportunity and wrote what Wriothesley wanted. Without solid evidence, it is impossible to know.

Shakespeare also dedicated the more serious and tragic poem *The Rape of Lucrece* to Wriothesley in 1594. It was about a Roman married woman who is raped by a Roman prince – she then commits suicide. The Rape of Lucrece was not quite as successful as Venus and Adonis but by now Shakespeare's reputation as a writer was established.

William returned to play writing once the Plague had died down again by the fall of 1594. A new theatrical company was formed by Lord Hunsdon (who was Queen Elizabeth's Lord Chamberlain), and called the Chamberlain's Men. Evidence has survived that indicate that Shakespeare was part of the company. Richard Burbage was also part of Chamberlain's Men – he became the company's star actor and would be the lead in many of the Shakespeare plays that they performed. Many of the actors who belonged to the company also had a financial stake in it.

The Chamberlain's Men did well from the start. They first performed for theatre-owner Philip Henslowe in 1594 and were on the bill at Court later that year over the Christmas season. The Chamberlain's Men main rival in London's theatre world was the Admiral's Men and between the two of them, they put on all theatrical performances in the city.

Lord Chamberlain's Men now had a base at the Shoreditch Theatre on the London side of the Thames River. This was an important factor for the rest of William's career – it now settled down to something of permanence. Shakespeare was an asset to the company – he brought in his body of work that could serve as part of the company's repertoire for years to come. William produced about two plays a year until he left London to live out his final days in Stratford.

The first Shakespeare play that was a success after the Plague years was *Richard III*, another history play that chronicled the downfall of the Plantagenet royal house and opened the door for the rise of the Tudor dynasty. No doubt this play was popularly supported by the monarch and her Court of the time. Three other well-regarded and often performed plays were thought to have been written during William's first years with the Chamberlain's Men – *A Midsummer Night's Dream, Romeo and Juliet, Love's Labour Lost*, and *Richard II*. The variety of comedy, tragedy, and history plays reflect Shakespeare's talent and versatility. Around this time Shakespeare garnered high praise from a fellow writer Francis Meres. Meres made reference to William's sonnets, which were not actually published for another eleven years.

Tragedy struck the Shakespeare family in 1596 when William and Anne's only son Hamnet. In 1597 William, obviously enjoying some material success with his writing career, purchased a larger house in Stratford, New Place, the second largest estate in the parish. Shakespeare still spent much of his time in London but as the years went on, he returned to Stratford more and more. The playwright was not only a creative type – he had a keen business sense, as well, or possibly good advisors. He invested in property, and by 1599 he was part owner of the Globe Theatre, forever afterward associated with Shakespeare.

After the Globe Theatre was built in 1599 Shakespeare became a prominent member of the King's Men – the company was sponsored by the King himself, James I, when he ascended the throne in 1603. The company was commanded to produce and perform plays "for our (the King's) solace and pleasure". Shakespeare produced a great body of work over the next ten years. The Globe burned down during a performance of Henry VIII (a fired canon caused the thatched roof to catch fire). No one was killed, and the Globe was rebuilt soon after. At about this time, after investing in the new theatre, Shakespeare retired to spend most of his time in Stratford. He died at New Place on his 52$^{nd}$ birthday. He was survived by his wife, two daughters, two sons-in-law, and a grandchild. His wife Anne outlived him, dying in 1623. One of the few official documentation of Shakepeare's to have survived is his will – in which he left his wife "his second-best bed" (by law, she would have also inherited one-third of his estate). William and Anne were survived by their two daughters, both married and who would leave descendants.

# Modern Version of the Play

# Characters

Claudius, King of Denmark.

Hamlet, Son to the former, and Nephew to the present King.

Polonius, Lord Chamberlain.

Horatio, Friend to Hamlet.

Laertes, Son to Polonius.

Voltimand, Courtier.

Cornelius, Courtier.

Rosencrantz, Courtier.

Guildenstern, Courtier.

Osric, Courtier.

A Gentleman, Courtier.

A Priest.

Marcellus, Officer.

Bernardo, Officer.

Francisco, a Soldier

Reynaldo, Servant to Polonius.

Players.

Two Clowns, Grave-diggers.

Fortinbras, Prince of Norway.

A Captain.

English Ambassadors.

Ghost of Hamlet's Father.

Gertrude, Queen of Denmark, and Mother of Hamlet.

Ophelia, Daughter to Polonius.

Lords, Ladies, Officers, Soldiers, Sailors, Messengers, and other Attendants.

# Act I

# Scene I
*Elsinore. A platform before the castle*

FRANCISCO at his post. Enter to him BERNARDO

**BERNARDO**

*Who's there?*

Who's there?

**FRANCISCO**

*No, you answer me. Identify yourself.*

Nay, answer me: stand, and unfold yourself.

**BERNARDO**

*I am an officer in the king's court.*

Long live the king!

**FRANCISCO**

*Bernardo, is that you?*

Bernardo?

**BERNARDO**

*Yes.*

He.

**FRANCISCO**

*You are late.*

You come most carefully upon your hour.

**BERNARDO**

*It's only twelve o' clock. Go to bed already, Francisco.*

'Tis now struck twelve; get thee to bed, Francisco.


**FRANCISCO**

*Thanks. It's cold and I am sick of it.*

For this relief much thanks: 'tis bitter cold,
And I am sick at heart.


**BERNARDO**

*Have things been quiet on your guard?*

Have you had quiet guard?


**FRANCISCO**

*Quiet as a mouse.*

Not a mouse stirring.


**BERNARDO**

*Well, good night. If you see Horatio and Marcellus, tell them to hurry up.*

Well, good night.
If you do meet Horatio and Marcellus,
The rivals of my watch, bid them make haste.


**FRANCISCO**

*I think I hear them now. Stop! Who's there?*

I think I hear them. Stand, ho! Who's there?


Enter HORATIO and MARCELLUS

## HORATIO

*We are friends.*

Friends to this ground.


## MARCELLUS

*And we work for the Dane.*

And liegemen to the Dane.


## FRANCISCO

*Be on your way then.*

Give you good night.


## MARCELLUS

*Goodbye, soldier. Who has relieved you?*

O, farewell, honest soldier:
Who hath relieved you?


## FRANCISCO

*Bernardo took my place. Good night.*

Bernardo has my place.
Give you good night.


Exit


## MARCELLUS

*Hey! Bernardo!*

Holla! Bernardo!

## BERNARDO

*What? Is that you, Horatio?*

Say,
What, is Horatio there?

## HORATIO

*A part of me is here.*

A piece of him.

## BERNARDO

*Welcome, Horatio and Marcellus.*

Welcome, Horatio: welcome, good Marcellus.

## MARCELLUS

*Has that thing appeared again tonight?*

What, has this thing appear'd again to-night?

## BERNARDO

*I haven't seen anything.*

I have seen nothing.

## MARCELLUS

*Horatio doesn't believe me; says it is all in my head. We have seen the ghost twice, so I invited him to stand guard with us tonight. If the apparition comes, he will see for himself.*

Horatio says 'tis but our fantasy,
And will not let belief take hold of him
Touching this dreaded sight, twice seen of us:
Therefore I have entreated him along
With us to watch the minutes of this night;
That if again this apparition come,
He may approve our eyes and speak to it.

## HORATIO

*Nonsense. It will not appear again.*

Tush, tush, 'twill not appear.

## BERNARDO

*Let's sit down and we will tell you, although you are skeptical, what we have seen the last two nights.*

Sit down awhile;
And let us once again assail your ears,
That are so fortified against our story
What we have two nights seen.

## HORATIO

*Ok, let's sit. I will listen to Bernardo's story.*

Well, sit we down,
And let us hear Bernardo speak of this.

## BERNARDO

*Last night, about one o'clock, with the light from that star in the west, Marcellus and I—*

Last night of all,
When yond same star that's westward from the pole
Had made his course to illume that part of heaven
Where now it burns, Marcellus and myself,
The bell then beating one,--

Enter Ghost

## MARCELLUS

*Be quiet. Look, here it comes again!*

Peace, break thee off; look, where it comes again!

**BERNARDO**

*It looks just like the dead king.*

In the same figure, like the king that's dead.

**MARCELLUS**

*You are smart, Horatio, speak to it.*

Thou art a scholar; speak to it, Horatio.

**BERNARDO**

*It does look like the king; doesn't it, Horatio?*

Looks it not like the king? mark it, Horatio.

**HORATIO**

*It does, and I'm both scared and curious.*

Most like: it harrows me with fear and wonder.

**BERNARDO**

*It acts like it wants to say something.*

It would be spoke to.

**MARCELLUS**

*Ask it something, Horatio.*

Question it, Horatio.

**HORATIO**

*What are you out at the time of night ready for war and resembling the dead king of Denmark? In the name of God, say something!*

What art thou that usurp'st this time of night,
Together with that fair and warlike form

In which the majesty of buried Denmark
Did sometimes march? by heaven I charge thee, speak!

## MARCELLUS

*It is offended.*

It is offended.

## BERNARDO

*See, it's going away!*

See, it stalks away!

## HORATIO

*Wait, stay. Speak! I command you to speak!*

Stay! speak, speak! I charge thee, speak!

Exit Ghost

## MARCELLUS

*It's gone and would not say anything.*

'Tis gone, and will not answer.

## BERNARDO

*What do you think now, Horatio? You look a little pale and scared. You think it's more than some fantasy?*

How now, Horatio! you tremble and look pale:
Is not this something more than fantasy?
What think you on't?

## HORATIO

*I swear, I never would have believed if I hadn't seen it with my own eyes.*

Before my God, I might not this believe
Without the sensible and true avouch
Of mine own eyes.


**MARCELLUS**

*Doesn't it look like the king?*

Is it not like the king?


**HORATIO**

*I know that armor as well as I know myself. He wore it during the battle with Norway when he killed the Polacks on their sleds. So strange.*

As thou art to thyself:
Such was the very armour he had on
When he the ambitious Norway combated;
So frown'd he once, when, in an angry parle,
He smote the sledded Polacks on the ice.
'Tis strange.


**MARCELLUS**

*This is the second time at this very hour that it has walked around like a soldier.*

Thus twice before, and jump at this dead hour,
With martial stalk hath he gone by our watch.


**HORATIO**

*I don't know what this means, but I have a funny feeling something is going to happen in our country.*

In what particular thought to work I know not;
But in the gross and scope of my opinion,
This bodes some strange eruption to our state.


**MARCELLUS**

*Okay, let's sit down and talk about what is going on. Why do we stand guard every night, and why are cannons being made? Why are we buying foreign weapons and ships are being built every day of the week. Do you think something is about to happen?*

Good now, sit down, and tell me, he that knows,
Why this same strict and most observant watch
So nightly toils the subject of the land,
And why such daily cast of brazen cannon,
And foreign mart for implements of war;
Why such impress of shipwrights, whose sore task
Does not divide the Sunday from the week;
What might be toward, that this sweaty haste
Doth make the night joint-labourer with the day:
Who is't that can inform me?


**HORATIO**

*I think I know. As you know, the king, we just saw in his ghostly form, was the enemy of Fortinbras, the king of Norway. Fortinbras dared the king to fight and was killed by the seemingly valiant Hamlet. According to a signed contract, Fortinbras forfeited his land, as well as his life, to his conqueror. Our king had signed a similar contract. Now, his son, the young Fortinbras, seeks revenge and the return of his father's land. He has commissioned the help of some lawless men. I think that is the reason for the frenzy of activity, including our watch and the procurement of weapons.*

That can I;
At least, the whisper goes so. Our last king,
Whose image even but now appear'd to us,
Was, as you know, by Fortinbras of Norway,
Thereto prick'd on by a most emulate pride,
Dared to the combat; in which our valiant Hamlet--
For so this side of our known world esteem'd him--
Did slay this Fortinbras; who by a seal'd compact,
Well ratified by law and heraldry,
Did forfeit, with his life, all those his lands
Which he stood seized of, to the conqueror:
Against the which, a moiety competent
Was gaged by our king; which had return'd
To the inheritance of Fortinbras,
Had he been vanquisher; as, by the same covenant,
And carriage of the article design'd,
His fell to Hamlet. Now, sir, young Fortinbras,
Of unimproved mettle hot and full,
Hath in the skirts of Norway here and there
Shark'd up a list of lawless resolutes,
For food and diet, to some enterprise
That hath a stomach in't; which is no other--
As it doth well appear unto our state--
But to recover of us, by strong hand
And terms compulsatory, those foresaid lands
So by his father lost: and this, I take it,

Is the main motive of our preparations,
The source of this our watch and the chief head
Of this post-haste and romage in the land.


**BERNARDO**

*I think you're right. That explains why the king, responsible for these wars, comes walking around in his armor on our watch.*

I think it be no other but e'en so:
Well may it sort that this portentous figure
Comes armed through our watch; so like the king
That was and is the question of these wars.


**HORATIO**

*There is definitely trouble brewing. Even in the great city of Rome, before the murder of Julius Caesar, the dead arose from their graves and walked the streets, speaking gibberish. There were other signs and omens, too, like shooting stars and solar eclipses. The fates are warning us. But wait! Here comes the ghost again! (Enter Ghost.) I'll go to it, even though I don't want to. Stay, ghost. If you can, speak to me. If there is anything I can do to ease your pain, tell me. Or, if you know something that would help our country, please speak. If you have some hidden treasure here on earth, which makes you uneasy, let us help you. (The cock crows.) Stay and speak! Stop the ghost, Marcellus.*

A mote it is to trouble the mind's eye.
In the most high and palmy state of Rome,
A little ere the mightiest Julius fell,
The graves stood tenantless and the sheeted dead
Did squeak and gibber in the Roman streets:
As stars with trains of fire and dews of blood,
Disasters in the sun; and the moist star
Upon whose influence Neptune's empire stands
Was sick almost to doomsday with eclipse:
And even the like precurse of fierce events,
As harbingers preceding still the fates
And prologue to the omen coming on,
Have heaven and earth together demonstrated
Unto our climatures and countrymen.--
But soft, behold! lo, where it comes again!

Re-enter Ghost

I'll cross it, though it blast me. Stay, illusion!
If thou hast any sound, or use of voice,
Speak to me:
If there be any good thing to be done,

That may to thee do ease and grace to me,
Speak to me:

Cock crows

If thou art privy to thy country's fate,
Which, happily, foreknowing may avoid, O, speak!
Or if thou hast uphoarded in thy life
Extorted treasure in the womb of earth,
For which, they say, you spirits oft walk in death,
Speak of it: stay, and speak! Stop it, Marcellus.


## MARCELLUS

*Should I hit it with my sword?*

Shall I strike at it with my partisan?


## HORATIO

*Yes, if it doesn't stop.*

Do, if it will not stand.


## BERNARDO

*It's here!*

'Tis here!


## HORATIO

*It's here!*

'Tis here!


## MARCELLUS

*It's gone! (Exit Ghost.) We shouldn't have used force on the ghost of the king. Anyway, it is an apparition and can't be touched. We were stupid to think otherwise.*

'Tis gone!

*Exit Ghost*

We do it wrong, being so majestical,
To offer it the show of violence;
For it is, as the air, invulnerable,
And our vain blows malicious mockery.

## BERNARDO

*It was about to speak when the cock crowed.*

It was about to speak, when the cock crew.

## HORATIO

*And then it started to act scared like someone guilty of a crime. I have heard when the cock crows, a sign that day is approaching, ghosts must return to where their spirits are confined. We just saw that for ourselves.*

And then it started like a guilty thing
Upon a fearful summons. I have heard,
The cock, that is the trumpet to the morn,
Doth with his lofty and shrill-sounding throat
Awake the god of day; and, at his warning,
Whether in sea or fire, in earth or air,
The extravagant and erring spirit his
To his confine: and of the truth herein
This present object made probation.

## MARCELLUS

*It also started to fade when the cock crowed. Some say, at Christmas, the rooster crows all night long, and ghosts, fairies, and witches are too fearful to work, because the time is so sacred.*

It faded on the crowing of the cock.
Some say that ever 'gainst that season comes
Wherein our Saviour's birth is celebrated,
The bird of dawning singeth all night long:
And then, they say, no spirit dares stir abroad;
The nights are wholesome; then no planets strike,
No fairy takes, nor witch hath power to charm,
So hallow'd and so gracious is the time.

## HORATIO

*I have heard that, too, and partially believe it. But, the morning is near, and I think we should tell Hamlet what we have seen. The spirit does not know us, but I bet my life, he will speak to him. Do you agree we should tell Hamlet about the ghost?*

So have I heard and do in part believe it.
But, look, the morn, in russet mantle clad,
Walks o'er the dew of yon high eastward hill:
Break we our watch up; and by my advice,
Let us impart what we have seen to-night
Unto young Hamlet; for, upon my life,
This spirit, dumb to us, will speak to him.
Do you consent we shall acquaint him with it,
As needful in our loves, fitting our duty?


**MARCELLUS**

*Let's do it, and I know where he is this morning, a most convenient place.*

Let's do't, I pray; and I this morning know
Where we shall find him most conveniently.

Exeunt

# Scene II
*A room of state in the castle*

Enter KING CLAUDIUS, QUEEN GERTRUDE, HAMLET, POLONIUS, LAERTES, VOLTIMAND, CORNELIUS, Lords, and Attendants

**KING CLAUDIUS**

*Although we are still mourning our dear brother Hamlet's death, and the country is joined by grief, we must remember to continue on in life. It is with both sadness and joy, that I have married my sister-in-law, as you all advised. For your wisdom, I thank you. Now, as you all know, the young Fortinbras thinks since the king has died, we are in vulnerable state. He has sent letters stating his desire to regain the land his father lost in battle to Hamlet. So, I have written a letter to his uncle, the poor bed-ridden fellow, to let him know what Fortinbras is planning. The letter asks his uncle, who in the head of Norway, to stop his nephew. I ask of you, Cornelius and Votimand, to deliver this letter and nothing else. Please be quick in fulfilling your duty.*

Though yet of Hamlet our dear brother's death
The memory be green, and that it us befitted
To bear our hearts in grief and our whole kingdom
To be contracted in one brow of woe,
Yet so far hath discretion fought with nature
That we with wisest sorrow think on him,
Together with remembrance of ourselves.
Therefore our sometime sister, now our queen,
The imperial jointress to this warlike state,
Have we, as 'twere with a defeated joy,--
With an auspicious and a dropping eye,
With mirth in funeral and with dirge in marriage,
In equal scale weighing delight and dole,--
Taken to wife: nor have we herein barr'd
Your better wisdoms, which have freely gone
With this affair along. For all, our thanks.
Now follows, that you know, young Fortinbras,
Holding a weak supposal of our worth,
Or thinking by our late dear brother's death
Our state to be disjoint and out of frame,
Colleagued with the dream of his advantage,
He hath not fail'd to pester us with message,
Importing the surrender of those lands
Lost by his father, with all bonds of law,
To our most valiant brother. So much for him.
Now for ourself and for this time of meeting:
Thus much the business is: we have here writ
To Norway, uncle of young Fortinbras,--

Who, impotent and bed-rid, scarcely hears
Of this his nephew's purpose,--to suppress
His further gait herein; in that the levies,
The lists and full proportions, are all made
Out of his subject: and we here dispatch
You, good Cornelius, and you, Voltimand,
For bearers of this greeting to old Norway;
Giving to you no further personal power
To business with the king, more than the scope
Of these delated articles allow.
Farewell, and let your haste commend your duty.


**CORNELIUS VOLTIMAND**

*We will do our best.*

In that and all things will we show our duty.


**KING CLAUDIUS**

*We have no doubt you will. Farewell. (Exit Voltimand and Cornelius.) And now, Laertes, what's new with you? You said you had something to ask me. What is it? Don't worry, you can ask me anything. Your father is an important man to the throne of Denmark. What do you want to ask?*

We doubt it nothing: heartily farewell.

Exeunt VOLTIMAND and CORNELIUS

And now, Laertes, what's the news with you?
You told us of some suit; what is't, Laertes?
You cannot speak of reason to the Dane,
And loose your voice: what wouldst thou beg, Laertes,
That shall not be my offer, not thy asking?
The head is not more native to the heart,
The hand more instrumental to the mouth,
Than is the throne of Denmark to thy father.
What wouldst thou have, Laertes?


**LAERTES**

*I would like to ask you, if I may return to France. Since, I came from France for the sole purpose of attending your coronation, and with that duty done, I would like to return. Please let me go back to France.*

*I would like to ask you, if I may return to France. Since, I came from France for the sole purpose of attending your coronation, and with that duty done, I would like to return. Please let me go back to France.*

My dread lord,
Your leave and favour to return to France;
From whence though willingly I came to Denmark,
To show my duty in your coronation,
Yet now, I must confess, that duty done,
My thoughts and wishes bend again toward France
And bow them to your gracious leave and pardon.

**KING CLAUDIUS**

*Do you have your father's permission? What does Polonius say about this?*

Have you your father's leave? What says Polonius?

**LORD POLONIUS**

*I have given him permission after he asked and asked. So, I ask you to allow him to return to France.*

He hath, my lord, wrung from me my slow leave
By laboursome petition, and at last
Upon his will I seal'd my hard consent:
I do beseech you, give him leave to go.

**KING CLAUDIUS**

*Then, I agree, too. This is the best time in your life, Laertes, spend it as you will. Now, my nephew, Hamlet, and my son--*

Take thy fair hour, Laertes; time be thine,
And thy best graces spend it at thy will!
But now, my cousin Hamlet, and my son,--

**HAMLET**

[Aside]

*I am more kin than I am kind.*

A little more than kin, and less than kind.

**KING CLAUDIUS**

*Why are you still sad? You look like a cloud is hanging over your head.*

How is it that the clouds still hang on you?

## HAMLET

*That's not true, sir. I am in the sun quite a bit.*

Not so, my lord; I am too much i' the sun.

## QUEEN GERTRUDE

*Dear Hamlet, you must stop being so dark and depressed. It's time you rejoin the living. You cannot bring your father back, as every living thing must die and enter eternity.*

Good Hamlet, cast thy nighted colour off,
And let thine eye look like a friend on Denmark.
Do not for ever with thy vailed lids
Seek for thy noble father in the dust:
Thou know'st 'tis common; all that lives must die,
Passing through nature to eternity.

## HAMLET

*Yes, ma'am. I know.*

Ay, madam, it is common.

## QUEEN GERTRUDE

*If you know, then why does it seem you don't?*

If it be,

Why seems it so particular with thee?

## HAMLET

*Seems, mother! It does not seem; it is. I may wear black clothes or behave sadly, but I do it because I am sad, not because I am pretending to be sad.*

Seems, madam! nay it is; I know not 'seems.'
'Tis not alone my inky cloak, good mother,
Nor customary suits of solemn black,
Nor windy suspiration of forced breath,

No, nor the fruitful river in the eye,
Nor the dejected 'havior of the visage,
Together with all forms, moods, shapes of grief,
That can denote me truly: these indeed seem,
For they are actions that a man might play:
But I have that within which passeth show;
These but the trappings and the suits of woe.


**KING CLAUDIUS**

*It is natural and proper for you to grieve over your father. Everyone loses a father, and the loved ones are sorrowful for some time. You have taken your mourning period too far. You are showing yourself to be stubborn and unmanly. You are going against the very nature of heaven and acting like a simple-minded, uneducated fool. It is a sin, continuing to act like this, so stop being so sad. We want you to think of me as your father, since you are heir to the throne. We want everyone to see that I love you like a son. We do not want you to go back to school in Wittenberg, but stay here where we can keep an eye on you, the best member of our court, my nephew and son.*

'Tis sweet and commendable in your nature, Hamlet,
To give these mourning duties to your father:
But, you must know, your father lost a father;
That father lost, lost his, and the survivor bound
In filial obligation for some term
To do obsequious sorrow: but to persever
In obstinate condolement is a course
Of impious stubbornness; 'tis unmanly grief;
It shows a will most incorrect to heaven,
A heart unfortified, a mind impatient,
An understanding simple and unschool'd:
For what we know must be and is as common
As any the most vulgar thing to sense,
Why should we in our peevish opposition
Take it to heart? Fie! 'tis a fault to heaven,
A fault against the dead, a fault to nature,
To reason most absurd: whose common theme
Is death of fathers, and who still hath cried,
From the first corse till he that died to-day,
'This must be so.' We pray you, throw to earth
This unprevailing woe, and think of us
As of a father: for let the world take note,
You are the most immediate to our throne;
And with no less nobility of love
Than that which dearest father bears his son,
Do I impart toward you. For your intent
In going back to school in Wittenberg,
It is most retrograde to our desire:
And we beseech you, bend you to remain

Here, in the cheer and comfort of our eye,
Our chiefest courtier, cousin, and our son.


## QUEEN GERTRUDE

*I pray you stay with us, Hamlet. Do not go back to Wittenberg.*

Let not thy mother lose her prayers, Hamlet:
I pray thee, stay with us; go not to Wittenberg.


## HAMLET

*I will do my best to not disappoint you, mother.*

I shall in all my best obey you, madam.


## KING CLAUDIUS

*That's a good answer: you are a true Dane. Dear wife, come. I am so happy with Hamlet's decision, I would like to drink a toast to his health. Let's tell all of Denmark the happy news. Let's shout it to the heavens. Let's go.*

Why, 'tis a loving and a fair reply:
Be as ourself in Denmark. Madam, come;
This gentle and unforced accord of Hamlet
Sits smiling to my heart: in grace whereof,
No jocund health that Denmark drinks to-day,
But the great cannon to the clouds shall tell,
And the king's rouse the heavens all bruit again,
Re-speaking earthly thunder. Come away.


Exeunt all but HAMLET


## HAMLET

*I feel as though my flesh will melt. I wish that God did not view suicide as a sin! Oh, God! Oh, God! This world is so unfair and it seems so useless. Damn this world! Damn, this world like a garden that grows weeds. How did it come to this? My father has only been dead two months, not even two months. He was so loving to my mother. He never raised a hand to her, and she clung to him; yet, within a month... I can't even think of it! Frailty is a woman. My shoes are not even a month old. She forgets my poor father and replaces him with another. An animal without reason would have mourned longer. She should not have married my uncle, my father's brother, who is no more like my father than I am like Hercules. Within a month, the salt of her tears had not even left her eyes, and she remarried. She sped with ease to make a bed of incest which can come to no good. But, even though it breaks my heart, I must hold my tongue!*

O, that this too too solid flesh would melt
Thaw and resolve itself into a dew!
Or that the Everlasting had not fix'd
His canon 'gainst self-slaughter! O God! God!
How weary, stale, flat and unprofitable,
Seem to me all the uses of this world!
Fie on't! ah fie! 'tis an unweeded garden,
That grows to seed; things rank and gross in nature
Possess it merely. That it should come to this!
But two months dead: nay, not so much, not two:
So excellent a king; that was, to this,
Hyperion to a satyr; so loving to my mother
That he might not beteem the winds of heaven
Visit her face too roughly. Heaven and earth!
Must I remember? why, she would hang on him,
As if increase of appetite had grown
By what it fed on: and yet, within a month--
Let me not think on't--Frailty, thy name is woman!--
A little month, or ere those shoes were old
With which she follow'd my poor father's body,
Like Niobe, all tears:--why she, even she--
O, God! a beast, that wants discourse of reason,
Would have mourn'd longer--married with my uncle,
My father's brother, but no more like my father
Than I to Hercules: within a month:
Ere yet the salt of most unrighteous tears
Had left the flushing in her galled eyes,
She married. O, most wicked speed, to post
With such dexterity to incestuous sheets!
It is not nor it cannot come to good:
But break, my heart; for I must hold my tongue.


Enter HORATIO, MARCELLUS, and BERNARDO


**HORATIO**

*Hello, my lord!*

Hail to your lordship!


**HAMLET**

*I am glad to see you are doing well, Horatio.*

I am glad to see you well:
Horatio,--or I do forget myself.


**HORATIO**

*I feel the same, my lord. I am forever your poor servant.*

The same, my lord, and your poor servant ever.


**HAMLET**

*Sir, my good friend, I'll change places with you. Horatio and Marcellus, what is going on in Wittenberg?*

Sir, my good friend; I'll change that name with you:
And what make you from Wittenberg, Horatio? Marcellus?


**MARCELLUS**

*My good lord...*

My good lord--


**HAMLET**

*I am very happy to see you. Very happy. But, tell me what is going on in Wittenberg.*

I am very glad to see you. Good even, sir.
But what, in faith, make you from Wittenberg?


**HORATIO**

*We are too late my lord.*

A truant disposition, good my lord.


**HAMLET**

*I don't think you enemy would say that, so I don't want to hear it, either. You are never too late. Why are you here in Elsinore? We'll teach you how to drink before you leave.*

I would not hear your enemy say so,
Nor shall you do mine ear that violence,
To make it truster of your own report
Against yourself: I know you are no truant.
But what is your affair in Elsinore?
We'll teach you to drink deep ere you depart.

## HORATIO

*My lord, I came to attend your father's funeral.*

My lord, I came to see your father's funeral.

## HAMLET

*Don't insult me. I think you came to see my mother's wedding.*

I pray thee, do not mock me, fellow-student;
I think it was to see my mother's wedding.

## HORATIO

*True, my lord, the wedding did happen quickly after the death of your father.*

Indeed, my lord, it follow'd hard upon.

## HAMLET

*Too quickly, Horatio! The food prepared for the funeral was served on the wedding tables. I would rather have died than live to see that day, Horatio! My father, I think I see him.*

Thrift, thrift, Horatio! the funeral baked meats
Did coldly furnish forth the marriage tables.
Would I had met my dearest foe in heaven
Or ever I had seen that day, Horatio!
My father!--methinks I see my father.

## HORATIO

*Where, my lord?*

Where, my lord?

**HAMLET**

*Only in my imagination, Horatio.*

In my mind's eye, Horatio.

**HORATIO**

*I saw him once. He was a good king.*

I saw him once; he was a goodly king.

**HAMLET**

*He was a man, one like I will never meet again.*

He was a man, take him for all in all,
I shall not look upon his like again.

**HORATIO**

*My lord, I think I saw him last night.*

My lord, I think I saw him yesternight.

**HAMLET**

*Saw who?*

Saw? who?

**HORATIO**

*My lord, the king, your father.*

My lord, the king your father.

**HAMLET**

*The king, my father!*

The king my father!


**HORATIO**

*Hold on. Don't get so excited, until you hear the whole crazy story, witnessed by these gentlemen.*

Season your admiration for awhile
With an attent ear, till I may deliver,
Upon the witness of these gentlemen,
This marvel to you.


**HAMLET**

*For the love of God, tell me.*

For God's love, let me hear.


**HORATIO**

*These gentlemen, Marcellus and Bernardo, on their watch in the middle of the night, were encountered by a figure like your father. It was armed and dressed exactly like him, and marched in front of their frightened eyes. They did not speak to him because they were so afraid. So, they told me about it and I went with them last night to keep watch. Just like they reported, I saw the apparition. I knew your father, and the ghost looked just like him.*

Two nights together had these gentlemen,
Marcellus and Bernardo, on their watch,
In the dead vast and middle of the night,
Been thus encounter'd. A figure like your father,
Armed at point exactly, cap-a-pe,
Appears before them, and with solemn march
Goes slow and stately by them: thrice he walk'd
By their oppress'd and fear-surprised eyes,
Within his truncheon's length; whilst they, distilled
Almost to jelly with the act of fear,
Stand dumb and speak not to him. This to me
In dreadful secrecy impart they did;
And I with them the third night kept the watch;
Where, as they had deliver'd, both in time,
Form of the thing, each word made true and good,
The apparition comes: I knew your father;
These hands are not more like.


**HAMLET**

*But, where was this?*

But where was this?

## MARCELLUS

*My lord, from the platform where they keep watch.*

My lord, upon the platform where we watch'd.

## HAMLET

*Did you speak to it?*

Did you not speak to it?

## HORATIO

*I did, my lord. But it did not answer. Although, I thought it lifted up its head and acted as if it were going to speak. Then, the morning cock crowed and the ghost quickly walked away and vanished from our sight.*

My lord, I did;
But answer made it none: yet once methought
It lifted up its head and did address
Itself to motion, like as it would speak;
But even then the morning cock crew loud,
And at the sound it shrunk in haste away,
And vanish'd from our sight.

## HAMLET

*This is very strange.*

'Tis very strange.

## HORATIO

*It is, but it is true, my lord. We thought it our duty to let you know.*

As I do live, my honour'd lord, 'tis true;
And we did think it writ down in our duty
To let you know of it.

**HAMLET**

*Yes, indeed, gentlemen, but this troubles me. Are you on watch tonight?*

Indeed, indeed, sirs, but this troubles me.
Hold you the watch to-night?


**MARCELLUS BERNARDO**

*Yes, my lord.*

We do, my lord.


**HAMLET**

*And you say he wore his armor?*

Arm'd, say you?


**MARCELLUS BERNARDO**

*Yes, my lord.*

Arm'd, my lord.


**HAMLET**

*From head to toe.*

From top to toe?


**MARCELLUS BERNARDO**

*My lord, completely.*

My lord, from head to foot.


**HAMLET**

*Then you didn't see his face.*

Then saw you not his face?

**HORATIO**

*Oh, yes, my lord. He wore his helmet up.*

O, yes, my lord; he wore his beaver up.

**HAMLET**

*Did he look angry?*

What, look'd he frowningly?

**HORATIO**

*He looked more sad than angry.*

A countenance more in sorrow than in anger.

**HAMLET**

*Was he pale or red?*

Pale or red?

**HORATIO**

*He was very pale.*

Nay, very pale.

**HAMLET**

*And he looked right at you?*

And fix'd his eyes upon you?

**HORATIO**

*He stared at us.*

Most constantly.

**HAMLET**

*I wish I would have been there.*

I would I had been there.

**HORATIO**

*You would have been amazed.*

It would have much amazed you.

**HAMLET**

*Likely so. Did it stay long?*

Very like, very like. Stay'd it long?

**HORATIO**

*Only a few minutes.*

While one with moderate haste might tell a hundred.

**MARCELLUS BERNARDO**

*It was longer than that.*

Longer, longer.

**HORATIO**

*I don't think so.*

Not when I saw't.

**HAMLET**

*Was his beard gray?*

His beard was grizzled--no?

## HORATIO

*It was just as I remember it, a silvery gray.*

It was, as I have seen it in his life,
A sable silver'd.


## HAMLET

*I will watch tonight and perhaps it will walk again.*

I will watch to-night;
Perchance 'twill walk again.


## HORATIO

*I think it will.*

I warrant it will.


## HAMLET

*If it looks like my noble father, I'll speak to it even if it is a sin and I should be quiet. I ask you if you have not told anyone else, to keep this a secret. Also, whatever happens tonight must remain between us. I require your faithfulness. So, goodbye. I will see you at the platform between eleven and twelve.*

If it assume my noble father's person,
I'll speak to it, though hell itself should gape
And bid me hold my peace. I pray you all,
If you have hitherto conceal'd this sight,
Let it be tenable in your silence still;
And whatsoever else shall hap to-night,
Give it an understanding, but no tongue:
I will requite your loves. So, fare you well:
Upon the platform, 'twixt eleven and twelve,
I'll visit you.


## All

*It is our duty and our honor.*

Our duty to your honour.

**HAMLET**

*It is my honor, too. Goodbye.*

Your loves, as mine to you: farewell.

Exeunt all but HAMLET

*My father's spirit in arms! It must mean things are not well and something terrible has happened. I wish the night were here. Until then, I must wait patiently. Bad things are surely coming.*

My father's spirit in arms! all is not well;
I doubt some foul play: would the night were come!
Till then sit still, my soul: foul deeds will rise,
Though all the earth o'erwhelm them, to men's eyes.

Exit

# Scene III
*A room in Polonius' house*

Enter LAERTES and OPHELIA

**LAERTES**

*It is time for me to return home, but do keep in touch, sister.*

My necessaries are embark'd: farewell:
And, sister, as the winds give benefit
And convoy is assistant, do not sleep,
But let me hear from you.

**OPHELIA**

*Do you doubt that I will?*

Do you doubt that?

**LAERTES**

*Do not believe Hamlet's ramblings of love. It is not permanent. It is sweet, but not everlasting. It will only last a minute.*

For Hamlet and the trifling of his favour,
Hold it a fashion and a toy in blood,
A violet in the youth of primy nature,
Forward, not permanent, sweet, not lasting,
The perfume and suppliance of a minute; No more.

**OPHELIA**

*So what?*

No more but so?

**LAERTES**

*It is natural for him to feel the way he does. Although, he is next in line to be king and he is beginning to think of the people of this state as his responsibility. He must prove his love to the queen mother to keep peace throughout the land. It is safer to be cautious, and lose his love. Just be weary, my dear sister, he is young and his ways are still inconsistent and unknown.*

Think it no more;
For nature, crescent, does not grow alone
In thews and bulk, but, as this temple waxes,
The inward service of the mind and soul
Grows wide withal. Perhaps he loves you now,
And now no soil nor cautel doth besmirch
The virtue of his will: but you must fear,
His greatness weigh'd, his will is not his own;
For he himself is subject to his birth:
He may not, as unvalued persons do,
Carve for himself; for on his choice depends
The safety and health of this whole state;
And therefore must his choice be circumscribed
Unto the voice and yielding of that body
Whereof he is the head. Then if he says he loves you,
It fits your wisdom so far to believe it
As he in his particular act and place
May give his saying deed; which is no further
Than the main voice of Denmark goes withal.
Then weigh what loss your honour may sustain,
If with too credent ear you list his songs,
Or lose your heart, or your chaste treasure open
To his unmaster'd importunity.
Fear it, Ophelia, fear it, my dear sister,
And keep you in the rear of your affection,
Out of the shot and danger of desire.
The chariest maid is prodigal enough,
If she unmask her beauty to the moon:
Virtue itself 'scapes not calumnious strokes:
The canker galls the infants of the spring,
Too oft before their buttons be disclosed,
And in the morn and liquid dew of youth
Contagious blastments are most imminent.
Be wary then; best safety lies in fear:
Youth to itself rebels, though none else near.


**OPHELIA**

*I shall keep what you say in mind. But, good brother, do not tell me one thing and turn around and do something else.*

I shall the effect of this good lesson keep,
As watchman to my heart. But, good my brother,

Do not, as some ungracious pastors do,
Show me the steep and thorny way to heaven;
Whiles, like a puff'd and reckless libertine,
Himself the primrose path of dalliance treads,
And recks not his own rede.


# LAERTES

*Oh, you need not fear me. I have stayed too long; here comes my father.*

O, fear me not.
I stay too long: but here my father comes.


Enter POLONIUS


*I am doubly blessed. It is time for me to leave.*

A double blessing is a double grace,
Occasion smiles upon a second leave.


# LORD POLONIUS

*Are you still here, Laertes? Shame on you! Everything is ready for your departure and you are still in Fortinbras. There, I give you my blessing! Keep these thoughts in mind. Be careful what you say and how you act. Be friendly, but not too friendly. Keep your old friends close, and be careful how you make new friends. Do not be quick to argue, but do not let anyone take you for a coward. Listen to your fellow man, but do not believe everything you hear. Dress your best, but do not overspend on fancy or gaudy clothes. Even the French dress according to their station. Do not borrow or lend money, because you will always lose, either the money or the friend or your sense of pride. And, most importantly, be true to yourself. That way no one can accuse you of being fake. Farewell and know you have my blessing!*

Yet here, Laertes! aboard, aboard, for shame!
The wind sits in the shoulder of your sail,
And you are stay'd for. There; my blessing with thee!
And these few precepts in thy memory
See thou character. Give thy thoughts no tongue,
Nor any unproportioned thought his act.
Be thou familiar, but by no means vulgar.
Those friends thou hast, and their adoption tried,
Grapple them to thy soul with hoops of steel;
But do not dull thy palm with entertainment
Of each new-hatch'd, unfledged comrade. Beware
Of entrance to a quarrel, but being in,

Bear't that the opposed may beware of thee.
Give every man thy ear, but few thy voice;
Take each man's censure, but reserve thy judgment.
Costly thy habit as thy purse can buy,
But not express'd in fancy; rich, not gaudy;
For the apparel oft proclaims the man,
And they in France of the best rank and station
Are of a most select and generous chief in that.
Neither a borrower nor a lender be;
For loan oft loses both itself and friend,
And borrowing dulls the edge of husbandry.
This above all: to thine ownself be true,
And it must follow, as the night the day,
Thou canst not then be false to any man.
Farewell: my blessing season this in thee!


### LAERTES

*I am most humble as I leave, my lord.*

Most humbly do I take my leave, my lord.


### LORD POLONIUS

*It is time. Go ahead. Your servants are waiting.*

The time invites you; go; your servants tend.


### LAERTES

*Goodbye, Ophelia, and remember what I said.*

Farewell, Ophelia; and remember well
What I have said to you.


### OPHELIA

*It is locked in my memory and only you have the key to unlock it.*

'Tis in my memory lock'd,
And you yourself shall keep the key of it.

## LAERTES

*Goodbye.*

Farewell.


Exit


## LORD POLONIUS

*What did he say to you, Ophelia?*

What is't, Ophelia, be hath said to you?


## OPHELIA

*If you must know, he said something about Lord Hamlet.*

So please you, something touching the Lord Hamlet.


## LORD POLONIUS

*Just as I thought. I have been told he has been spending time with you. But, I must tell you be careful and protect yourself. What is going on between you? Tell me the truth.*

Marry, well bethought:
'Tis told me, he hath very oft of late
Given private time to you; and you yourself
Have of your audience been most free and bounteous:
If it be so, as so 'tis put on me,
And that in way of caution, I must tell you,
You do not understand yourself so clearly
As it behoves my daughter and your honour.
What is between you? give me up the truth.


## OPHELIA

*He has, my lord, shown me how much he loves me, lately.*

He hath, my lord, of late made many tenders
Of his affection to me.

**LORD POLONIUS**

*Love! That's worthless! You sound like a foolish girl who has no experience with danger. Do you believe him?*

Affection! pooh! you speak like a green girl,
Unsifted in such perilous circumstance.
Do you believe his tenders, as you call them?


**OPHELIA**

*I don't know what to think, my lord.*

I do not know, my lord, what I should think.


**LORD POLONIUS**

*Love! That's worthless! You sound like a foolish girl who has no experience with danger. Do you believe him?*

Marry, I'll teach you: think yourself a baby;
That you have ta'en these tenders for true pay,
Which are not sterling. Tender yourself more dearly;
Or--not to crack the wind of the poor phrase,
Running it thus--you'll tender me a fool.


**OPHELIA**

*Father, he has treated me with love in an honorable fashion.*

My lord, he hath importuned me with love
In honourable fashion.


**LORD POLONIUS**

*Yes, you can call it fashion, something that changes often. Go ahead.*

Ay, fashion you may call it; go to, go to.


**OPHELIA**

*He swears he is being honest.*

And hath given countenance to his speech, my lord,
With almost all the holy vows of heaven.

**LORD POLONIUS**

*Bologna! I know when lust burns in the blood, how quickly one is to take vows of any kind. His heart may burn for you, but do not be deceived by what stokes the fire. Act like a grown woman and don't believe Lord Hamlet's vows. Do not be alone with him anymore. I demand you listen to me and change your ways.*

Ay, springes to catch woodcocks. I do know,
When the blood burns, how prodigal the soul
Lends the tongue vows: these blazes, daughter,
Giving more light than heat, extinct in both,
Even in their promise, as it is a-making,
You must not take for fire. From this time
Be somewhat scanter of your maiden presence;
Set your entreatments at a higher rate
Than a command to parley. For Lord Hamlet,
Believe so much in him, that he is young
And with a larger tether may he walk
Than may be given you: in few, Ophelia,
Do not believe his vows; for they are brokers,
Not of that dye which their investments show,
But mere implorators of unholy suits,
Breathing like sanctified and pious bawds,
The better to beguile. This is for all:
I would not, in plain terms, from this time forth,
Have you so slander any moment leisure,
As to give words or talk with the Lord Hamlet.
Look to't, I charge you: come your ways.

**OPHELIA**

*I will obey, my lord.*

I shall obey, my lord.

Exeunt

# Scene IV
*The platform*

Enter HAMLET, HORATIO, and MARCELLUS

**HAMLET**

*The air is bitterly cold.*

The air bites shrewdly; it is very cold.

**HORATIO**

*It is nippy in the air.*

It is a nipping and an eager air.

**HAMLET**

*What time is it now?*

What hour now?

**HORATIO**

*I think it is almost twelve.*

I think it lacks of twelve.

**HAMLET**

*No, it is already struck twelve.*

No, it is struck.

**HORATIO**

*It is? I didn't hear it. Then, the time is near for the spirit to hold his walk.*

Indeed? I heard it not: then it draws near the season
    Wherein the spirit held his wont to walk.

A flourish of trumpets, and ordnance shot off, within

*What is that? What does it mean, my lord?*

What does this mean, my lord?

**HAMLET**

*It means the king is awake tonight and is up drinking. The drum and trumpet play to show a pledge to be triumphant.*

The king doth wake to-night and takes his rouse,
Keeps wassail, and the swaggering up-spring reels;
And, as he drains his draughts of Rhenish down,
The kettle-drum and trumpet thus bray out
The triumph of his pledge.

**HORATIO**

*Is it a custom?*

Is it a custom?

**HAMLET**

*Yes, it is. But, although I am from here, I don't think it is a good one. Many countries think we are drunks. They do not think we are capable of great achievements, like someone who is born with an affliction they cannot control or someone with a bad habit. It is unfortunate, but people are judged by these things. A little problem can mar a whole man's life.*

Ay, marry, is't:
But to my mind, though I am native here
And to the manner born, it is a custom
More honour'd in the breach than the observance.
This heavy-headed revel east and west
Makes us traduced and tax'd of other nations:
They clepe us drunkards, and with swinish phrase
Soil our addition; and indeed it takes
From our achievements, though perform'd at height,
The pith and marrow of our attribute.
So, oft it chances in particular men,
That for some vicious mole of nature in them,

As, in their birth--wherein they are not guilty,
Since nature cannot choose his origin--
By the o'ergrowth of some complexion,
Oft breaking down the pales and forts of reason,
Or by some habit that too much o'er-leavens
The form of plausive manners, that these men,
Carrying, I say, the stamp of one defect,
Being nature's livery, or fortune's star,--
Their virtues else--be they as pure as grace,
As infinite as man may undergo--
Shall in the general censure take corruption
From that particular fault: the dram of eale
Doth all the noble substance of a doubt
To his own scandal.


**HORATIO**

*Look, my lord, here it comes!*

Look, my lord, it comes!


Enter Ghost


**HAMLET**

*God help us! Whether you are an angel or demon, from heaven or hell, good or bad, I will speak to you. I'll call you Hamlet, King, father, royal Dane. Oh, answer me! Tell me why you are here. What does it mean the dead walking? Why are you in your battle armor and making us doubt our minds? Why? What do you want?*

Angels and ministers of grace defend us!
Be thou a spirit of health or goblin damn'd,
Bring with thee airs from heaven or blasts from hell,
Be thy intents wicked or charitable,
Thou comest in such a questionable shape
That I will speak to thee: I'll call thee Hamlet,
King, father, royal Dane: O, answer me!
Let me not burst in ignorance; but tell
Why thy canonized bones, hearsed in death,
Have burst their cerements; why the sepulchre,
Wherein we saw thee quietly inurn'd,
Hath oped his ponderous and marble jaws,
To cast thee up again. What may this mean,
That thou, dead corse, again in complete steel
Revisit'st thus the glimpses of the moon,

Making night hideous; and we fools of nature
So horridly to shake our disposition
With thoughts beyond the reaches of our souls?
Say, why is this? wherefore? what should we do?

Ghost beckons HAMLET

## HORATIO

*It beckons for you to go with it, as if it wants to be with you alone.*

It beckons you to go away with it,
As if it some impartment did desire
To you alone.

## MARCELLUS

*Look, it wants you to go over there, but don't go!*

Look, with what courteous action
It waves you to a more removed ground:
But do not go with it.

## HORATIO

*No, by no means.*

No, by no means.

## HAMLET

*It will not speak, if I don't follow.*

It will not speak; then I will follow it.

## HORATIO

*Do not, my lord.*

Do not, my lord.

**HAMLET**

*Why not? What do I have to fear? It cannot hurt me or take my soul. It waves at me, again. I'll follow.*

Why, what should be the fear?
I do not set my life in a pin's fee;
And for my soul, what can it do to that,
Being a thing immortal as itself?
It waves me forth again: I'll follow it.


**HORATIO**

*What if it tempts you toward the water, my lord, or to the end of the cliff or assumes some other horrible form which drives you insane.*

What if it tempt you toward the flood, my lord,
Or to the dreadful summit of the cliff
That beetles o'er his base into the sea,
And there assume some other horrible form,
Which might deprive your sovereignty of reason
And draw you into madness? think of it:
The very place puts toys of desperation,
Without more motive, into every brain
That looks so many fathoms to the sea
And hears it roar beneath.


**HAMLET**

*It still waves at me. Go on. I'll follow you.*

It waves me still.
Go on; I'll follow thee.


**MARCELLUS**

*You will not, my lord.*

You shall not go, my lord.


**HAMLET**

*Take your hands off of me.*

Hold off your hands.

### HORATIO

*Be sensible. You will not go.*

Be ruled; you shall not go.

### HAMLET

*This is my fate and I am not afraid. Now, take your hands off, gentlemen. I swear, I'll make a ghost of you, if you don't. I say, go on. I'll follow you.*

My fate cries out,
And makes each petty artery in this body
As hardy as the Nemean lion's nerve.
Still am I call'd. Unhand me, gentlemen.
By heaven, I'll make a ghost of him that lets me!
I say, away! Go on; I'll follow thee.

Exeunt Ghost and HAMLET

### HORATIO

*He is desperate and not thinking sensibly.*

He waxes desperate with imagination.

### MARCELLUS

*Let's follow him. It is not right for us to let him go alone.*

Let's follow; 'tis not fit thus to obey him.

### HORATIO

*Go ahead. What good can come of this?*

Have after. To what issue will this come?

### MARCELLUS

*Something terrible is definitely happening in Denmark.*

Something is rotten in the state of Denmark.

**HORATIO**

*God will protect him.*

Heaven will direct it.

**MARCELLUS**

*No, let's follow him.*

Nay, let's follow him.

Exeunt

# SCENE V
### Another part of the platform.

Enter GHOST and HAMLET

**HAMLET**

*Where are you leading me? Speak or I'll stop.*

Where wilt thou lead me? speak; I'll go no further.

**Ghost**

*Listen to me.*

Mark me.

**HAMLET**

*I will.*

I will.

**Ghost**

*My time is almost up, and I have to return to the sulfurous fire and tormenting flames.*

My hour is almost come,
When I to sulphurous and tormenting flames
Must render up myself.

**HAMLET**

*You poor ghost!*

Alas, poor ghost!

**Ghost**

*Don't pity me, but listen to what I have to say.*

Pity me not, but lend thy serious hearing
To what I shall unfold.

## HAMLET

*Speak. I am listening.*

Speak; I am bound to hear.

## Ghost

*You will want revenge when you hear my story.*

So art thou to revenge, when thou shalt hear.

## HAMLET

*What?*

What?

## Ghost

*I am the spirit of your father, and I am doomed to walk the night and confined by day to waste in the fires, until I have paid for the crimes of my life. But, I am forbidden to tell the secrets of hell, although I could tell a small story that would freeze your blood, make your eyes pop out of your head, or make your hair stand on end like the quills of a porcupine. However, I cannot tell you. Listen, if you ever loved your dear father--*

I am thy father's spirit,
Doom'd for a certain term to walk the night,
And for the day confined to fast in fires,
Till the foul crimes done in my days of nature
Are burnt and purged away. But that I am forbid
To tell the secrets of my prison-house,
I could a tale unfold whose lightest word
Would harrow up thy soul, freeze thy young blood,
Make thy two eyes, like stars, start from their spheres,
Thy knotted and combined locks to part
And each particular hair to stand on end,
Like quills upon the fretful porpentine:
But this eternal blazon must not be
To ears of flesh and blood. List, list, O, list!
If thou didst ever thy dear father love--

**HAMLET**

*Oh, God!*

O God!


**Ghost**

*You will seek revenge for his foul murder.*

Revenge his foul and most unnatural murder.


**HAMLET**

*Murder!*

Murder!


**Ghost**

*Yes, murder, in the most unnatural sense.*

Murder most foul, as in the best it is;
But this most foul, strange and unnatural.


**HAMLET**

*Hurry and tell me, so I can seek revenge quickly.*

Haste me to know't, that I, with wings as swift
As meditation or the thoughts of love,
May sweep to my revenge.


**Ghost**

*I know you are capable and no one would suspect you. Now, listen Hamlet. It was told throughout Denmark that while I was sleeping in my orchard, I was bitten by a serpent, but I want you to the serpent that bit me now wears my crown.*

*I know you are capable and no one would suspect you. Now, listen Hamlet. It was told throughout Denmark that while I was sleeping in my orchard, I was bitten by a serpent, but I want you to the serpent that bit me now wears my crown.*

I find thee apt;
And duller shouldst thou be than the fat weed
That roots itself in ease on Lethe wharf,
Wouldst thou not stir in this. Now, Hamlet, hear:
'Tis given out that, sleeping in my orchard,
A serpent stung me; so the whole ear of Denmark
Is by a forged process of my death
Rankly abused: but know, thou noble youth,
The serpent that did sting thy father's life
Now wears his crown.


**HAMLET**

*I knew it! My uncle!*

O my prophetic soul! My uncle!


**Ghost**

*Yes, that incestuous beast of adultery and witchcraft. He is traitorous and has the powers of seduction, which won him my most seemingly virtuous queen. Oh, Hamlet, what a terrible blow. My wife, whom I loved with dignity from the day we married, falls for the likes of him. But, perhaps her virtue was not as solid as I thought to fall so quickly into the bed of another. Wait! I think the morning is approaching, and I must be brief. Your uncle, while I was sleeping in the orchard like every afternoon, came and poured some poison into my ear. The poison worked quickly and my body became crusty with death, and I was not given the opportunity to confess my sins. Oh, horrible! Horrible! Most horrible! Protect yourself against sin, and however you go about getting your revenge, leave your mother alone. Let heaven deal with her. Living with the truth will prick and sting her enough. Now, I must go. The sun is rising. Goodbye. Goodbye. Hamlet, remember me!*

Ay, that incestuous, that adulterate beast,
With witchcraft of his wit, with traitorous gifts,--
O wicked wit and gifts, that have the power
So to seduce!--won to his shameful lust
The will of my most seeming-virtuous queen:
O Hamlet, what a falling-off was there!
From me, whose love was of that dignity
That it went hand in hand even with the vow
I made to her in marriage, and to decline
Upon a wretch whose natural gifts were poor
To those of mine!
But virtue, as it never will be moved,
Though lewdness court it in a shape of heaven,
So lust, though to a radiant angel link'd,
Will sate itself in a celestial bed,
And prey on garbage.

But, soft! methinks I scent the morning air;
Brief let me be. Sleeping within my orchard,
My custom always of the afternoon,
Upon my secure hour thy uncle stole,
With juice of cursed hebenon in a vial,
And in the porches of my ears did pour
The leperous distilment; whose effect
Holds such an enmity with blood of man
That swift as quicksilver it courses through
The natural gates and alleys of the body,
And with a sudden vigour doth posset
And curd, like eager droppings into milk,
The thin and wholesome blood: so did it mine;
And a most instant tetter bark'd about,
Most lazar-like, with vile and loathsome crust,
All my smooth body.
Thus was I, sleeping, by a brother's hand
Of life, of crown, of queen, at once dispatch'd:
Cut off even in the blossoms of my sin,
Unhousel'd, disappointed, unanel'd,
No reckoning made, but sent to my account
With all my imperfections on my head:
O, horrible! O, horrible! most horrible!
If thou hast nature in thee, bear it not;
Let not the royal bed of Denmark be
A couch for luxury and damned incest.
But, howsoever thou pursuest this act,
Taint not thy mind, nor let thy soul contrive
Against thy mother aught: leave her to heaven
And to those thorns that in her bosom lodge,
To prick and sting her. Fare thee well at once!
The glow-worm shows the matin to be near,
And 'gins to pale his uneffectual fire:
Adieu, adieu! Hamlet, remember me.


Exit


## HAMLET

*Oh, God of heaven and earth! What else can I bear? I swear! Be still, my heart and body give me strength. Remember you! You poor ghost, I will remember you. I will think of nothing else. Oh, villainous woman! Oh, villain, damned villain! How can one sit and smile and know he is a villain? I know it is possible in Denmark.*

O all you host of heaven! O earth! what else?

And shall I couple hell? O, fie! Hold, hold, my heart;
And you, my sinews, grow not instant old,
But bear me stiffly up. Remember thee!
Ay, thou poor ghost, while memory holds a seat
In this distracted globe. Remember thee!
Yea, from the table of my memory
I'll wipe away all trivial fond records,
All saws of books, all forms, all pressures past,
That youth and observation copied there;
And thy commandment all alone shall live
Within the book and volume of my brain,
Unmix'd with baser matter: yes, by heaven!
O most pernicious woman!
O villain, villain, smiling, damned villain!
My tables,--meet it is I set it down,
That one may smile, and smile, and be a villain;
At least I'm sure it may be so in Denmark:


*Writing*

*So, uncle, there you are. I will keep my word and remember my father. I have sworn it.*

So, uncle, there you are. Now to my word;
It is 'Adieu, adieu! remember me.'
I have sworn 't.


## MARCELLUS HORATIO

[Within]

*My lord, my lord,--*

My lord, my lord,--


## MARCELLUS

[Within]

*Lord Hamlet,--*

Lord Hamlet,--


## HORATIO

[Within]

*Heaven protect him!*

Heaven secure him!

**HAMLET**

*So be it!*

So be it!

**HORATIO**

[Within]

*Hello, my lord!*

Hillo, ho, ho, my lord!

**HAMLET**

*Hello, boy! Come here, come.*

Hillo, ho, ho, boy! come, bird, come.

Enter HORATIO and MARCELLUS

**MARCELLUS**

*How are you, my noble lord?*

How is't, my noble lord?

**HORATIO**

*What happened, my lord?*

What news, my lord?

**HAMLET**

*It was wonderful!*

O, wonderful!

## HORATIO

*Good my lord, tell us.*

Good my lord, tell it.

## HAMLET

*No, you'll tell someone.*

No; you'll reveal it.

## HORATIO

*Not me, my lord, I swear.*

Not I, my lord, by heaven.

## MARCELLUS

*Nor me, my lord.*

Nor I, my lord.

## HAMLET

*Can you keep a secret?*

How say you, then; would heart of man once think it?
But you'll be secret?

## HORATIO MARCELLUS

*Yes, we swear, my lord.*

Ay, by heaven, my lord.

**HAMLET**

*There's a villain living in Denmark, an awful scoundrel.*

There's ne'er a villain dwelling in all Denmark
But he's an arrant knave.


**HORATIO**

*No ghost needed to tell us that, my lord.*

There needs no ghost, my lord, come from the grave
To tell us this.


**HAMLET**

*You are so right. So, I think we should shake hands and go our separate ways, you to your business and me, well, I need to go pray.*

Why, right; you are i' the right;
And so, without more circumstance at all,
I hold it fit that we shake hands and part:
You, as your business and desire shall point you;
For every man has business and desire,
Such as it is; and for mine own poor part,
Look you, I'll go pray.


**HORATIO**

*You aren't making much sense, my lord.*

These are but wild and whirling words, my lord.


**HAMLET**

*I'm sorry they offend you. I truly am.*

I'm sorry they offend you, heartily;
Yes, 'faith heartily.


**HORATIO**

*I'm not offended, my lord.*

There's no offence, my lord.

**HAMLET**

*Oh, but there has been an offense, I swear by Saint Patrick, Horatio. From what the honest ghost says, a large offense, too. I know you want to know what was said, but I must keep it to myself. Now, good friends, you are friends, scholars, and soldiers; I ask but one thing.*

Yes, by Saint Patrick, but there is, Horatio,
And much offence too. Touching this vision here,
It is an honest ghost, that let me tell you:
For your desire to know what is between us,
O'ermaster 't as you may. And now, good friends,
As you are friends, scholars and soldiers,
Give me one poor request.

**HORATIO**

*What is it, my lord? We will.*

What is't, my lord? we will.

**HAMLET**

*Never tell anyone what you have seen tonight.*

Never make known what you have seen to-night.

**HORATIO MARCELLUS**

*My lord, we will not tell anyone.*

My lord, we will not.

**HAMLET**

*No, swear it.*

Nay, but swear't.

**HORATIO**

*I swear, my lord, I will never tell.*

In faith,
My lord, not I.


**MARCELLUS**

*Nor I, my lord, I swear.*

Nor I, my lord, in faith.


**HAMLET**

*Swear upon my sword.*

Upon my sword.


**MARCELLUS**

*We have already sworn, my lord.*

We have sworn, my lord, already.


**HAMLET**

*You have, but I want you to swear upon my sword.*

Indeed, upon my sword, indeed.


**Ghost**

[Beneath]

*Swear.*

Swear.


**HAMLET**

*Ha, ha boy! Is that right? Aren't you helpful? Come on! You hear the fellow down below. Swear.*

Ah, ha, boy! say'st thou so? art thou there,
truepenny?
Come on--you hear this fellow in the cellarage--
Consent to swear.

**HORATIO**

*Say the oath, my lord.*

Propose the oath, my lord.

**HAMLET**

*Swear by my sword, you will never speak of what you have seen.*

Never to speak of this that you have seen,
Swear by my sword.

**Ghost**

[Beneath]

*Swear.*

Swear.

**HAMLET**

*He is everywhere. Let's move. Come over here, gentlemen, and lay your hands upon my sword. Swear you will never tell anyone what you have heard. Swear by my sword.*

Hic et ubique? then we'll shift our ground.
Come hither, gentlemen,
And lay your hands again upon my sword:
Never to speak of this that you have heard,
Swear by my sword.

**Ghost**

[Beneath]

*Swear.*

Swear.

## HAMLET

*Well said, old mole! I wished I could move that fast. He is a worthy pioneer! Try again, good friends.*

Well said, old mole! canst work i' the earth so fast?
A worthy pioner! Once more remove, good friends.

## HORATIO

*I swear this is weird.*

O day and night, but this is wondrous strange!

## HAMLET

*Yes, it is strange, but you want to know. First, there are more things in heaven and earth, Horatio, than you know about. But, listen to what I am about to say. No matter how I act or what I say, and undoubtedly, I will act crazy and say inane things in the future, you must not let on you know what is going on. You may never say, "Oh, just as I thought," or "If you only knew." Swear it!*

And therefore as a stranger give it welcome.
There are more things in heaven and earth, Horatio,
Than are dreamt of in your philosophy. But come;
Here, as before, never, so help you mercy,
How strange or odd soe'er I bear myself,
As I perchance hereafter shall think meet
To put an antic disposition on,
That you, at such times seeing me, never shall,
With arms encumber'd thus, or this headshake,
Or by pronouncing of some doubtful phrase,
As 'Well, well, we know,' or 'We could, an if we would,'
Or 'If we list to speak,' or 'There be, an if they might,'
Or such ambiguous giving out, to note
That you know aught of me: this not to do,
So grace and mercy at your most need help you, Swear.

## **Ghost**

[Beneath]

*Swear.*

165

Swear.

**HAMLET**

*Rest, poor spirit. So, gentlemen, I give you all my love and will repay you for your friendship. Let's go back inside together, but you must stay quiet, please. You must not talk about any of this. I know it is extremely strange, and I curse the day I am supposed to set everything straight. Come on, let's go inside.*

Rest, rest, perturbed spirit!

So, gentlemen,
With all my love I do commend me to you:
And what so poor a man as Hamlet is
May do, to express his love and friending to you,
God willing, shall not lack. Let us go in together;
And still your fingers on your lips, I pray.
The time is out of joint: O cursed spite,
That ever I was born to set it right!
Nay, come, let's go together.

Exeunt

**Act II**

# Scene I
*A room in **POLONIUS'** house*

Enter POLONIUS and REYNALDO

**LORD POLONIUS**

*Give him this money and these notes, Reynaldo.*

Give him this money and these notes, Reynaldo.

**REYNALDO**

*I will, my lord.*

I will, my lord.

**LORD POLONIUS**

*It would be wise, Reynaldo, before you visit him, to find out what he's been up to.*

You shall do marvellous wisely, good Reynaldo,
Before you visit him, to make inquire
Of his behavior.

**REYNALDO**

*Those were my intentions, my lord.*

My lord, I did intend it.

**LORD POLONIUS**

*Good, well said. Ask around and find out what Danes are in Paris—who they are, where they live, how they make money and who their friends are? Also, find out if they know my son. You will find out more by asking these questions than if you enquired directly about him. Just say you are a friend of his father and vaguely know him. Understand, Reynaldo?*

Marry, well said; very well said. Look you, sir,
Inquire me first what Danskers are in Paris;
And how, and who, what means, and where they keep,

What company, at what expense; and finding
By this encompassment and drift of question
That they do know my son, come you more nearer
Than your particular demands will touch it:
Take you, as 'twere, some distant knowledge of him;
As thus, 'I know his father and his friends,
And in part him: ' do you mark this, Reynaldo?

## REYNALDO

*No problem, sir.*

Ay, very well, my lord.

## LORD POLONIUS

*And you may make up stories about him like he acts wildly or likes to drink, et cetera, but don't make up anything that would be shameful. You know, make up something believable about someone of his age and position.*

'And in part him; but' you may say 'not well:
But, if't be he I mean, he's very wild;
Addicted so and so:' and there put on him
What forgeries you please; marry, none so rank
As may dishonour him; take heed of that;
But, sir, such wanton, wild and usual slips
As are companions noted and most known
To youth and liberty.

## REYNALDO

*Like gambling?*

As gaming, my lord.

## LORD POLONIUS

*Yes, or drinking, fencing, swearing, fighting, or visiting brothels.*

Ay, or drinking, fencing, swearing, quarrelling,
Drabbing: you may go so far.

## REYNALDO

*But that would bring him shame.*

My lord, that would dishonour him.

## LORD POLONIUS

*Oh, heavens no, not if you say it the right way. You may say what you need to but do not make him seem scandalous. Just mention his faults in a way that seem usual of someone like Laertes, a fiery youth from a long-line of fiery men.*

'Faith, no; as you may season it in the charge
You must not put another scandal on him,
That he is open to incontinency;
That's not my meaning: but breathe his faults so quaintly
That they may seem the taints of liberty,
The flash and outbreak of a fiery mind,
A savageness in unreclaimed blood,
Of general assault.

## REYNALDO

*But, my good sir--*

But, my good lord,--

## LORD POLONIUS

*You want to know why I want you to do this?*

Wherefore should you do this?

## REYNALDO

*Yes, my lord, I would.*

Ay, my lord,
I would know that.

## LORD POLONIUS

*Okay, sir, this is what I think and if I say so myself, it is very clever. I think if you mention my son's faults in vague conversation as if it was nothing, the other person will agree with you saying, 'Yes, my good sir,' or 'No, my friend.'*

Marry, sir, here's my drift;
And I believe, it is a fetch of wit:
You laying these slight sullies on my son,
As 'twere a thing a little soil'd i' the working, Mark you,
Your party in converse, him you would sound,
Having ever seen in the prenominate crimes
The youth you breathe of guilty, be assured
He closes with you in this consequence;
'Good sir,' or so, or 'friend,' or 'gentleman,'
According to the phrase or the addition
Of man and country.


## REYNALDO

*I understand, my lord.*

Very good, my lord.


## LORD POLONIUS

*And then sir, he will—what was I about to say?—Good lord, I was about to say something. Where did I leave off?*

And then, sir, does he this--he does--what was I
about to say? By the mass, I was about to say
something: where did I leave?


## REYNALDO

*You were saying how the other person would respond.*

At 'closes in the consequence,' at 'friend or so,'
and 'gentleman.'


## LORD POLONIUS

*Oh yes, the other person. He'll say, "Yes, I know that gentlemen; I saw him yesterday. He was gambling or he was fighting." You see what I mean? See, your little lie will actually reveal the truth. That's how you'll find out what Laertes is doing in Paris. Understand?*

At 'closes in the consequence,' ay, marry;
He closes thus: 'I know the gentleman;
I saw him yesterday, or t' other day,
Or then, or then; with such, or such; and, as you say,
There was a' gaming; there o'ertook in's rouse;

There falling out at tennis:' or perchance,
'I saw him enter such a house of sale,'
Videlicet, a brothel, or so forth.
See you now;
Your bait of falsehood takes this carp of truth:
And thus do we of wisdom and of reach,
With windlasses and with assays of bias,
By indirections find directions out:
So by my former lecture and advice,
Shall you my son. You have me, have you not?

**REYNALDO**

*I understand, sir.*

My lord, I have.

**LORD POLONIUS**

*May God be with you.*

God be wi' you; fare you well.

**REYNALDO**

*Thank you, my lord!*

Good my lord!

**LORD POLONIUS**

*Don't forget to observe his actions for yourself.*

Observe his inclination in yourself.

**REYNALDO**

*I will, sir.*

I shall, my lord.

**LORD POLONIUS**

*Make sure he is studying his music.*

And let him ply his music.

**REYNALDO**

*No problem, sir.*

Well, my lord.

**LORD POLONIUS**

*Goodbye!*

Farewell!

Exit REYNALDO

Enter OPHELIA

*Ophelia, what is wrong?*

How now, Ophelia! what's the matter?

**OPHELIA**

*Oh, father, I have been so scared!*

O, my lord, my lord, I have been so affrighted!

**LORD POLONIUS**

*By what, in the name of God?*

With what, i' the name of God?

**OPHELIA**

*My lord, as I was sewing in my bedroom, Lord Hamlet appeared. His vest was unbuttoned, there was no hat on his head, his socks were dirty and down around his ankles, and he was as pale as his shirt. He was pitiful looking with his knees knocking together, as if he had seen the demons in hell.*

My lord, as I was sewing in my closet,
Lord Hamlet, with his doublet all unbraced;
No hat upon his head; his stockings foul'd,
Ungarter'd, and down-gyved to his ancle;
Pale as his shirt; his knees knocking each other;
And with a look so piteous in purport
As if he had been loosed out of hell
To speak of horrors,--he comes before me.


### LORD POLONIUS

*Was he insane with love for you?*

Mad for thy love?


### OPHELIA

*I don't know, but that is what I'm afraid of.*

My lord, I do not know;
But truly, I do fear it.


### LORD POLONIUS

*What did he say?*

What said he?


### OPHELIA

*He took me by the wrist with a hard grip. Then, he holds me at arm's length and stares at me like an artist preparing to draw a portrait. He stayed like that for so long, my arm began to shake. He shook his head three times and sighed so loudly and pitifully, it seemed he was about to die. Then he let me go and without opening his eyes he left, like I was the last thing he wanted to see.*

He took me by the wrist and held me hard;
Then goes he to the length of all his arm;
And, with his other hand thus o'er his brow,
He falls to such perusal of my face
As he would draw it. Long stay'd he so;

At last, a little shaking of mine arm
And thrice his head thus waving up and down,
He raised a sigh so piteous and profound
As it did seem to shatter all his bulk
And end his being: that done, he lets me go:
And, with his head over his shoulder turn'd,
He seem'd to find his way without his eyes;
For out o' doors he went without their helps,
And, to the last, bended their light on me.


**LORD POLONIUS**

*Come on, let's go see the king. He is acting like he is in love with you and I am afraid of what he might do in the name of passion. I am sorry, but have you spoken harshly to him lately?*

Come, go with me: I will go seek the king.
This is the very ecstasy of love,
Whose violent property fordoes itself
And leads the will to desperate undertakings
As oft as any passion under heaven
That does afflict our natures. I am sorry.
What, have you given him any hard words of late?


**OPHELIA**

*No, father. I did as you told me. I wouldn't receive his letters or let him visit me.*

No, my good lord, but, as you did command,
I did repel his fetters and denied
His access to me.


**LORD POLONIUS**

*That is probably what made him angry. I'm sorry. I should have monitored him more closely before I gave you such advice, but I thought he was just trying to use you. I guess people my age think we know more. Let's go see the king and tell him what is going on. It is better to have this out in the open.*

That hath made him mad.
I am sorry that with better heed and judgment
I had not quoted him: I fear'd he did but trifle,
And meant to wreck thee; but, beshrew my jealousy!
By heaven, it is as proper to our age
To cast beyond ourselves in our opinions
As it is common for the younger sort

To lack discretion. Come, go we to the king:
This must be known; which, being kept close, might move
More grief to hide than hate to utter love.


Exeunt

# Scene II
*A room in the castle*

Enter KING CLAUDIUS, QUEEN GERTRUDE, ROSENCRANTZ, GUILDENSTERN, and

Attendants

## KING CLAUDIUS

*Welcome Rosencratntz and Guildenstern. We have looked so forward to seeing you, but we sent for you so hastily, because we need your assistance. I'm sure you have heard of Hamlet's "transformation," or at least that's what I call it. He is not like he used to be. He doesn't even look the same. I have no idea what has caused this change other than his father's death. So, I am asking for both of you, being so close in age to Hamlet, to stay here and spend some time with him. Try to figure out what is wrong with him and let us know, so we may help him.*

Welcome, dear Rosencrantz and Guildenstern!
Moreover that we much did long to see you,
The need we have to use you did provoke
Our hasty sending. Something have you heard
Of Hamlet's transformation; so call it,
Sith nor the exterior nor the inward man
Resembles that it was. What it should be,
More than his father's death, that thus hath put him
So much from the understanding of himself,
I cannot dream of: I entreat you both,
That, being of so young days brought up with him,
And sith so neighbour'd to his youth and havior,
That you vouchsafe your rest here in our court
Some little time: so by your companies
To draw him on to pleasures, and to gather,
So much as from occasion you may glean,
Whether aught, to us unknown, afflicts him thus,
That, open'd, lies within our remedy.

## QUEEN GERTRUDE

*Gentlemen, Hamlet has talked so much about you, I am sure there are no others alive to whom he is as close. If you would be so kind to spend some time with us and help us with Hamlet, I am sure your visit would be compensated befitting a king.*

Good gentlemen, he hath much talk'd of you;
And sure I am two men there are not living

To whom he more adheres. If it will please you
To show us so much gentry and good will
As to expend your time with us awhile,
For the supply and profit of our hope,
Your visitation shall receive such thanks
As fits a king's remembrance.


## ROSENCRANTZ

*I beg your pardon, your majesties, but knowing the power you have over us, it seems as if your request is more of a command than a question.*

Both your majesties
Might, by the sovereign power you have of us,
Put your dread pleasures more into command
Than to entreaty.


## GUILDENSTERN

*It would be our pleasure to be of service. We are at your command.*

But we both obey,
And here give up ourselves, in the full bent
To lay our service freely at your feet,
To be commanded.


## KING CLAUDIUS

*Thanks, Rosencrantz and Guildenstern.*

Thanks, Rosencrantz and gentle Guildenstern.


## QUEEN GERTRUDE

*Thank you, Guildenstern and gentle Rosencrantz. I ask you to go to Hamlet, who has changed so much lately. Attendants, some of you take these gentlemen to Hamlet.*

Thanks, Guildenstern and gentle Rosencrantz:
And I beseech you instantly to visit
My too much changed son. Go, some of you,
And bring these gentlemen where Hamlet is.

**GUILDENSTERN**

*May God bless us in helping Hamlet!*

Heavens make our presence and our practises
Pleasant and helpful to him!


**QUEEN GERTRUDE**

*Amen!*

Ay, amen!


Exeunt ROSENCRANTZ, GUILDENSTERN, and some Attendants


Enter POLONIUS


**LORD POLONIUS**

*I see the ambassadors from Norway have happily returned.*

The ambassadors from Norway, my good lord,
Are joyfully return'd.


**KING CLAUDIUS**

*You are still the bearer of good news.*

Thou still hast been the father of good news.


**LORD POLONIUS**

*Am I, my lord? I assure you I take my duty to the King as seriously as my soul to God. I think I know what may be wrong with Hamlet and causing him to act so crazily.*

Have I, my lord? I assure my good liege,
I hold my duty, as I hold my soul,
Both to my God and to my gracious king:
And I do think, or else this brain of mine
Hunts not the trail of policy so sure
As it hath used to do, that I have found

The very cause of Hamlet's lunacy.

### KING CLAUDIUS

*Do tell me what I long to hear.*

O, speak of that; that do I long to hear.

### LORD POLONIUS

*First, let me get the ambassadors. My news will be the cherry on top of what they have to say.*

Give first admittance to the ambassadors;
My news shall be the fruit to that great feast.

### KING CLAUDIUS

*Sure. Bring them in.*

Thyself do grace to them, and bring them in.

Exit POLONIUS

*Polonius tells me, my sweet queen, he may know what is wrong with your son.*

He tells me, my dear Gertrude, he hath found
The head and source of all your son's distemper.

### QUEEN GERTRUDE

*I doubt it is anything other than the death of his father and our hasty marriage.*

I doubt it is no other but the main;
His father's death, and our o'erhasty marriage.

### KING CLAUDIUS

*Well, we will hear him out.*

Well, we shall sift him.

Re-enter POLONIUS, with VOLTIMAND and CORNELIUS

*Welcome, good friends! What do you know, Voltimand, about our neighbor Norway?*

Welcome, my good friends!
Say, Voltimand, what from our brother Norway?


**VOLTIMAND**

*Thank you, your highness. When we first visited Norway, your brother sent out soldiers to stop his nephew. He thought Fortinbras was preparing to attack the Poles, but at a second look, he discovered the attack was meant for you. This news made him sick, so he arrested Fortinbras, who in turn, vowed to his uncle to not send arms against Denmark. His uncle, being so overjoyed by his nephew's vows, gave him an increase in his annual salary and permission to employ soldiers to attack the Poles.*

Most fair return of greetings and desires.
Upon our first, he sent out to suppress
His nephew's levies; which to him appear'd
To be a preparation 'gainst the Polack;
But, better look'd into, he truly found
It was against your highness: whereat grieved,
That so his sickness, age and impotence
Was falsely borne in hand, sends out arrests
On Fortinbras; which he, in brief, obeys;
Receives rebuke from Norway, and in fine
Makes vow before his uncle never more
To give the assay of arms against your majesty.
Whereon old Norway, overcome with joy,
Gives him three thousand crowns in annual fee,
And his commission to employ those soldiers,
So levied as before, against the Polack:
With an entreaty, herein further shown,


Giving a paper


*He asks for safe passage through Denmark for this mission.*

That it might please you to give quiet pass
Through your dominions for this enterprise,
On such regards of safety and allowance
As therein are set down.

## KING CLAUDIUS

*I think that will be fine but I will read it later and make my decision. In the meantime, thank you for your work. Go get some rest for tonight we will feast together. Welcome home!*

It likes us well;
And at our more consider'd time well read,
Answer, and think upon this business.
Meantime we thank you for your well-took labour:
Go to your rest; at night we'll feast together:
Most welcome home!


Exeunt VOLTIMAND and CORNELIUS


## LORD POLONIUS

*Well, that turned out well. My liege and madam, to think about what is majestic, what duty is, why day is day, night is night, and time is time, is a waste of time. To be serious for a moment, and I will be brief, I think your son is crazy. I call it crazy, because I don't know a better word to describe his actions. But, let's put madness aside.*

This business is well ended.
My liege, and madam, to expostulate
What majesty should be, what duty is,
Why day is day, night night, and time is time,
Were nothing but to waste night, day and time.
Therefore, since brevity is the soul of wit,
And tediousness the limbs and outward flourishes,
I will be brief: your noble son is mad:
Mad call I it; for, to define true madness,
What is't but to be nothing else but mad?
But let that go.


## QUEEN GERTRUDE

*Get to the point and don't embellish the truth.*

More matter, with less art.


## LORD POLONIUS

*Madam, I swear I am telling the truth. Hamlet is mad. It is pitiful and true. I am not embellishing the truth. If he is mad, and I think he is, then we must find the cause of his craziness, because it must be caused by something. You see, I have a daughter, for now, who is dutiful and obedient in giving me this. Now listen and see what you think.*

Madam, I swear I use no art at all.
That he is mad, 'tis true: 'tis true 'tis pity;
And pity 'tis 'tis true: a foolish figure;
But farewell it, for I will use no art.
Mad let us grant him, then: and now remains
That we find out the cause of this effect,
Or rather say, the cause of this defect,
For this effect defective comes by cause:
Thus it remains, and the remainder thus. Perpend.
I have a daughter--have while she is mine--
Who, in her duty and obedience, mark,
Hath given me this: now gather, and surmise.


Reads


*"To the heavenly idol of my soul, the most beautiful Ophelia,"—That's a little forward and calling her beautiful is definitely bold. But listen.*

'To the celestial and my soul's idol, the most
beautified Ophelia,'--
That's an ill phrase, a vile phrase; 'beautified' is
a vile phrase: but you shall hear. Thus:


Reads


*"In her excellent white bosom, et cetera."*

'In her excellent white bosom, these, & c.'


**QUEEN GERTRUDE**

*Hamlet sent this to her?*

Came this from Hamlet to her?


**LORD POLONIUS**

*Yes madam, listen for there is more.*

183

Good madam, stay awhile; I will be faithful.


Reads


*"You may doubt the stars are made of fire, the sun moves, or truth is a liar, but never doubt my love for you. "Oh dear Ophelia, I am not good at putting my feelings into words, but know I love you best, the best of all. Believe it. Goodbye." "Yours truly, my dear lady, as long as I live." My daughter in her obedience gave me this letter and told me how he has wooed her.*

'Doubt thou the stars are fire;
Doubt that the sun doth move;
Doubt truth to be a liar;
But never doubt I love.
'O dear Ophelia, I am ill at these numbers;
I have not art to reckon my groans: but that
I love thee best, O most best, believe it. Adieu.
'Thine evermore most dear lady, whilst
this machine is to him, HAMLET.'
This, in obedience, hath my daughter shown me,
And more above, hath his solicitings,
As they fell out by time, by means and place,
All given to mine ear.


### KING CLAUDIUS

*How does she feel about him?*

But how hath she
Received his love?


### LORD POLONIUS

*What do you take me for?*

What do you think of me?


### KING CLAUDIUS

*I think you are a faithful and honorable man.*

As of a man faithful and honourable.

## LORD POLONIUS

*I should hope so. But, what would you have thought of me if I had turned my head when I saw this blossoming love? What would you or your majesty the queen thought if I had not acted on what I saw? No, I took action. I told my daughter, "Lord Hamlet is a prince and not of your same position in life." Then, I ordered her to stay away from him, take no messages from him, or any gifts. When she did this, he fell into such a sadness that he could not eat, which led to a weak state that turned into madness. All of this took place while we were preoccupied by the situation with Fortinbras.*

I would fain prove so. But what might you think,
When I had seen this hot love on the wing--
As I perceived it, I must tell you that,
Before my daughter told me--what might you,
Or my dear majesty your queen here, think,
If I had play'd the desk or table-book,
Or given my heart a winking, mute and dumb,
Or look'd upon this love with idle sight;
What might you think? No, I went round to work,
And my young mistress thus I did bespeak:
'Lord Hamlet is a prince, out of thy star;
This must not be:' and then I precepts gave her,
That she should lock herself from his resort,
Admit no messengers, receive no tokens.
Which done, she took the fruits of my advice;
And he, repulsed--a short tale to make--
Fell into a sadness, then into a fast,
Thence to a watch, thence into a weakness,
Thence to a lightness, and, by this declension,
Into the madness wherein now he raves,
And all we mourn for.


## KING CLAUDIUS

*Do you think this is possible?*

Do you think 'tis this?


## QUEEN GERTRUDE

*It is possible and quite possible.*

It may be, very likely.

**LORD POLONIUS**

*Have I ever told you something I thought was true and it turned out not to be?*

Hath there been such a time--I'd fain know that--
That I have positively said 'Tis so,'
When it proved otherwise?


**KING CLAUDIUS**

*Not that I know of.*

Not that I know.


**LORD POLONIUS**

[Pointing to his head and shoulder]
*Not that I know of.*

*If it is not the truth, I will find out what is if I have to go the center of the world.*

Take this from this, if this be otherwise:
If circumstances lead me, I will find
Where truth is hid, though it were hid indeed
Within the centre.


**KING CLAUDIUS**

*What can we do to find out?*

How may we try it further?


**LORD POLONIUS**

*Sometimes he walks for hours here in the lobby.*

You know, sometimes he walks four hours together
Here in the lobby.


**QUEEN GERTRUDE**

*He does indeed.*

So he does indeed.

**LORD POLONIUS**

*When he is walking, I will allow my daughter to go to him. We will hide and watch what happens. If he doesn't love her and his love is not the reason for his breakdown then I will no longer be an assistant for the state, but a farmer.*

At such a time I'll loose my daughter to him:
Be you and I behind an arras then;
Mark the encounter: if he love her not
And be not from his reason fall'n thereon,
Let me be no assistant for a state,
But keep a farm and carters.


**KING CLAUDIUS**

*Okay, we will try it.*

We will try it.


**QUEEN GERTRUDE**

*Here he comes, the sad fellow, walking and reading.*

But, look, where sadly the poor wretch comes reading.


**LORD POLONIUS**

*Go. Both of you go away and I'll talk to him.*

Away, I do beseech you, both away:
I'll board him presently.


Exeunt KING CLAUDIUS, QUEEN GERTRUDE, and Attendants


Enter HAMLET, reading


*How are you Hamlet?*

O, give me leave:

How does my good Lord Hamlet?

**HAMLET**

*I'm well, thanks be to God.*

Well, God-a-mercy.

**LORD POLONIUS**

*Do you recognize me, my lord?*

Do you know me, my lord?

**HAMLET**

*Of course; you're a fishmonger.*

Excellent well; you are a fishmonger.

**LORD POLONIUS**

*No, not me, my lord.*

Not I, my lord.

**HAMLET**

*Well, I hope you are an honest man.*

Then I would you were so honest a man.

**LORD POLONIUS**

*Oh yes, I am honest, sir.*

Honest, my lord!

**HAMLET**

*Yes, it is rare to be honest in this world. Only one out of ten thousand men are honest.*

Ay, sir; to be honest, as this world goes, is to be
one man picked out of ten thousand.

**LORD POLONIUS**

*That's very true, my lord.*

That's very true, my lord.

**HAMLET**

*For if the sun causes maggots in a dead dog,--Have you a daughter?*

For if the sun breed maggots in a dead dog, being a
god kissing carrion,--Have you a daughter?

**LORD POLONIUS**

*I do, my lord.*

I have, my lord.

**HAMLET**

*Don't let her walk in the sun. Conception is a blessing, but don't let your daughter conceive that way, friend.*

Let her not walk i' the sun: conception is a
blessing: but not as your daughter may conceive.
Friend, look to 't.

**LORD POLONIUS**

[Aside]

*What do you mean? He is still hung up on my daughter. Yet, he didn't know me at first. He thought I was a fishmonger. He is far gone, and I remember suffering from love's sting in my youth. I'll try to talk to him again. What are you reading, my lord?*

How say you by that? Still harping on my
daughter: yet he knew me not at first; he said I
was a fishmonger: he is far gone, far gone: and
truly in my youth I suffered much extremity for
love; very near this. I'll speak to him again.

What do you read, my lord?

**HAMLET**

*Words, words, words.*

Words, words, words.

**LORD POLONIUS**

*What is the matter, my lord?*

What is the matter, my lord?

**HAMLET**

*Between who?*

Between who?

**LORD POLONIUS**

*I mean, the subject matter that you read, my lord.*

I mean, the matter that you read, my lord.

**HAMLET**

*Lies, sir. The slave to satire says here that old men have gray beards and wrinkled faces, their cloudy eyes are blood-shot, and they have lost their minds as well as their strength. Although, I believe it to be true, I think it is wrong to write it down. Don't you agree, you being as old as I am, if you could go back in time?*

Slanders, sir: for the satirical rogue says here
that old men have grey beards, that their faces are
wrinkled, their eyes purging thick amber and
plum-tree gum and that they have a plentiful lack of
wit, together with most weak hams: all which, sir,
though I most powerfully and potently believe, yet
I hold it not honesty to have it thus set down, for
yourself, sir, should be old as I am, if like a crab
you could go backward.

**LORD POLONIUS**

[Aside]

*There is some sense in his madness. Will you come outside, my lord?*

Though this be madness, yet there is method
in 't. Will you walk out of the air, my lord?


**HAMLET**

*To my grave?*

Into my grave.


**LORD POLONIUS**

*Well, that is outside.*

Indeed, that is out o' the air.


Aside


*He seems to be hinting at something with his answers. He seems so happy, too; a happiness only possible through insanity. I will leave him and arrange a later meeting between him and my daughter.—My honorable lord, I am leaving now.*

How pregnant sometimes his replies are! a happiness
that often madness hits on, which reason and sanity
could not so prosperously be delivered of. I will
leave him, and suddenly contrive the means of
meeting between him and my daughter.--My honourable
lord, I will most humbly take my leave of you.


**HAMLET**

*You cannot, sir. Take anything from me except my life, except my life, except my life.*

You cannot, sir, take from me any thing that I will
more willingly part withal: except my life, except
my life, except my life.

**LORD POLONIUS**

*Goodbye, my lord.*

Fare you well, my lord.

**HAMLET**

*These are some worrisome old fools!*

These tedious old fools!

Enter ROSENCRANTZ and GUILDENSTERN

**LORD POLONIUS**

*If you are looking for the Lord Hamlet, he is over there.*

You go to seek the Lord Hamlet; there he is.

**ROSENCRANTZ**

[To POLONIUS]

*Thank you, sir!*

God save you, sir!

Exit POLONIUS

**GUILDENSTERN**

*My honored lord!*

My honoured lord!

**ROSENCRANTZ**

*My most dear sir!*

My most dear lord!

**HAMLET**

*Well, look who it is, my excellent friends! How are you, Guildenstern? And, Rosencrantz! Gentlemen, how are you?*

My excellent good friends! How dost thou,
Guildenstern? Ah, Rosencrantz! Good lads, how do ye both?


**ROSENCRANTZ**

*We are well, happy and carefree.*

As the indifferent children of the earth.


**GUILDENSTERN**

*Happy, but not overly happy. We have been lucky, but not the luckiest.*

Happy, in that we are not over-happy;
On fortune's cap we are not the very button.


**HAMLET**

*But, you haven't been unlucky?*

Nor the soles of her shoe?


**ROSENCRANTZ**

*No, we are fine.*

Neither, my lord.


**HAMLET**

*So you live about the waist of Lady Luck.*

Then you live about her waist, or in the middle of
her favours?

**GUILDENSTERN**

*Yes, by God, we live somewhere in the middle.*

'Faith, her privates we.


**HAMLET**

*Near her secret parts? Oh, she is a whore. What's going on?*

In the secret parts of fortune? O, most true; she
is a strumpet. What's the news?


**ROSENCRANTZ**

*Nothing, my lord, since there is peace in the world.*

None, my lord, but that the world's grown honest.


**HAMLET**

*I guess that means that the end of the world is soon. Let me be more specific: What are doing here in this prison?*

Then is doomsday near: but your news is not true.
Let me question more in particular: what have you,
my good friends, deserved at the hands of fortune,
that she sends you to prison hither?


**GUILDENSTERN**

*Prison, my lord!*

Prison, my lord!


**HAMLET**

*Denmark's a prison.*

Denmark's a prison.


**ROSENCRANTZ**

*So is the world.*

Then is the world one.


**HAMLET**

*Yes, the world has many prisons, and Denmark is the worst.*

A goodly one; in which there are many confines,
wards and dungeons, Denmark being one o' the worst.


**ROSENCRANTZ**

*We don't think so, my lord.*

We think not so, my lord.


**HAMLET**

*Well, you may not think so, but it is definitely a prison to me.*

Why, then, 'tis none to you; for there is nothing
either good or bad, but thinking makes it so: to me
it is a prison.


**ROSENCRANTZ**

*That is because you are so ambitious. You are too big for such a small country.*

Why then, your ambition makes it one; 'tis too
narrow for your mind.


**HAMLET**

*Oh, God, I could live in a nut shell and feel like a king, but I have bad dreams.*

O God, I could be bounded in a nut shell and count
myself a king of infinite space, were it not that I
have bad dreams.


**GUILDENSTERN**

*Dreams and ambition are one in the same; ambition is the shadow of a dream.*

Which dreams indeed are ambition, for the very
substance of the ambitious is merely the shadow of a dream.


### HAMLET

*A dream is just a shadow.*

A dream itself is but a shadow.


### ROSENCRANTZ

*That is true that I think a dream is just a shadow of a shadow.*

Truly, and I hold ambition of so airy and light a
quality that it is but a shadow's shadow.


### HAMLET

*In that case, beggars are real and kings or heroes are the shadows of beggars. Let's go inside. I can't think anymore.*

Then are our beggars bodies, and our monarchs and
outstretched heroes the beggars' shadows. Shall we
to the court? for, by my fay, I cannot reason.


### ROSENCRANTZ GUILDENSTERN

*We're waiting on you.*

We'll wait upon you.


### HAMLET

*No way. I will not put you with the rest of my servants, because they are dreadful. But, tell me friends, why are you in Elsinore?*

No such matter: I will not sort you with the rest
of my servants, for, to speak to you like an honest
man, I am most dreadfully attended. But, in the
beaten way of friendship, what make you at Elsinore?

## ROSENCRANTZ

*Just to visit you, my lord; no other reason.*

To visit you, my lord; no other occasion.


## HAMLET

*I am a beggar now and am poor in thanks, but, I thank you. My thanks are not even worth very much. Weren't you sent for? Or was it your own decision? Is this visitation without some purpose? Just tell me, straight.*

Beggar that I am, I am even poor in thanks; but I
thank you: and sure, dear friends, my thanks are
too dear a halfpenny. Were you not sent for? Is it
your own inclining? Is it a free visitation? Come,
deal justly with me: come, come; nay, speak.


## GUILDENSTERN

*What do you want us to say, my lord?*

What should we say, my lord?


## HAMLET

*Tell me whatever you wish, but answer my question. You were sent for. I can tell by the look on your face. You are not good at lying. I know the good king and queen sent for you.*

Why, any thing, but to the purpose. You were sent
for; and there is a kind of confession in your looks
which your modesties have not craft enough to colour:
I know the good king and queen have sent for you.


## ROSENCRANTZ

*Why would they do that, my lord?*

To what end, my lord?


## HAMLET

*You tell me. But let me remind you of our friendship, starting in our youth, and our love for one another. Tell me directly, if you were sent for.*

That you must teach me. But let me conjure you, by
the rights of our fellowship, by the consonancy of
our youth, by the obligation of our ever-preserved
love, and by what more dear a better proposer could
charge you withal, be even and direct with me,
whether you were sent for, or no?

## ROSENCRANTZ

[Aside to GUILDENSTERN]

*What should we say?*

What say you?

## HAMLET

[Aside]

*I am watching you.—If you love me, don't lie.*

Nay, then, I have an eye of you.--If you
love me, hold not off.

## GUILDENSTERN

*My lord, we were sent for.*

My lord, we were sent for.

## HAMLET

*Well, I will tell you why you were asked to come. Then, your allegiance to the king and queen will not be broken. Lately, I have been depressed. You know, lost my zeal for life. I did not want to exercise or have any fun. The world is just a foul place. And, man! What a joke! I have no interest in men or manly things, or women, for that matter. I guess you still do, by the smile on your face.*

I will tell you why; so shall my anticipation
prevent your discovery, and your secrecy to the king
and queen moult no feather. I have of late--but
wherefore I know not--lost all my mirth, forgone all

custom of exercises; and indeed it goes so heavily
with my disposition that this goodly frame, the
earth, seems to me a sterile promontory, this most
excellent canopy, the air, look you, this brave
o'erhanging firmament, this majestical roof fretted
with golden fire, why, it appears no other thing to
me than a foul and pestilent congregation of vapours.
What a piece of work is a man! how noble in reason!
how infinite in faculty! in form and moving how
express and admirable! in action how like an angel!
in apprehension how like a god! the beauty of the
world! the paragon of animals! And yet, to me,
what is this quintessence of dust? man delights not
me: no, nor woman neither, though by your smiling
you seem to say so.


## ROSENCRANTZ

*I wasn't thinking anything like that.*

My lord, there was no such stuff in my thoughts.


## HAMLET

*Why did you laugh then, when I said "I do not have any in interest in things of men?"*

Why did you laugh then, when I said 'man delights not me'?


## ROSENCRANTZ

*I was just thinking, if you don't like the things that make men happy, you're going to be pretty bored by the actors we passed on the way here. They are coming to entertain you.*

To think, my lord, if you delight not in man, what
lenten entertainment the players shall receive from
you: we coted them on the way; and hither are they
coming, to offer you service.


## HAMLET

*I'll welcome the actor who plays the king and watch the knight as he waves around his weapons. I will show the lover gratitude and laugh at the clown, and I'll listen to the lady character babble on. Which actors are coming?*

He that plays the king shall be welcome; his majesty

shall have tribute of me; the adventurous knight
shall use his foil and target; the lover shall not
sigh gratis; the humourous man shall end his part
in peace; the clown shall make those laugh whose
lungs are tickled o' the sere; and the lady shall
say her mind freely, or the blank verse shall halt
for't. What players are they?

## ROSENCRANTZ

*The tragic group from the city.*

Even those you were wont to take delight in, the
tragedians of the city.

## HAMLET

*What are they doing on the road? They were very popular and profitable.*

How chances it they travel? their residence, both
in reputation and profit, was better both ways.

## ROSENCRANTZ

*Things change and now they travel.*

I think their inhibition comes by the means of the
late innovation.

## HAMLET

*Are they still popular as they used to be? Do they still pull a crowd?*

Do they hold the same estimation they did when I was
in the city? are they so followed?

## ROSENCRANTZ

*No, not anymore.*

No, indeed, are they not.

**HAMLET**

*Why? Are they getting old?*

How comes it? do they grow rusty?


**ROSENCRANTZ**

*No, they are the same, but there is a group of children who yell out their lines the crowd loves. They are all the rage. The rich theater-goers don't come out for fear they will be teased by the writers.*

Nay, their endeavour keeps in the wonted pace: but
there is, sir, an aery of children, little eyases,
that cry out on the top of question, and are most
tyrannically clapped for't: these are now the
fashion, and so berattle the common stages--so they
call them--that many wearing rapiers are afraid of
goose-quills and dare scarce come thither.


**HAMLET**

*Children actors? Who takes care of them? How do they get around? Will they stay actors when they grow up? Won't they be used up by the time they are adults? Or do they have money?*

What, are they children? who maintains 'em? how are
they escoted? Will they pursue the quality no
longer than they can sing? will they not say
afterwards, if they should grow themselves to common
players--as it is most like, if their means are no
better--their writers do them wrong, to make them
exclaim against their own succession?


**ROSENCRANTZ**

*True, there has been a lot of controversy over the subject. For awhile, no plays were being held without a big fight over who was going to act.*

'Faith, there has been much to do on both sides; and
the nation holds it no sin to tarre them to
controversy: there was, for a while, no money bid
for argument, unless the poet and the player went to
cuffs in the question.


**HAMLET**

*Really?*

Is't possible?

## GUILDENSTERN

*Oh, there has been much arguing about it.*

O, there has been much throwing about of brains.

## HAMLET

*Can the boys carry it off?*

Do the boys carry it away?

## ROSENCRANTZ

*Yes, they do. And they handle an adult load, too.*

Ay, that they do, my lord; Hercules and his load too.

## HAMLET

*I guess it is not very strange. For example, my uncle, the king of Denmark, was made fun of when my father lived. Now, those same people who made fun of him are paying for a little picture of him. It certainly is something to think about.*

It is not very strange; for mine uncle is king of
Denmark, and those that would make mows at him while
my father lived, give twenty, forty, fifty, an
hundred ducats a-piece for his picture in little.
'Sblood, there is something in this more than
natural, if philosophy could find it out.

Flourish of trumpets within

## GUILDENSTERN

*Here come the actors.*

There are the players.

## HAMLET

*Gentlemen, welcome to Elsinore. Shake my hand and let me keep up with fashion and customs. You are welcome. But, let me deceive my uncle-father and aunt-mother.*

Gentlemen, you are welcome to Elsinore. Your hands, come then: the appurtenance of welcome is fashion and ceremony: let me comply with you in this garb, lest my extent to the players, which, I tell you, must show fairly outward, should more appear like entertainment than yours. You are welcome: but my uncle-father and aunt-mother are deceived.


## GUILDENSTERN

*In what, my dear lord?*

In what, my dear lord?


## HAMLET

*I am completely crazy, sometimes. But, other times I am straight as an arrow.*

I am but mad north-north-west: when the wind is southerly I know a hawk from a handsaw.


Enter POLONIUS


## LORD POLONIUS

*Gentlemen, I hope you are well!*

Well be with you, gentlemen!


## HAMLET

*Hey, listen Guilderstern and Rosencrantz. There's a great big baby who is still in diapers.*

Hark you, Guildenstern; and you too: at each ear a hearer: that great baby you see there is not yet out of his swaddling-clouts.

**ROSENCRANTZ**

*He must be in his second childhood; once a man, twice a child, they say.*

Happily he's the second time come to them; for they
say an old man is twice a child.


**HAMLET**

*I believe he is coming to tell me about the actors. Watch. Oh, yes, you were right about Monday.*

I will prophesy he comes to tell me of the players;
mark it. You say right, sir: o' Monday morning;
'twas so indeed.


**LORD POLONIUS**

*My lord, I have news for you.*

My lord, I have news to tell you.


**HAMLET**

*My lord, I have news for you. When Roscius was an actor in Rome…*

My lord, I have news to tell you.
When Roscius was an actor in Rome,--


**LORD POLONIUS**

*The actors are here, my lord.*

The actors are come hither, my lord.


**HAMLET**

*Whatever!*

Buz, buz!


**LORD POLONIUS**

*My word...*

Upon mine honour,--

## HAMLET

*Each one coming in on his ass...*

Then came each actor on his ass,--

## LORD POLONIUS

*These are the best actors in the world. They can perform anything from Seneca to Plautus. There is nothing too difficult for these actors.*

The best actors in the world, either for tragedy, comedy, history, pastoral, pastoral-comical, historical-pastoral, tragical-historical, tragical-comical-historical-pastoral, scene individable, or poem unlimited: Seneca cannot be too heavy, nor Plautus too light. For the law of writ and the liberty, these are the only men.

## HAMLET

*Oh, Jephthah, judge of Israel, what a treasure you have!*

O Jephthah, judge of Israel, what a treasure hadst thou!

## LORD POLONIUS

*What treasure are you talking about?*

What a treasure had he, my lord?

## HAMLET

*Well, "One fair daughter, and no more; that he loved so well."*

Why,
'One fair daughter and no more,
The which he loved passing well.'

**LORD POLONIUS**

[Aside]

*Still hung up on my daughter.*

Still on my daughter.

**HAMLET**

*Am I not telling it right, old Jephthah?*

Am I not i' the right, old Jephthah?

**LORD POLONIUS**

*I do have a daughter like Japhthath, my lord, and I love her very much.*If you call me Jephthah, my lord, I have a daughter
that I love passing well.

**HAMLET**

*No, that can't be right?*

Nay, that follows not.

**LORD POLONIUS**

*What is right, then?*

What follows, then, my lord?

**HAMLET**

*Why, only God knows what is right. Listen to the words. Wait, here comes the actors.*

Why,
'As by lot, God wot,'
and then, you know,
'It came to pass, as most like it was,'--
the first row of the pious chanson will show you
more; for look, where my abridgement comes.

Enter four or five Players

*You are welcome friends. I am glad to see you doing so well. Oh, I know you. You've grown a beard, since I saw you last. Have you come to put a beard on me, too? And, my young lady, you've grown, since I saw you. I hope your voice hasn't changed. Actors, you are welcome. Give us a speech, a passionate one to peak our interests.*

You are welcome, masters; welcome, all. I am glad
to see thee well. Welcome, good friends. O, my old
friend! thy face is valenced since I saw thee last:
comest thou to beard me in Denmark? What, my young
lady and mistress! By'r lady, your ladyship is
nearer to heaven than when I saw you last, by the
altitude of a chopine. Pray God, your voice, like
apiece of uncurrent gold, be not cracked within the
ring. Masters, you are all welcome. We'll e'en
to't like French falconers, fly at any thing we see:
we'll have a speech straight: come, give us a taste
of your quality; come, a passionate speech.


**First Player**

*What kind of speech, my lord?*

What speech, my lord?


**HAMLET**

*I heard you once make a speech, but you never acted it out. Or if it was, it wasn't very popular. It was like caviar to the poor. But, the critics and I thought it was excellent. I remember one said it was not fancy but clever. Another said it was truly honest. One speech I loved was from Aeneas to Dido, talking about the death of Priam. If you remember it, start with "The rugged Pyrrhus, like the Hyrcanian beast." No, that's not right. It started with "The rugged Pyrrhus, with black arms and purpose, resembling the night on his horse, is now covered in red blood of fathers, mothers, daughters, and sons. The blood is baked with the burning streets from fires he lit that illuminate the murders he committed. Drenched in gore, he goes in search of old Priam." Start from there.*

I heard thee speak me a speech once, but it was
never acted; or, if it was, not above once; for the
play, I remember, pleased not the million; 'twas
caviare to the general: but it was--as I received
it, and others, whose judgments in such matters
cried in the top of mine--an excellent play, well
digested in the scenes, set down with as much

modesty as cunning. I remember, one said there
were no sallets in the lines to make the matter
savoury, nor no matter in the phrase that might
indict the author of affectation; but called it an
honest method, as wholesome as sweet, and by very
much more handsome than fine. One speech in it I
chiefly loved: 'twas Aeneas' tale to Dido; and
thereabout of it especially, where he speaks of
Priam's slaughter: if it live in your memory, begin
at this line: let me see, let me see--
'The rugged Pyrrhus, like the Hyrcanian beast,'--
it is not so:--it begins with Pyrrhus:--
'The rugged Pyrrhus, he whose sable arms,
Black as his purpose, did the night resemble
When he lay couched in the ominous horse,
Hath now this dread and black complexion smear'd
With heraldry more dismal; head to foot
Now is he total gules; horridly trick'd
With blood of fathers, mothers, daughters, sons,
Baked and impasted with the parching streets,
That lend a tyrannous and damned light
To their lord's murder: roasted in wrath and fire,
And thus o'er-sized with coagulate gore,
With eyes like carbuncles, the hellish Pyrrhus
Old grandsire Priam seeks.'
So, proceed you.


**LORD POLONIUS**

*I swear to God, my lord, you said that so well and with the proper accent and pauses.*

'Fore God, my lord, well spoken, with good accent and
good discretion.


**First Player**

*Soon, he finds him, after his fall to the Greeks. With his old sword he is unable to bear, young Pyrrhus drives at Priam. His rage leaves him unbalanced but the force of his blow knocks Priam to the ground. Just before taking the head of Priam, Pyrrhus hears the roar of flames in the city of Ilium. He stands frozen as if in a painting. Like the quiet before the storm, Pyrrhus took back up his sword and with newly found fury wielded a deathly blow on Priam.—Out, out Fortune, you whore. Gods of heaven, take away her power and break her wheel of fortune. Send her and it to the depths of hell.*

'Anon he finds him
Striking too short at Greeks; his antique sword,

Rebellious to his arm, lies where it falls,
Repugnant to command: unequal match'd,
Pyrrhus at Priam drives; in rage strikes wide;
But with the whiff and wind of his fell sword
The unnerved father falls. Then senseless Ilium,
Seeming to feel this blow, with flaming top
Stoops to his base, and with a hideous crash
Takes prisoner Pyrrhus' ear: for, lo! his sword,
Which was declining on the milky head
Of reverend Priam, seem'd i' the air to stick:
So, as a painted tyrant, Pyrrhus stood,
And like a neutral to his will and matter,
Did nothing.
But, as we often see, against some storm,
A silence in the heavens, the rack stand still,
The bold winds speechless and the orb below
As hush as death, anon the dreadful thunder
Doth rend the region, so, after Pyrrhus' pause,
Aroused vengeance sets him new a-work;
And never did the Cyclops' hammers fall
On Mars's armour forged for proof eterne
With less remorse than Pyrrhus' bleeding sword
Now falls on Priam.
Out, out, thou strumpet, Fortune! All you gods,
In general synod 'take away her power;
Break all the spokes and fellies from her wheel,
And bowl the round nave down the hill of heaven,
As low as to the fiends!'


## LORD POLONIUS

*This is too long.*

This is too long.


## HAMLET

*We'll let the barber cut it, as well as your beard.—Please go on.—He only likes the crude scenes, or else he falls asleep.—Go to the part about Hecuba.*

It shall to the barber's, with your beard. Prithee, say on: he's for a jig or a tale of bawdry, or he sleeps: say on: come to Hecuba.

### First Player

*But who had seen the quiet queen,--*

'But who, O, who had seen the mobled queen--'

### HAMLET

*The "quiet queen?"*

'The mobled queen?'

### LORD POLONIUS

*That sounds good! "Quiet queen!"*

That's good; 'mobled queen' is good.

### First Player

*She runs barefoot throughout the city threatening to put out the flames with her tears, a cloth on her head which once bore a crown and a blanket around her where once she wore a robe. Someone seeing her like this would have cursed Fortune. Even the gods, themselves, would have pity on her if they had seen her watch Pyrrhus murder her husband, unless the gods have no care for humans.*

'Run barefoot up and down, threatening the flames
With bisson rheum; a clout upon that head
Where late the diadem stood, and for a robe,
About her lank and all o'er-teemed loins,
A blanket, in the alarm of fear caught up;
Who this had seen, with tongue in venom steep'd,
'Gainst Fortune's state would treason have pronounced:
But if the gods themselves did see her then
When she saw Pyrrhus make malicious sport
In mincing with his sword her husband's limbs,
The instant burst of clamour that she made,
Unless things mortal move them not at all,
Would have made milch the burning eyes of heaven,
And passion in the gods.'

### LORD POLONIUS

*Look, the actor has turned colors and has tears in his eyes. Please let him stop!*

Look, whether he has not turned his colour and has
tears in's eyes. Pray you, no more.

## HAMLET

*Very well. I'll have you tell me the rest, soon.—Polonius, will you see the players are taken care of? Do you understand? Be good to them, for it would be better to have a bad epitaph than have them angry with you.*

'Tis well: I'll have thee speak out the rest soon.
Good my lord, will you see the players well
bestowed? Do you hear, let them be well used; for
they are the abstract and brief chronicles of the
time: after your death you were better have a bad
epitaph than their ill report while you live.

## LORD POLONIUS

*My lord, I will treat them as they deserve.*

My lord, I will use them according to their desert.

## HAMLET

*Oh no man, if every man were treated as he deserved, no one would escape punishment. Treat them as you would want to be treated with respect and honor. The less deserving, the more the generosity. Take them inside.*

God's bodykins, man, much better: use every man
after his desert, and who should 'scape whipping?
Use them after your own honour and dignity: the less
they deserve, the more merit is in your bounty.
Take them in.

## LORD POLONIUS

*Come along, sirs.*

Come, sirs.

## HAMLET

*Go with him, my friends. We'll hear a play tomorrow.*

Follow him, friends: we'll hear a play to-morrow.

Exit POLONIUS with all the Players but the First

*Do you know the play, "The Murder of Gonzago?"*

Dost thou hear me, old friend; can you play the
Murder of Gonzago?


**First Player**

*Yes, my lord.*

Ay, my lord.


**HAMLET**

*We would like to hear it tomorrow night. Could you add a few lines for me?*

We'll ha't to-morrow night. You could, for a need,
study a speech of some dozen or sixteen lines, which
I would set down and insert in't, could you not?


**First Player**

*Yes, my lord.*

Ay, my lord.


**HAMLET**

*Good.—Follow that man; and do not mock him.*

Very well. Follow that lord; and look you mock him
not.


Exit First Player


*My friends, I must leave now. I will see you tonight. Welcome to Elsinore.*

My good friends, I'll leave you till night: you are
welcome to Elsinore.

**ROSENCRANTZ**

*Okay, my lord.*

Good my lord!


**HAMLET**

*Good, go with God.*

Ay, so, God be wi' ye;


Exeunt ROSENCRANTZ and GUILDENSTERN


*Thank God, I am alone. What a mischievous man I am! Aren't I terrible to make the actor feel something so powerful in his soul that it brought tears to his eyes and made his voice crack. And, for what? Nothing! For Hecuba? What's Hecuba to him or vice-versa? What would he do if her were in my shoes? He would probably cry and make horrible speeches, drive the guilty crazy and appall the little ones. He would confuse the ignorant spectators and amaze them. But I am not so brave and so I say nothing against a king who stole his position and property. Am I a coward? Would someone call me a villain, hit me, pull off my beard and blow it back in my face, or tweak my nose? Would someone call me a liar and I not respond? I wouldn't do anything because I'm afraid or else I would have already killed the king, that bloody villain! That remorseless, treacherous villain. I want vengeance! I am such an ass! I, the son of a dear murdered father, with all rights to seek revenge, stand around and do nothing! I need to get control! I have heard that some people are so driven by watching a play they confess their sins out loud. I know! I'll have the players put on a play similar to the murder of my father and I will watch my uncle's reaction. If he flinches or becomes pale I will know for sure what to do because all I have to go on are the words of a ghost. If the ghost is the devil who is trying to condemn my soul, I need to be careful before I act. The play will reveal the true conscience of the king.*

Now I am alone.
O, what a rogue and peasant slave am I!
Is it not monstrous that this player here,
But in a fiction, in a dream of passion,
Could force his soul so to his own conceit
That from her working all his visage wann'd,
Tears in his eyes, distraction in's aspect,
A broken voice, and his whole function suiting
With forms to his conceit? and all for nothing!
For Hecuba!
What's Hecuba to him, or he to Hecuba,
That he should weep for her? What would he do,
Had he the motive and the cue for passion

That I have? He would drown the stage with tears
And cleave the general ear with horrid speech,
Make mad the guilty and appal the free,
Confound the ignorant, and amaze indeed
The very faculties of eyes and ears. Yet I,
A dull and muddy-mettled rascal, peak,
Like John-a-dreams, unpregnant of my cause,
And can say nothing; no, not for a king,
Upon whose property and most dear life
A damn'd defeat was made. Am I a coward?
Who calls me villain? breaks my pate across?
Plucks off my beard, and blows it in my face?
Tweaks me by the nose? gives me the lie i' the throat,
As deep as to the lungs? who does me this?
Ha!
'Swounds, I should take it: for it cannot be
But I am pigeon-liver'd and lack gall
To make oppression bitter, or ere this
I should have fatted all the region kites
With this slave's offal: bloody, bawdy villain!
Remorseless, treacherous, lecherous, kindless villain!
O, vengeance!
Why, what an ass am I! This is most brave,
That I, the son of a dear father murder'd,
Prompted to my revenge by heaven and hell,
Must, like a whore, unpack my heart with words,
And fall a-cursing, like a very drab,
A scullion!
Fie upon't! foh! About, my brain! I have heard
That guilty creatures sitting at a play
Have by the very cunning of the scene
Been struck so to the soul that presently
They have proclaim'd their malefactions;
For murder, though it have no tongue, will speak
With most miraculous organ. I'll have these players
Play something like the murder of my father
Before mine uncle: I'll observe his looks;
I'll tent him to the quick: if he but blench,
I know my course. The spirit that I have seen
May be the devil: and the devil hath power
To assume a pleasing shape; yea, and perhaps
Out of my weakness and my melancholy,
As he is very potent with such spirits,
Abuses me to damn me: I'll have grounds
More relative than this: the play 's the thing
Wherein I'll catch the conscience of the king.

Exit

# Act III

# Scene I
*A room in the castle*

Enter KING CLAUDIUS, QUEEN GERTRUDE, POLONIUS, OPHELIA, ROSENCRANTZ, and GUILDENSTERN

**KING CLAUDIUS**

*Have you figured out why he is acting so crazy?*

And can you, by no drift of circumstance,
Get from him why he puts on this confusion,
Grating so harshly all his days of quiet
With turbulent and dangerous lunacy?

**ROSENCRANTZ**

*He does say he feels distracted, but he did not explain the cause.*

He does confess he feels himself distracted;
But from what cause he will by no means speak.

**GUILDENSTERN**

*He doesn't seem to want to be questioned. He skirts around the issue of how he feels.*

Nor do we find him forward to be sounded,
But, with a crafty madness, keeps aloof,
When we would bring him on to some confession
Of his true state.

**QUEEN GERTRUDE**

*Did he treat you well?*

Did he receive you well?

**ROSENCRANTZ**

*Yes, he was a gentleman.*

Most like a gentleman.

**GUILDENSTERN**

*But, it seemed forced, like he had to try to be nice.*

But with much forcing of his disposition.

**ROSENCRANTZ**

*He didn't ask us any questions, but he answered all of ours.*

Niggard of question; but, of our demands,
Most free in his reply.

**QUEEN GERTRUDE**

*Did you ask him to hang out with you?*

Did you assay him?
To any pastime?

**ROSENCRANTZ**

*Madam, it just so happened that a group of actors we knew came up, and when we told Hamlet about them, it seemed to cheer him up. They are supposed to play for him tonight.*

Madam, it so fell out, that certain players
We o'er-raught on the way: of these we told him;
And there did seem in him a kind of joy
To hear of it: they are about the court,
And, as I think, they have already order
This night to play before him.

**LORD POLONIUS**

*It's true, and he asked me to ask you, your majesties, to come and join him.*

'Tis most true:
And he beseech'd me to entreat your majesties
To hear and see the matter.

**KING CLAUDIUS**

*This does my heart good to hear he is interested in something. Gentlemen, please encourage him to attend the play, and maybe it will make him happier.*

With all my heart; and it doth much content me
To hear him so inclined.
Good gentlemen, give him a further edge,
And drive his purpose on to these delights.


**ROSENCRANTZ**

*We will, my lord.*

We shall, my lord.

Exeunt ROSENCRANTZ and GUILDENSTERN

**KING CLAUDIUS**

*Sweet Gertrude, please leave us alone a minute. We have sent for Hamlet to come here so he may bump into Ophelia. Her father and I are acting as spies. We are trying to see if it is love that is making him act so strangely.*

Sweet Gertrude, leave us too;
For we have closely sent for Hamlet hither,
That he, as 'twere by accident, may here
Affront Ophelia:
Her father and myself, lawful espials,
Will so bestow ourselves that, seeing, unseen,
We may of their encounter frankly judge,
And gather by him, as he is behaved,
If 't be the affliction of his love or no
That thus he suffers for.


**QUEEN GERTRUDE**

*Yes, I'll go. As for you, Ophelia, I do hope it is his infatuation with your beauty that makes him crazy. I also hope your virtue will help him return to his normal state, for both your sakes.*

I shall obey you.
And for your part, Ophelia, I do wish
That your good beauties be the happy cause
Of Hamlet's wildness: so shall I hope your virtues
Will bring him to his wonted way again,
To both your honours.

**OPHELIA**

*Madam, I wish it, too.*

Madam, I wish it may.

Exit QUEEN GERTRUDE

**LORD POLONIUS**

*Ophelia, walk over here. We will hide over there.*

Ophelia, walk you here. Gracious, so please you,
We will bestow ourselves.

To OPHELIA

*Read this book and act as if you are alone, like people who act righteous to cover up their evil ways.*

Read on this book;
That show of such an exercise may colour
Your loneliness. We are oft to blame in this,--
'Tis too much proved--that with devotion's visage
And pious action we do sugar o'er
The devil himself.


**KING CLAUDIUS**

[Aside]

*That's true! His words are like daggers to my conscience! The harlot's cheek, covered with makeup is as ugly as the actions I am trying to hide with pretty words. Oh, my heavy heart!*

O, 'tis too true!
How smart a lash that speech doth give my conscience!
The harlot's cheek, beautied with plastering art,
Is not more ugly to the thing that helps it
Than is my deed to my most painted word:
O heavy burthen!


**LORD POLONIUS**

*I hear him coming: Let's hide, my lord.*

I hear him coming: let's withdraw, my lord.

Exeunt KING CLAUDIUS and POLONIUS

Enter HAMLET

**HAMLET**

*To live or to die…That is the question. Is it more courageous to suffer through life's horrors or to fight them and perhaps end them? Should I die or like death, sleep, and perhaps dream? Now there's the problem. By sleeping, I would put an end to the torment life offers. Why should anyone choose to live when you must suffer the hands of time, the evil of men, the pain of unreturned love, or the unjust government? Who would endure such struggles in life, but those that dread the unknown of death, the undiscovered country from where travelers never return. Our fear of death makes us all cowards, and we consider our choices too much, keeping us from acting at all. But, wait! The beautiful Ophelia!—Angel, do pray for me.*

To be, or not to be: that is the question:
Whether 'tis nobler in the mind to suffer
The slings and arrows of outrageous fortune,
Or to take arms against a sea of troubles,
And by opposing end them? To die: to sleep;
No more; and by a sleep to say we end
The heart-ache and the thousand natural shocks
That flesh is heir to, 'tis a consummation
Devoutly to be wish'd. To die, to sleep;
To sleep: perchance to dream: ay, there's the rub;
For in that sleep of death what dreams may come
When we have shuffled off this mortal coil,
Must give us pause: there's the respect
That makes calamity of so long life;
For who would bear the whips and scorns of time,
The oppressor's wrong, the proud man's contumely,
The pangs of despised love, the law's delay,
The insolence of office and the spurns
That patient merit of the unworthy takes,
When he himself might his quietus make
With a bare bodkin? who would fardels bear,
To grunt and sweat under a weary life,
But that the dread of something after death,
The undiscover'd country from whose bourn
No traveller returns, puzzles the will
And makes us rather bear those ills we have
Than fly to others that we know not of?
Thus conscience does make cowards of us all;
And thus the native hue of resolution
Is sicklied o'er with the pale cast of thought,
And enterprises of great pith and moment
With this regard their currents turn awry,
And lose the name of action.--Soft you now!
The fair Ophelia! Nymph, in thy orisons
Be all my sins remember'd.

**OPHELIA**

*Oh, hello, my lord. How have you been doing?*

Good my lord,
How does your honour for this many a day?


**HAMLET**

*Very well, thank you.*

I humbly thank you; well, well, well.


**OPHELIA**

*My lord, I have some things that belong to you that I have been wanting to return. Please take them.*

My lord, I have remembrances of yours,
That I have longed long to re-deliver;
I pray you, now receive them.


**HAMLET**

*No, it's not mine. I never gave you anything.*

No, not I;
I never gave you aught.


**OPHELIA**

*My lord, you know very well you did. You gave me the sweetest letters, but they mean nothing to me now. Here they are.*

My honour'd lord, you know right well you did;
And, with them, words of so sweet breath composed
As made the things more rich: their perfume lost,
Take these again; for to the noble mind
Rich gifts wax poor when givers prove unkind.
There, my lord.


**HAMLET**

*Ha, ha! Are you telling the truth?*

Ha, ha! are you honest?

**OPHELIA**

*What?*

My lord?

**HAMLET**

*Are you beautiful?*

Are you fair?

**OPHELIA**

*What are you talking about?*

What means your lordship?

**HAMLET**

*I am saying, if you are honest and beautiful, then your honesty should not affect your beauty.*

That if you be honest and fair, your honesty should
admit no discourse to your beauty.

**OPHELIA**

*Is beauty, my lord, more important than honesty?*

Could beauty, my lord, have better commerce than
with honesty?

**HAMLET**

*Yes, because beauty can change a person, but honesty cannot change anything. I used to be confused by this, but I understand now. I used to love you.*

Ay, truly; for the power of beauty will sooner

transform honesty from what it is to a bawd than the
force of honesty can translate beauty into his
likeness: this was sometime a paradox, but now the
time gives it proof. I did love you once.


**OPHELIA**

*You made me think you did.*

Indeed, my lord, you made me believe so.


**HAMLET**

*You should not have believed me, because we are all evil beings. I did not love you.* You should not have believed me; for virtue cannot
so inoculate our old stock but we shall relish of
it: I loved you not.


**OPHELIA**

*I was fooled.*

I was the more deceived.


**HAMLET**

*Get to a convent or would you rather be a mother to more sinners? I am an honest person, but even I am guilty of sin and it would have been better if I had never been born. I am proud, vengeful, and ambitious, with more sin in my heart than I have time to put into thoughts or actions. What should a man, like me, do? We are all sinners; don't believe any of us. Go find a convent. Where's your father?*

Get thee to a nunnery: why wouldst thou be a
breeder of sinners? I am myself indifferent honest;
but yet I could accuse me of such things that it
were better my mother had not borne me: I am very
proud, revengeful, ambitious, with more offences at
my beck than I have thoughts to put them in,
imagination to give them shape, or time to act them
in. What should such fellows as I do crawling
between earth and heaven? We are arrant knaves,
all; believe none of us. Go thy ways to a nunnery.
Where's your father?

**OPHELIA**

*At home, my lord.*

At home, my lord.


**HAMLET**

*May he stay there and pretend to be a fool. Goodbye.*

Let the doors be shut upon him, that he may play the fool no where but in's own house. Farewell.


**OPHELIA**

*O, help him, Lord!*

O, help him, you sweet heavens!


**HAMLET**

*If you do marry, I'll give you this curse as a gift,--Be as cold as ice, pure as snow, but you will not escape trouble. Now, go to a convent. Goodbye. Or, if you need to marry, marry a fool. Smart men know what women will do. Go to a convent, and go quickly. Goodbye.*

If thou dost marry, I'll give thee this plague for thy dowry: be thou as chaste as ice, as pure as snow, thou shalt not escape calumny. Get thee to a nunnery, go: farewell. Or, if thou wilt needs marry, marry a fool; for wise men know well enough what monsters you make of them. To a nunnery, go, and quickly too. Farewell.


**OPHELIA**

*Oh God, help him!*

O heavenly powers, restore him!


**HAMLET**

*I have heard of how you put on makeup and dance and walk about talking like high society. I have heard of your loose ways. It's driven me crazy. Go on. I declare there will be no more marriages: those that already are married may stay that way, but there will be no more. Take yourself to a convent.*

I have heard of your paintings too, well enough; God
has given you one face, and you make yourselves
another: you jig, you amble, and you lisp, and
nick-name God's creatures, and make your wantonness
your ignorance. Go to, I'll no more on't; it hath
made me mad. I say, we will have no more marriages:
those that are married already, all but one, shall
live; the rest shall keep as they are. To a
nunnery, go.

Exit

**OPHELIA**

*Oh, what a wonderful mind has been lost! He was such a gentleman, a scholar, and soldier. He used to be the pride of the state with his perfect charm and sense of taste. Everyone loved him, wanted to be like him! Now he is so low! And I, of all the ladies who loved to hear his voice, have seen him at his worst. His youthfulness has been killed by madness. Oh, how terrible to see what I have seen, to see what I see, now.*

O, what a noble mind is here o'erthrown!
The courtier's, soldier's, scholar's, eye, tongue, sword;
The expectancy and rose of the fair state,
The glass of fashion and the mould of form,
The observed of all observers, quite, quite down!
And I, of ladies most deject and wretched,
That suck'd the honey of his music vows,
Now see that noble and most sovereign reason,
Like sweet bells jangled, out of tune and harsh;
That unmatch'd form and feature of blown youth
Blasted with ecstasy: O, woe is me,
To have seen what I have seen, see what I see!

Re-enter KING CLAUDIUS and POLONIUS

**KING CLAUDIUS**

*Oh, what a wonderful mind has been lost! He was such a gentleman, a scholar, and soldier. He used to be the pride of the state with his perfect charm and sense of taste. Everyone loved him, wanted to be like him! Now he is so low! And I, of all the ladies who loved to hear his voice, have seen him at his worst. His youthfulness has been killed by madness. Oh, how terrible to see what I have seen, to see what I see, now.*

Love! his affections do not that way tend;
Nor what he spake, though it lack'd form a little,
Was not like madness. There's something in his soul,
O'er which his melancholy sits on brood;
And I do doubt the hatch and the disclose

Will be some danger: which for to prevent,
I have in quick determination
Thus set it down: he shall with speed to England,
For the demand of our neglected tribute
Haply the seas and countries different
With variable objects shall expel
This something-settled matter in his heart,
Whereon his brains still beating puts him thus
From fashion of himself. What think you on't?


**LORD POLONIUS**

*It may work, but I still believe his behavior was caused by his unreturned love for Ophelia. Hello, Ophelia. We heard what Hamlet said. My lord, do whatever pleases you, but if you don't mind, let his mother talk with him alone tonight after the play to see if she can find out what is bothering him. I'll listen to what they say. If she can't get it out of him, then send him to England or wherever you think is best.*

It shall do well: but yet do I believe
The origin and commencement of his grief
Sprung from neglected love. How now, Ophelia!
You need not tell us what Lord Hamlet said;
We heard it all. My lord, do as you please;
But, if you hold it fit, after the play
Let his queen mother all alone entreat him
To show his grief: let her be round with him;
And I'll be placed, so please you, in the ear
Of all their conference. If she find him not,
To England send him, or confine him where
Your wisdom best shall think.


**KING CLAUDIUS**

*Okay. We must be watchful of insanity among great men.* It shall be so:
Madness in great ones must not unwatch'd go.

Exeunt

# Scene II
*A hall in the castle*

Enter HAMLET and Players

**HAMLET**

*Please say the speech like I told you, smoothly and flowingly. If you start saying it like the other players do, I might as well have the town crier do it. Don't use your hands too much, either. You must not get too emotional, because nothing bothers me more than to hear a fellow in a wig ruin a passionate story with loud, showy actions to please to the crowd. I would rather whip a man for performing like the old plays where King Herod went on and on. Please avoid doing that.*

Speak the speech, I pray you, as I pronounced it to
you, trippingly on the tongue: but if you mouth it,
as many of your players do, I had as lief the
town-crier spoke my lines. Nor do not saw the air
too much with your hand, thus, but use all gently;
for in the very torrent, tempest, and, as I may say,
the whirlwind of passion, you must acquire and beget
a temperance that may give it smoothness. O, it
offends me to the soul to hear a robustious
periwig-pated fellow tear a passion to tatters, to
very rags, to split the ears of the groundlings, who
for the most part are capable of nothing but
inexplicable dumbshows and noise: I would have such
a fellow whipped for o'erdoing Termagant; it
out-herods Herod: pray you, avoid it.

**First Player**

*I will try, your honor.*

I warrant your honour.

**HAMLET**

*Don't be too tame, either. Use your instincts. Make sure the action suits the word and vice-versa. Just be natural and don't overdo it. I want this play to be believable. Don't perform just to make the commoners laugh, while the other listeners must suffer. I have seen plays performed like that, and I couldn't stand it; the performers were so inept.*

Be not too tame neither, but let your own discretion

be your tutor: suit the action to the word, the
word to the action; with this special o'erstep not
the modesty of nature: for any thing so overdone is
from the purpose of playing, whose end, both at the
first and now, was and is, to hold, as 'twere, the
mirror up to nature; to show virtue her own feature,
scorn her own image, and the very age and body of
the time his form and pressure. Now this overdone,
or come tardy off, though it make the unskilful
laugh, cannot but make the judicious grieve; the
censure of the which one must in your allowance
o'erweigh a whole theatre of others. O, there be
players that I have seen play, and heard others
praise, and that highly, not to speak it profanely,
that, neither having the accent of Christians nor
the gait of Christian, pagan, nor man, have so
strutted and bellowed that I have thought some of
nature's journeymen had made men and not made them
well, they imitated humanity so abominably.


**First Player**

*I hope we please you, sir.*

I hope we have reformed that indifferently with us,
sir.


**HAMLET**

*I'm sure you will. And don't let your comedians improvise and ruin the play. Only amateurs attempt to win over the audience with vile humor. Go get ready.*

O, reform it altogether. And let those that play
your clowns speak no more than is set down for them;
for there be of them that will themselves laugh, to
set on some quantity of barren spectators to laugh
too; though, in the mean time, some necessary
question of the play be then to be considered:
that's villanous, and shows a most pitiful ambition
in the fool that uses it. Go, make you ready.

Exeunt Players

Enter POLONIUS, ROSENCRANTZ, and GUILDENSTERN

*Hello, my lord! Is the king attending the play?*

How now, my lord! I will the king hear this piece of work?

**LORD POLONIUS**

*The queen is coming, too. They should be here soon.*

And the queen too, and that presently.

**HAMLET**

*Tell the actors to hurry.*

Bid the players make haste.

Exit POLONIUS

*Will you two go hurry them along?*

Will you two help to hasten them?

**ROSENCRANTZ GUILDENSTERN**

*We will, my lord.*

We will, my lord.

Exeunt ROSENCRANTZ and GUILDENSTERN

**HAMLET**

*Hey, Horatio? What's up?*

What ho! Horatio!

Enter HORATIO

**HORATIO**

*I am here to serve you, lord.*

Here, sweet lord, at your service.

**HAMLET**

*You are just the man with whom I need to speak.*

Horatio, thou art e'en as just a man
As e'er my conversation coped withal.


## HORATIO

*O, my lord,--*

O, my dear lord,--


## HAMLET

*I'm not trying to flatter you. I don't want anything. I am being sincere. A play is being held tonight resembling the situation of which you are aware. When the similar scene takes place, look at my uncle. If he does not look guilty, then I will know the ghost was a fake and I am a fool. I will be looking, too. Afterwards, we will compare what we saw.*

Nay, do not think I flatter;
For what advancement may I hope from thee
That no revenue hast but thy good spirits,
To feed and clothe thee? Why should the poor be flatter'd?
No, let the candied tongue lick absurd pomp,
And crook the pregnant hinges of the knee
Where thrift may follow fawning. Dost thou hear?
Since my dear soul was mistress of her choice
And could of men distinguish, her election
Hath seal'd thee for herself; for thou hast been
As one, in suffering all, that suffers nothing,
A man that fortune's buffets and rewards
Hast ta'en with equal thanks: and blest are those
Whose blood and judgment are so well commingled,
That they are not a pipe for fortune's finger
To sound what stop she please. Give me that man
That is not passion's slave, and I will wear him
In my heart's core, ay, in my heart of heart,
As I do thee.--Something too much of this.--
There is a play to-night before the king;
One scene of it comes near the circumstance
Which I have told thee of my father's death:
I prithee, when thou seest that act afoot,
Even with the very comment of thy soul
Observe mine uncle: if his occulted guilt
Do not itself unkennel in one speech,
It is a damned ghost that we have seen,

And my imaginations are as foul
As Vulcan's stithy. Give him heedful note;
For I mine eyes will rivet to his face,
And after we will both our judgments join
In censure of his seeming.

## HORATIO

*I will watch him, my lord. His reaction will not escape me.*

Well, my lord:
If he steal aught the whilst this play is playing,
And 'scape detecting, I will pay the theft.

## HAMLET

*Here they come. I have to look normal. Go get a seat.*

They are coming to the play; I must be idle:
Get you a place.

Danish march. A flourish. Enter KING CLAUDIUS, QUEEN GERTRUDE, POLONIUS, OPHELIA, ROSENCRANTZ, GUILDENSTERN, and others

## KING CLAUDIUS

*How is our cousin Hamlet?*

How fares our cousin Hamlet?

## HAMLET

*I am as excellent as can be. I eat the air like the chameleons.*

Excellent, i' faith; of the chameleon's dish: I eat
the air, promise-crammed: you cannot feed capons so.

## KING CLAUDIUS

*I don't know what to say, Hamlet. I don't understand you.*

I have nothing with this answer, Hamlet; these words
are not mine.

**HAMLET**

*Me either.*

No, nor mine now.

To POLONIUS

*My lord, didn't you perform once at the university?*

My lord, you played once i' the university, you say?


**LORD POLONIUS**

*Yes I did, my lord, and I was pretty good.*

That did I, my lord; and was accounted a good actor.


**HAMLET**

*What play did you perform?*

What did you enact?


**LORD POLONIUS**

*I was in Julius Caesar. I was killed in the Capitol by Brutus.*

I did enact Julius Caesar: I was killed i' the
Capitol; Brutus killed me.


**HAMLET**

*What a brute to slaughter such a capital calf. Are the performers ready?*

It was a brute part of him to kill so capital a calf
there. Be the players ready?


**ROSENCRANTZ**

*Yes, sir, they are waiting for you.*

Ay, my lord; they stay upon your patience.

**QUEEN GERTRUDE**

*Come here, Hamlet, and sit by me.*

Come hither, my dear Hamlet, sit by me.

**HAMLET**

*No, Mother, this seat is better.*

No, good mother, here's metal more attractive.

**LORD POLONIUS**

[To KING CLAUDIUS]

*Did you hear that? What do you make of it?*

O, ho! do you mark that?

**HAMLET**

*Lady, may I lie in your lap?*

Lady, shall I lie in your lap?

Lying down at OPHELIA's feet

**OPHELIA**

*No, my lord.*

No, my lord.

**HAMLET**

*I mean with my head in your lap.*

I mean, my head upon your lap?

**OPHELIA**

*Yes, my lord.*

Ay, my lord.

**HAMLET**

*Did you think I meant something inappropriate?*

Do you think I meant country matters?

**OPHELIA**

*I wasn't thinking anything, my lord.*

I think nothing, my lord.

**HAMLET**

*That's a nice thought to lie between a girl's legs.*

That's a fair thought to lie between maids' legs.

**OPHELIA**

*What is, sir?*

What is, my lord?

**HAMLET**

*Nothing.*

Nothing.

**OPHELIA**

*You are happy, my lord.*

You are merry, my lord.

**HAMLET**

*Who, me?*

Who, I?

**OPHELIA**

*Yes, my lord.*

Ay, my lord.

**HAMLET**

*Oh, you silly girl! What man wouldn't be happy? Just look at my mother, how happy she looks, with my father only dead a couple of hours.*

O God, your only jig-maker. What should a man do
but be merry? for, look you, how cheerfully my
mother looks, and my father died within these two hours.

**OPHELIA**

*It's been over four months, my lord.*

Nay, 'tis twice two months, my lord.

**HAMLET**

*That long? Well then, for whom am I mourning? Oh God! Dead two months, and not quite forgotten. There is hope for a man's memory, that it may outlive him. But, he's got to build churches for that to happen. Otherwise, he will be like the carnival, soon forgotten.*

So long? Nay then, let the devil wear black, for
I'll have a suit of sables. O heavens! die two
months ago, and not forgotten yet? Then there's
hope a great man's memory may outlive his life half
a year: but, by'r lady, he must build churches,
then; or else shall he suffer not thinking on, with
the hobby-horse, whose epitaph is 'For, O, for, O,
the hobby-horse is forgot.'

Hautboys play. The dumb-show enters

Enter a King and a Queen very lovingly; the Queen embracing him, and he her. She kneels, and makes show of protestation unto him. He takes her up, and declines his head upon her neck: lays him down upon a bank of flowers: she, seeing him asleep, leaves him. Anon comes in a fellow, takes off his crown, kisses it, and pours poison in the King's ears, and exit. The Queen returns; finds the King dead, and makes passionate action. The Poisoner, with some two or three Mutes, comes in again, seeming to lament with her. The dead body is carried away. The Poisoner wooes the Queen with gifts: she seems loath and unwilling awhile, but in the end accepts his love

Exeunt

**OPHELIA**

*What do you mean, my lord?*

What means this, my lord?

**HAMLET**

*It means mischief is brewing.*

Marry, this is miching mallecho; it means mischief.

**OPHELIA**

*The play is about to begin.*

Belike this show imports the argument of the play.

Enter Prologue

**HAMLET**

*Here comes the players. They are about to begin.*

We shall know by this fellow: the players cannot keep counsel; they'll tell all.

**OPHELIA**

*Will he give us an introduction?*

Will he tell us what this show meant?

**HAMLET**

*Yes, or you can put a play on for him. Don't be ashamed to play and let him tell the story.*

Ay, or any show that you'll show him: be not you
ashamed to show, he'll not shame to tell you what it means.

**OPHELIA**

*You are naughty. I'll watch the actors.*

You are naught, you are naught: I'll mark the play.

**Prologue**

*We humbly present our tragedy for your enjoyment. Please listen.*

For us, and for our tragedy,
Here stooping to your clemency,
We beg your hearing patiently.

Exit

**HAMLET**

*Was that the prologue or an inscription on a ring?*

Is this a prologue, or the posy of a ring?

**OPHELIA**

*It was brief, my lord.*

'Tis brief, my lord.

**HAMLET**

*As a woman's love.*

As woman's love.

Enter two Players, King and Queen

**Player King**

*We have been married now for thirty years.*

Full thirty times hath Phoebus' cart gone round
Neptune's salt wash and Tellus' orbed ground,

And thirty dozen moons with borrow'd sheen
About the world have times twelve thirties been,
Since love our hearts and Hymen did our hands
Unite commutual in most sacred bands.


**Player Queen**

*I hope we have thirty more, but you have not been yourself lately. You seem sad. But, I am just a woman who fears the loss of her love.*

So many journeys may the sun and moon
Make us again count o'er ere love be done!
But, woe is me, you are so sick of late,
So far from cheer and from your former state,
That I distrust you. Yet, though I distrust,
Discomfort you, my lord, it nothing must:
For women's fear and love holds quantity;
In neither aught, or in extremity.
Now, what my love is, proof hath made you know;
And as my love is sized, my fear is so:
Where love is great, the littlest doubts are fear;
Where little fears grow great, great love grows there.


**Player King**

*I am afraid I must leave you soon. My body is old and does not work like it used to. You will probably find another husband.*

'Faith, I must leave thee, love, and shortly too;
My operant powers their functions leave to do:
And thou shalt live in this fair world behind,
Honour'd, beloved; and haply one as kind
For husband shalt thou--


**Player Queen**

*No man compares to you. I would rather be cursed than to marry again. When a woman marries a second time, she surely was responsible for the first husband's death.*

O, confound the rest!
Such love must needs be treason in my breast:
In second husband let me be accurst!
None wed the second but who kill'd the first.

**HAMLET**

[Aside]

*Ouch!*

Wormwood, wormwood.


**Player Queen**

*A second marriage may be for money, but not for love. If I were to kiss my second husband, it would be like killing my first all over again.*

The instances that second marriage move
Are base respects of thrift, but none of love:
A second time I kill my husband dead,
When second husband kisses me in bed.


**Player King**

*I know you believe what you are saying, now, but, you may change your mind. What we promise ourselves during times of great emotion, we may not keep when the emotions subside. After I am gone, your love and grief will run its course and then you may remarry.*

I do believe you think what now you speak;
But what we do determine oft we break.
Purpose is but the slave to memory,
Of violent birth, but poor validity;
Which now, like fruit unripe, sticks on the tree;
But fall, unshaken, when they mellow be.
Most necessary 'tis that we forget
To pay ourselves what to ourselves is debt:
What to ourselves in passion we propose,
The passion ending, doth the purpose lose.
The violence of either grief or joy
Their own enactures with themselves destroy:
Where joy most revels, grief doth most lament;
Grief joys, joy grieves, on slender accident.
This world is not for aye, nor 'tis not strange
That even our loves should with our fortunes change;
For 'tis a question left us yet to prove,
Whether love lead fortune, or else fortune love.
The great man down, you mark his favourite flies;
The poor advanced makes friends of enemies.
And hitherto doth love on fortune tend;
For who not needs shall never lack a friend,

And who in want a hollow friend doth try,
Directly seasons him his enemy.
But, orderly to end where I begun,
Our wills and fates do so contrary run
That our devices still are overthrown;
Our thoughts are ours, their ends none of our own:
So think thou wilt no second husband wed;
But die thy thoughts when thy first lord is dead.


**Player Queen**

*I will starve first! I will lock myself away in prison before I remarry. I will be a widow forever.*

Nor earth to me give food, nor heaven light!
Sport and repose lock from me day and night!
To desperation turn my trust and hope!
An anchor's cheer in prison be my scope!
Each opposite that blanks the face of joy
Meet what I would have well and it destroy!
Both here and hence pursue me lasting strife,
If, once a widow, ever I be wife!


**HAMLET**

*She will break that vow!*

If she should break it now!


**Player King**

*You have sworn with great passion. Leave me for awhile. I would like to take a nap.*

'Tis deeply sworn. Sweet, leave me here awhile;
My spirits grow dull, and fain I would beguile
The tedious day with sleep.

Sleeps

**Player Queen**

*Sleep tight and let nothing ever come between us!*

Sleep rock thy brain,
And never come mischance between us twain!

Exit

**HAMLET**

*Madam, how are you liking this play?*

Madam, how like you this play?

**QUEEN GERTRUDE**

*I think the lady is overplaying it.*

The lady protests too much, methinks.

**HAMLET**

*Oh, but she'll keep her word.*

O, but she'll keep her word.

**KING CLAUDIUS**

*Have you seen this play before? Is there anything offensive in it?*

Have you heard the argument? Is there no offence in 't?

**HAMLET**

*No, no! It's just a joke. I don't think it is offensive at all.*

No, no, they do but jest, poison in jest; no offence
i' the world.

**KING CLAUDIUS**

*What is the name of the play?*

What do you call the play?

**HAMLET**

*The Mouse-trap. Why? The play is about a murder in Vienna. Gonzago is the duke and his wife is Baptista. You will see, it's just a common play. It might be uncomfortable for some, but we are guilt-free, so we can watch it without it bothering us.*

The Mouse-trap. Marry, how? Tropically. This play is the image of a murder done in Vienna: Gonzago is the duke's name; his wife, Baptista: you shall see anon; 'tis a knavish piece of work: but what o' that? your majesty and we that have free souls, it touches us not: let the galled jade wince, our withers are unwrung.

Enter LUCIANUS

*This is Lucianus, the king's nephew.*

This is one Lucianus, nephew to the king.


**OPHELIA**

*You are a good interpreter, my lord.*

You are as good as a chorus, my lord.


**HAMLET**

*I could even interpret your relationship with your lover, if ever I saw you together.* I could interpret between you and your love, if I
could see the puppets dallying.


**OPHELIA**

*You're so smart, my lord, so smart.*

You are keen, my lord, you are keen.


**HAMLET**

*You could make me relax, but it may make you groan a little.*

It would cost you a groaning to take off my edge.


**OPHELIA**

*You are so funny! Not!*

Still better, and worse.


### HAMLET

*That's what women get when they get married.—But, let the murdering begin. Hurry up! "The croaking raven doth bellow for revenge."*

So you must take your husbands. Begin, murderer;
pox, leave thy damnable faces, and begin. Come:
'the croaking raven doth bellow for revenge.'


### LUCIANUS

*I am ready. My thoughts are dark, my hands are still, the drugs are here, and it is time. The darkness obscures my actions. Let the magic do its work and take life quickly.*

Thoughts black, hands apt, drugs fit, and time agreeing;
Confederate season, else no creature seeing;
Thou mixture rank, of midnight weeds collected,
With Hecate's ban thrice blasted, thrice infected,
Thy natural magic and dire property,
On wholesome life usurp immediately.

Pours the poison into the sleeper's ears

### HAMLET

*He poisons him in the estates' garden. His name's Gonzago. The story is in the finest Italian. Now, you will see how the murderer seduces the duke's wife.*

He poisons him i' the garden for's estate. His
name's Gonzago: the story is extant, and writ in
choice Italian: you shall see anon how the murderer
gets the love of Gonzago's wife.


### OPHELIA

*The King is getting up.*

The king rises.


### HAMLET

*What? Is he scared of this pretend play?*

What, frighted with false fire!

## QUEEN GERTRUDE

*Are you feeling okay, my lord?*

How fares my lord?

## LORD POLONIUS

*Stop the play.*

Give o'er the play.

## KING CLAUDIUS

*Someone turn on the lights. I've got to get out of here!*

Give me some light: away!

## All

*Lights! Lights!*

Lights, lights, lights!

Exeunt all but HAMLET and HORATIO

## HAMLET

*Oh, let the hunted deer go weep, and let everyone else watch the play. I am putting up such a fine act, I may have to become an actor one day.*

Why, let the stricken deer go weep,
The hart ungalled play;
For some must watch, while some must sleep:
So runs the world away.
Would not this, sir, and a forest of feathers-- if
the rest of my fortunes turn Turk with me--with two
Provincial roses on my razed shoes, get me a
fellowship in a cry of players, sir?

**HORATIO**

*They might pay you half of the profits.*

Half a share.


**HAMLET**

*I want all of it.*

    *For you know, my dear friend.*

    *This realm was rid of God, himself. And now*

        *reigns a peacock.*

A whole one, I.
For thou dost know, O Damon dear,
This realm dismantled was
Of Jove himself; and now reigns here
A very, very--pajock.

**HORATIO**

*You might have rhymed.*

You might have rhymed.


**HAMLET**

*Oh Horatio, I'll take the ghost's word for the truth. What did you think?*

O good Horatio, I'll take the ghost's word for a
thousand pound. Didst perceive?


**HORATIO**

*I agree, my lord.*

Very well, my lord.


**HAMLET**

*Did you see how he acted when they mentioned poison?*

Upon the talk of the poisoning?

## HORATIO

*I did, sir.*

I did very well note him.


## HAMLET

*Ah ha! Let's have some music. Let the musicians play their instruments! If the king doesn't like the comedy, oh well! Come on, music!*

Ah, ha! Come, some music! come, the recorders!
For if the king like not the comedy,
Why then, belike, he likes it not, perdy.
Come, some music!

Re-enter ROSENCRANTZ and GUILDENSTERN

## GUILDENSTERN

*My lord, could I have a word with you?*

Good my lord, vouchsafe me a word with you.


## HAMLET

*You can have many words, a whole history.*

Sir, a whole history.


## GUILDENSTERN

*Well, the king, sir...*

The king, sir,--


## HAMLET

*Yes, what of him?*

Ay, sir, what of him?

**GUILDENSTERN**

*He is resting and he is very upset.*

Is in his retirement marvellous distempered.


**HAMLET**

*Is he drunk, sir?*

With drink, sir?


**GUILDENSTERN**

*No, my lord, he is angry.*

No, my lord, rather with choler.


**HAMLET**

*You would be wise to tell his doctor. If I were to help, I would only make him angrier.*

Your wisdom should show itself more richer to
signify this to his doctor; for, for me to put him
to his purgation would perhaps plunge him into far
more choler.


**GUILDENSTERN**

*Please, my lord, try to be sensible.*

Good my lord, put your discourse into some frame and
start not so wildly from my affair.


**HAMLET**

*Okay, I'm listening.*

I am tame, sir: pronounce.


**GUILDENSTERN**

*The queen, your mother, is very upset and has sent for you.*

The queen, your mother, in most great affliction of
spirit, hath sent me to you.


### HAMLET

*Glad you could come.*

You are welcome.


### GUILDENSTERN

*You are not being good, my lord. If you cannot give me an answer, then I will excuse myself and return to your mother.*

Nay, good my lord, this courtesy is not of the right
breed. If it shall please you to make me a
wholesome answer, I will do your mother's
commandment: if not, your pardon and my return
shall be the end of my business.


### HAMLET

*Sir, I can't.*

Sir, I cannot.


### GUILDENSTERN

*Can't what, my lord?*

What, my lord?


### HAMLET

*I can't give you a good answer because my mind is not right, but, I'll be as honest as possible. So, what did my mother want?*

Make you a wholesome answer; my wit's diseased: but,
sir, such answer as I can make, you shall command;
or, rather, as you say, my mother: therefore no
more, but to the matter: my mother, you say,--

**ROSENCRANTZ**

*She says your behavior has amazed her and she is very proud of you.*

Then thus she says; your behavior hath struck her
into amazement and admiration.


**HAMLET**

*Oh, what a wonderful son who can fill his mother with pride. But, what does she want?*

O wonderful son, that can so astonish a mother! But
is there no sequel at the heels of this mother's
admiration? Impart.


**ROSENCRANTZ**

*She wants to speak with you in her room before you go to bed.*

She desires to speak with you in her closet, ere you
go to bed.


**HAMLET**

*We shall obey ten times over. Anything else?*

We shall obey, were she ten times our mother. Have
you any further trade with us?


**ROSENCRANTZ**

*My lord, we were once friends.*

My lord, you once did love me.


**HAMLET**

*We still are. I swear by these hands.*

So I do still, by these pickers and stealers.

## ROSENCRANTZ

*Good, my lord. What is wrong with you? You can't be a free man with all of your grief locked up inside.*

Good my lord, what is your cause of distemper? you do, surely, bar the door upon your own liberty, if you deny your griefs to your friend.


## HAMLET

*Sir, I can't see any future for myself.*

Sir, I lack advancement.


## ROSENCRANTZ

*How is that possible, when you will be the next king of Denmark?*

How can that be, when you have the voice of the king himself for your succession in Denmark?


## HAMLET

*Yes, but how does the old proverb go: 'While the grass grows…' Oh, that is an old one.*

Ay, but sir, 'While the grass grows,'--the proverb is something musty.

Re-enter Players with recorders

*Oh, the recorders are here. Let me see one. Hey, why are you standing so close, as if you would like to kill me?*

O, the recorders! let me see one. To withdraw with you:--why do you go about to recover the wind of me, as if you would drive me into a toil?


## GUILDENSTERN

*Oh, sorry, my lord. I just am concerned about you.*

O, my lord, if my duty be too bold, my love is too unmannerly.

## HAMLET

*I don't understand why. Here play this.*

I do not well understand that. Will you play upon this pipe?

## GUILDENSTERN

*My lord, I can't.*

My lord, I cannot.

## HAMLET

*Come on. I am begging.*

I pray you.

## GUILDENSTERN

*Believe me, I can't.*

Believe me, I cannot.

## HAMLET

*Please, for me.*

I do beseech you.

## GUILDENSTERN

*I don't know how.*

I know no touch of it, my lord.

## HAMLET

*It's as easy as lying. Put your fingers and thumb here and blow. It will make the most beautiful music. Here are the holes.*

'Tis as easy as lying: govern these ventages with

your lingers and thumb, give it breath with your
mouth, and it will discourse most eloquent music.
Look you, these are the stops.

**GUILDENSTERN**

*I don't have the skill to make music.*

But these cannot I command to any utterance of
harmony; I have not the skill.

**HAMLET**

*Who do you think I am? You try to play me. You seem to know my holes. You wish to know my secrets, and try to search my soul. Yet, you cannot play a single note from this little instrument. How is it you think you can manipulate me, but not this pipe? You will not play me for a fool.*

Why, look you now, how unworthy a thing you make of
me! You would play upon me; you would seem to know
my stops; you would pluck out the heart of my
mystery; you would sound me from my lowest note to
the top of my compass: and there is much music,
excellent voice, in this little organ; yet cannot
you make it speak. 'Sblood, do you think I am
easier to be played on than a pipe? Call me what
instrument you will, though you can fret me, yet you
cannot play upon me.

Enter POLONIUS

*God bless you, sir!*

God bless you, sir!

**LORD POLONIUS**

*My lord, the queen wants to speak with you now.*

My lord, the queen would speak with you, and
presently.

**HAMLET**

*Do you see the cloud over there, shaped like a camel?*

Do you see yonder cloud that's almost in shape of a camel?

**LORD POLONIUS**

*I do and it does look like a camel.*

By the mass, and 'tis like a camel, indeed.

**HAMLET**

*I think it looks more like a weasel.*

Methinks it is like a weasel.

**LORD POLONIUS**

*Its back is like a weasel.*

It is backed like a weasel.

**HAMLET**

*Or like a whale?*

Or like a whale?

**LORD POLONIUS**

*It is very much like a whale.*

Very like a whale.

**HAMLET**

*Now I will go see my mother, if you will stop messing with me.*

Then I will come to my mother by and by. They fool
me to the top of my bent. I will come by and by.

**LORD POLONIUS**

*I will tell her.*

I will say so.

**HAMLET**

*That is easy to say.*

By and by is easily said.

Exit POLONIUS

*Please leave me alone.*

Leave me, friends.

Exeunt all but HAMLET

*Now is the time when witches come out, graves open, and hell releases its demons into the world. The time to seek revenge is here. I must go to my mother, but I mustn't lose my nerve. I must be cruel but not murderous. I must speak with bitter words, but not poison her. So, I will be in internal conflict.*

Tis now the very witching time of night,
When churchyards yawn and hell itself breathes out
Contagion to this world: now could I drink hot blood,
And do such bitter business as the day
Would quake to look on. Soft! now to my mother.
O heart, lose not thy nature; let not ever
The soul of Nero enter this firm bosom:
Let me be cruel, not unnatural:
I will speak daggers to her, but use none;
My tongue and soul in this be hypocrites;
How in my words soever she be shent,
To give them seals never, my soul, consent!

Exit

# Scene III.
*A room in the castle*

Enter KING CLAUDIUS, ROSENCRANTZ, and GUILDENSTERN

**KING CLAUDIUS**

*I don't like the way he's acting and it's not safe for this madness to go on. Therefore, get ready. I'm sending you and Hamlet to England.*

I like him not, nor stands it safe with us
To let his madness range. Therefore prepare you;
I your commission will forthwith dispatch,
And he to England shall along with you:
The terms of our estate may not endure
Hazard so dangerous as doth hourly grow
Out of his lunacies.

**GUILDENSTERN**

*We will gladly do our duty to all the people who depend on your majesty.*

We will ourselves provide:
Most holy and religious fear it is
To keep those many many bodies safe
That live and feed upon your majesty.

**ROSENCRANTZ**

*Everyone's existence depends on the strength of the mind and thus, requires some protection. But the life of a king, that many lives depend upon, requires far stronger protection. A king is like a wheel on top of a mountain, and when it falls, everything in its path falls, too. When a king feels pain, everyone hurts.*

The single and peculiar life is bound,
With all the strength and armour of the mind,
To keep itself from noyance; but much more
That spirit upon whose weal depend and rest
The lives of many. The cease of majesty
Dies not alone; but, like a gulf, doth draw
What's near it with it: it is a massy wheel,
Fix'd on the summit of the highest mount,
To whose huge spokes ten thousand lesser things
Are mortised and adjoin'd; which, when it falls,

Each small annexment, petty consequence,
Attends the boisterous ruin. Never alone
Did the king sigh, but with a general groan.


## KING CLAUDIUS

*Please get ready quickly for this trip. We must put an end to this craziness.*

Arm you, I pray you, to this speedy voyage;
For we will fetters put upon this fear,
Which now goes too free-footed.


## ROSENCRANTZ GUILDENSTERN

*We will hurry.*

We will haste us.

Exeunt ROSENCRANTZ and GUILDENSTERN

Enter POLONIUS

## LORD POLONIUS

*My lord, he's going to his mother's bedroom. I'll hide behind the curtain and listen. I'll bet she gives him an earful. And, as you wisely said, 'It is better to have someone listen to the conversation other than a mother who may be bias.' I'll come back before you go to bed to tell you what I heard.*

My lord, he's going to his mother's closet:
Behind the arras I'll convey myself,
To hear the process; and warrant she'll tax him home:
And, as you said, and wisely was it said,
'Tis meet that some more audience than a mother,
Since nature makes them partial, should o'erhear
The speech, of vantage. Fare you well, my liege:
I'll call upon you ere you go to bed,
And tell you what I know.


## KING CLAUDIUS

*Thanks, my lord.*

Thanks, dear my lord.

Exit POLONIUS

*Oh, my crime is so awful, it smells to high heavens. It has the mark of a brother's murder. I can't pray, even though I want. I am like a man with so much to do, not knowing where to start, I stand still. If this hand is covered in my brother's blood, is there not enough rain to rinse it clean? Isn't this what God's mercy is for? And, isn't this what prayer is for, to protect us from sin and forgiveness? So, I'll pray. I have already sinned. But, what kind of prayer? Forgive me Lord for my horrible crime? That won't work since I am still reaping the rewards of my sin, the crown and the queen. Can one be forgiven and still keep the rewards of sin. What passes in this world does not in heaven. Nothing goes unseen. So what can I do? Maybe I can offer repentance. It couldn't hurt, but it won't help either. My heart is black as death and my soul is full of sin. Help me angels! Come on knees and bend. Heart, be as soft as a newborn, so I can pray.*

O, my offence is rank it smells to heaven;
It hath the primal eldest curse upon't,
A brother's murder. Pray can I not,
Though inclination be as sharp as will:
My stronger guilt defeats my strong intent;
And, like a man to double business bound,
I stand in pause where I shall first begin,
And both neglect. What if this cursed hand
Were thicker than itself with brother's blood,
Is there not rain enough in the sweet heavens
To wash it white as snow? Whereto serves mercy
But to confront the visage of offence?
And what's in prayer but this two-fold force,
To be forestalled ere we come to fall,
Or pardon'd being down? Then I'll look up;
My fault is past. But, O, what form of prayer
Can serve my turn? 'Forgive me my foul murder'?
That cannot be; since I am still possess'd
Of those effects for which I did the murder,
My crown, mine own ambition and my queen.
May one be pardon'd and retain the offence?
In the corrupted currents of this world
Offence's gilded hand may shove by justice,
And oft 'tis seen the wicked prize itself
Buys out the law: but 'tis not so above;
There is no shuffling, there the action lies
In his true nature; and we ourselves compell'd,
Even to the teeth and forehead of our faults,
To give in evidence. What then? what rests?
Try what repentance can: what can it not?
Yet what can it when one can not repent?
O wretched state! O bosom black as death!
O limed soul, that, struggling to be free,
Art more engaged! Help, angels! Make assay!
Bow, stubborn knees; and, heart with strings of steel,
Be soft as sinews of the newborn babe!
All may be well.

Retires and kneels

Enter HAMLET

**HAMLET**

*I could do it easily now; he is praying. He goes to heaven and I have my revenge. The villain who killed my father, I put to death. But, that is too good for him, to kill him when he is ready. He killed my father in the prime of his life without thought to his afterlife, which doesn't appear to be so good. Not now, sword. We will wait until he is drunk or in a rage or in his incestuous bed. Perhaps, we will kill while he is gambling, swearing, or some other sinful act for which there is no forgiveness. Then, we will kill him so his soul may be damned to hell where it belongs. My mother waits for me. Death waits for the king.*

Now might I do it pat, now he is praying;
And now I'll do't. And so he goes to heaven;
And so am I revenged. That would be scann'd:
A villain kills my father; and for that,
I, his sole son, do this same villain send
To heaven.
O, this is hire and salary, not revenge.
He took my father grossly, full of bread;
With all his crimes broad blown, as flush as May;
And how his audit stands who knows save heaven?
But in our circumstance and course of thought,
'Tis heavy with him: and am I then revenged,
To take him in the purging of his soul,
When he is fit and season'd for his passage?
No!
Up, sword; and know thou a more horrid hent:
When he is drunk asleep, or in his rage,
Or in the incestuous pleasure of his bed;
At gaming, swearing, or about some act
That has no relish of salvation in't;
Then trip him, that his heels may kick at heaven,
And that his soul may be as damn'd and black
As hell, whereto it goes. My mother stays:
This physic but prolongs thy sickly days.

Exit

**KING CLAUDIUS**

[Rising]

*My prayers are just words without meaning. They will never be heard.*

My words fly up, my thoughts remain below:
Words without thoughts never to heaven go.

Exit

# Scene IV
*The Queen's closet*

Enter QUEEN GERTRUDE and POLONIUS

**LORD POLONIUS**

*He is coming soon. Make sure you give him a good talking to about his pranks. Tell him how you have protected him. I'll be here, but he won't know it. Be firm with him!*

He will come straight. Look you lay home to him:
Tell him his pranks have been too broad to bear with,
And that your grace hath screen'd and stood between
Much heat and him. I'll sconce me even here.
Pray you, be round with him.

**HAMLET**

[Within]

*Mother, mother, mother!*

Mother, mother, mother!

**QUEEN GERTRUDE**

*I will. Hide, he is coming.*

I will, don't worry. Hide, I hear him coming.

I'll warrant you,
Fear me not: withdraw, I hear him coming.

POLONIUS hides behind the arras

Enter HAMLET

**HAMLET**

*Now, mother, what's the matter?*

Now, mother, what's the matter?

## QUEEN GERTRUDE

*Hamlet, you have offended your father.*

Hamlet, thou hast thy father much offended.


## HAMLET

*Mother, you are the one who has offended my father*

Mother, you have my father much offended.


## QUEEN GERTRUDE

*Come now. Talk sensibly.*

Come, come, you answer with an idle tongue.


## HAMLET

*Go on. You are questioning me angrily.*

Go, go, you question with a wicked tongue.


## QUEEN GERTRUDE

*What are you talking about, Hamlet?*

Why, how now, Hamlet!


## HAMLET

*What's the matter now!*

What's the matter now?


## QUEEN GERTRUDE

*Have you forgotten who I am?*

Have you forgot me?

## HAMLET

*Of course not. You are the queen; your husband's brother's wife. And although I wish it were not true, you are my mother.*

No, by the rood, not so:
You are the queen, your husband's brother's wife;
And--would it were not so!--you are my mother.


## QUEEN GERTRUDE

*Alright then, I'll bring in someone who can speak some sense into you.*

Nay, then, I'll set those to you that can speak.


## HAMLET

*No. Sit down. You will not leave until I give you a mirror and show you your true self.*

Come, come, and sit you down; you shall not budge;
You go not till I set you up a glass
Where you may see the inmost part of you.


## QUEEN GERTRUDE

*What are you going to do? Murder me? Help, help!*

What wilt thou do? thou wilt not murder me?
Help, help, ho!


## LORD POLONIUS

[Behind]

*Help! Help!*

What is going on? Help! Help!

What, ho! help, help, help!


## HAMLET

[Drawing]

*What now?*

What now? A rat? He'll be a dead rat, I bet!

How now! a rat? Dead, for a ducat, dead!

Makes a pass through the arras

**LORD POLONIUS**

[Behind]

*Oh, I am killed!*

O, I am slain!

Falls and dies

**QUEEN GERTRUDE**

*Oh no! What have you done?*

O me, what hast thou done?


**HAMLET**

*I do not know. Is it the king?*

Nay, I know not:
Is it the king?


**QUEEN GERTRUDE**

*Oh what a horrible, bloody deed this is!*

O, what a rash and bloody deed is this!


**HAMLET**

*It is a bloody deed; almost as bad, good mother, as killing a king and marrying his brother.*

A bloody deed! almost as bad, good mother,
As kill a king, and marry with his brother.


**QUEEN GERTRUDE**

*As killing a king!*

As kill a king!


## HAMLET

*Yes, lady, that's what I said.*

Ay, lady, 'twas my word.

Lifts up the array and discovers POLONIUS

*You stupid fool! Goodbye! I thought you were better. Take what you deserve. Now mother. Stop wringing your hands. Be still and sit down. Let me lay something on your heart, if it is not made of brass.*

Thou wretched, rash, intruding fool, farewell!
I took thee for thy better: take thy fortune;
Thou find'st to be too busy is some danger.
Leave wringing of your hands: peace! sit you down,
And let me wring your heart; for so I shall,
If it be made of penetrable stuff,
If damned custom have not brass'd it so
That it is proof and bulwark against sense.


## QUEEN GERTRUDE

*What have I done so terribly that you dare talk to me this way?*

What have I done, that thou darest wag thy tongue
In noise so rude against me?


## HAMLET

*You have done such an awful act that is unforgiveable.*

Such an act
That blurs the grace and blush of modesty,
Calls virtue hypocrite, takes off the rose
From the fair forehead of an innocent love
And sets a blister there, makes marriage-vows
As false as dicers' oaths: O, such a deed
As from the body of contraction plucks
The very soul, and sweet religion makes
A rhapsody of words: heaven's face doth glow:
Yea, this solidity and compound mass,

With tristful visage, as against the doom,
Is thought-sick at the act.


**QUEEN GERTRUDE**

*What have I done that is so awful?*

Ay me, what act,
That roars so loud, and thunders in the index?


**HAMLET**

*Imagine this…Two brothers sitting side-by-side where one is blessed by God and in the eyes of man. This man was your husband. Now the other man is horrid and capable of evil. He is your current husband. Don't you see? Why are with this man? Don't say it is love, because love fades with age and is replaced with wisdom. What persuaded you to marry this man? Don't you have any sense? You aren't even ashamed. Perhaps, I will not be ashamed either.*

Look here, upon this picture, and on this,
The counterfeit presentment of two brothers.
See, what a grace was seated on this brow;
Hyperion's curls; the front of Jove himself;
An eye like Mars, to threaten and command;
A station like the herald Mercury
New-lighted on a heaven-kissing hill;
A combination and a form indeed,
Where every god did seem to set his seal,
To give the world assurance of a man:
This was your husband. Look you now, what follows:
Here is your husband; like a mildew'd ear,
Blasting his wholesome brother. Have you eyes?
Could you on this fair mountain leave to feed,
And batten on this moor? Ha! have you eyes?
You cannot call it love; for at your age
The hey-day in the blood is tame, it's humble,
And waits upon the judgment: and what judgment
Would step from this to this? Sense, sure, you have,
Else could you not have motion; but sure, that sense
Is apoplex'd; for madness would not err,
Nor sense to ecstasy was ne'er so thrall'd
But it reserved some quantity of choice,
To serve in such a difference. What devil was't
That thus hath cozen'd you at hoodman-blind?
Eyes without feeling, feeling without sight,
Ears without hands or eyes, smelling sans all,

Or but a sickly part of one true sense
Could not so mope.
O shame! where is thy blush? Rebellious hell,
If thou canst mutine in a matron's bones,
To flaming youth let virtue be as wax,
And melt in her own fire: proclaim no shame
When the compulsive ardour gives the charge,
Since frost itself as actively doth burn
And reason panders will.


**QUEEN GERTRUDE**

*Oh, Hamlet, stop saying those things. I am looking into my own wretched soul, black with sin.*

O Hamlet, speak no more:
Thou turn'st mine eyes into my very soul;
And there I see such black and grained spots
As will not leave their tinct.


**HAMLET**

*Yes, and you live in a bed of sin, corrupt with love making.*

Nay, but to live
In the rank sweat of an enseamed bed,
Stew'd in corruption, honeying and making love
Over the nasty sty,--


**QUEEN GERTRUDE**

*Say no more. You're killing me! No more, please, Hamlet!*

O, speak to me no more;
These words, like daggers, enter in mine ears;
No more, sweet Hamlet!


**HAMLET**

*You are married to a murderer and a villain, a shadow of your first husband, who stole the crown.*

A murderer and a villain;
A slave that is not twentieth part the tithe
Of your precedent lord; a vice of kings;
A cutpurse of the empire and the rule,

That from a shelf the precious diadem stole,
And put it in his pocket!


**QUEEN GERTRUDE**

*No more!*

No more!


**HAMLET**

*He is a pathetic king...*

A king of shreds and patches,--

Enter Ghost

*Oh, God, sending your angel to save me. What do you want?*

Save me, and hover o'er me with your wings,
You heavenly guards! What would your gracious figure?


**QUEEN GERTRUDE**

*Finally, he's gone crazy!*

Alas, he's mad!


**HAMLET**

*Please don't be upset that it has taken me so long to obey you. Tell me?*

Do you not come your tardy son to chide,
That, lapsed in time and passion, lets go by
The important acting of your dread command? O, say!


**Ghost**

*Don't forget your purpose. Your mother is close to breaking. Keep talking to her.*

Do not forget: this visitation
Is but to whet thy almost blunted purpose.
But, look, amazement on thy mother sits:

O, step between her and her fighting soul:
Conceit in weakest bodies strongest works:
Speak to her, Hamlet.

## HAMLET

*How are you doing, mother?*

How is it with you, lady?

## QUEEN GERTRUDE

*How are you? Who are you talking to? Your hair is standing on end. Calm down and tell me what are you looking at?*

Alas, how is't with you,
That you do bend your eye on vacancy
And with the incorporal air do hold discourse?
Forth at your eyes your spirits wildly peep;
And, as the sleeping soldiers in the alarm,
Your bedded hair, like life in excrements,
Starts up, and stands on end. O gentle son,
Upon the heat and flame of thy distemper
Sprinkle cool patience. Whereon do you look?

## HAMLET

*At him, at him! Look how pale he is. He could make the stones move. Don't look at me or else I will cry and be unable to kill.*

On him, on him! Look you, how pale he glares!
His form and cause conjoin'd, preaching to stones,
Would make them capable. Do not look upon me;
Lest with this piteous action you convert
My stern effects: then what I have to do
Will want true colour; tears perchance for blood.

## QUEEN GERTRUDE

*Who are you talking to?*

To whom do you speak this?

## HAMLET

*Do you not see anything?*

Do you see nothing there?

**QUEEN GERTRUDE**

*I don't see anything unusual.*

Nothing at all; yet all that is I see.

**HAMLET**

*And you don't hear anything?*

Nor did you nothing hear?

**QUEEN GERTRUDE**

*Nothing but us talking.*

No, nothing but ourselves.

**HAMLET**

*Look over there. See how he is going away. It is my father. He looks just like he did when he was alive. Look, he's going out the door.*

Why, look you there! look, how it steals away!
My father, in his habit as he lived!
Look, where he goes, even now, out at the portal!

Exit Ghost

**QUEEN GERTRUDE**

*It is only your imagination playing tricks on you.*

This the very coinage of your brain:
This bodiless creation ecstasy
Is very cunning in.

**HAMLET**

*You think I am crazy! My heart beats as well as yours. I am not mad; test me. I know exactly what I am saying. Mother, for the love of the Lord, don't blame your crimes on my madness. You will only suffer. Confess your sins to heaven and repent. Avoid the obvious outcome of your sins. Don't let this go on any longer and forgive me for trying to do good in these horrible times.*

Ecstasy!
My pulse, as yours, doth temperately keep time,
And makes as healthful music: it is not madness
That I have utter'd: bring me to the test,
And I the matter will re-word; which madness
Would gambol from. Mother, for love of grace,
Lay not that mattering unction to your soul,
That not your trespass, but my madness speaks:
It will but skin and film the ulcerous place,
Whilst rank corruption, mining all within,
Infects unseen. Confess yourself to heaven;
Repent what's past; avoid what is to come;
And do not spread the compost on the weeds,
To make them ranker. Forgive me this my virtue;
For in the fatness of these pursy times
Virtue itself of vice must pardon beg,
Yea, curb and woo for leave to do him good.


## QUEEN GERTRUDE

*Oh Hamlet, you have torn my heart in two.*

O Hamlet, thou hast cleft my heart in twain.


## HAMLET

*Throw away the worst part of your life and live more purely. Have a good night, but do not go to my uncle's bed. Pretend to be virtuous, if you have none. Do not give in to temptation. Start saying no to my uncle tonight. Once again, have a good night.*

O, throw away the worser part of it,
And live the purer with the other half.
Good night: but go not to mine uncle's bed;
Assume a virtue, if you have it not.
That monster, custom, who all sense doth eat,
Of habits devil, is angel yet in this,
That to the use of actions fair and good
He likewise gives a frock or livery,
That aptly is put on. Refrain to-night,
And that shall lend a kind of easiness
To the next abstinence: the next more easy;
For use almost can change the stamp of nature,

And either rein the devil, or throw him out
With wondrous potency. Once more, good night:
And when you are desirous to be bless'd,
I'll blessing beg of you. For this same lord,

Pointing to POLONIUS

*I will repent for this murder, even though it was God's will. I am only God's instrument. I know I will have to pay in the end. One other thing…*

I do repent: but heaven hath pleased it so,
To punish me with this and this with me,
That I must be their scourge and minister.
I will bestow him, and will answer well
The death I gave him. So, again, good night.
I must be cruel, only to be kind:
Thus bad begins and worse remains behind.
One word more, good lady.


**QUEEN GERTRUDE**

*What would you have me do?*

What shall I do?


**HAMLET**

*Whatever you do, do not let that bloated king tempt you into his bed again, call you his mouse, or pinch your cheek. Don't let him touch you with his damned fingers or convince you to think badly of me. But, what wise queen would do fall for a pig like him. Go ahead and tell him what's what, even if it means the end for you.*

Not this, by no means, that I bid you do:
Let the bloat king tempt you again to bed;
Pinch wanton on your cheek; call you his mouse;
And let him, for a pair of reechy kisses,
Or paddling in your neck with his damn'd fingers,
Make you to ravel all this matter out,
That I essentially am not in madness,
But mad in craft. 'Twere good you let him know;
For who, that's but a queen, fair, sober, wise,
Would from a paddock, from a bat, a gib,
Such dear concernings hide? who would do so?
No, in despite of sense and secrecy,
Unpeg the basket on the house's top.
Let the birds fly, and, like the famous ape,

To try conclusions, in the basket creep,
And break your own neck down.


## QUEEN GERTRUDE

*Rest assure that I will not breathe a word of what you said tonight.*

Be thou assured, if words be made of breath,
And breath of life, I have no life to breathe
What thou hast said to me.


## HAMLET

*Did you know I have to go to England?*

I must to England; you know that?


## QUEEN GERTRUDE

*Oh yes, I had forgotten that, but it has been decided.*

Alack,
I had forgot: 'tis so concluded on.


## HAMLET

*There are two sealed letters that state my two friends from school, whom I do not trust any more than a snake, will take me to England. So what? Let them try. His plan is going to blow up in his face. However, I will come out just fine. I am going to have to leave in a hurry now. I'll carry the body into the other room. Good night, Mother. This man is indeed a great counselor; he can keep secrets forever. Good night.*

There's letters seal'd: and my two schoolfellows,
Whom I will trust as I will adders fang'd,
They bear the mandate; they must sweep my way,
And marshal me to knavery. Let it work;
For 'tis the sport to have the engineer
Hoist with his own petard: and 't shall go hard
But I will delve one yard below their mines,
And blow them at the moon: O, 'tis most sweet,
When in one line two crafts directly meet.
This man shall set me packing:
I'll lug the guts into the neighbour room.
Mother, good night. Indeed this counsellor
Is now most still, most secret and most grave,

Who was in life a foolish prating knave.
Come, sir, to draw toward an end with you.
Good night, mother.

Exeunt severally; HAMLET dragging in POLONIUS

# Act IV

# Scene I
*A room in the castle*

Enter KING CLAUDIUS, QUEEN GERTRUDE, ROSENCRANTZ, and GUILDENSTERN

**KING CLAUDIUS**

*What's wrong with you, making these deep sighs? You must tell me what's going on. Where is Hamlet?*

There's matter in these sighs, these profound heaves:
You must translate: 'tis fit we understand them.
Where is your son?

**QUEEN GERTRUDE**

*Let us have some privacy for a bit.*

Bestow this place on us a little while.

*Exeunt ROSENCRANTZ and GUILDENSTERN*

*You won't believe what I have seen tonight!*

Ah, my good lord, what have I seen to-night!

**KING CLAUDIUS**

*What Gertrude? How is Hamlet?*

What, Gertrude? How does Hamlet?

**QUEEN GERTRUDE**

*He is completely crazy. He heard something behind the curtains and in a rage he drew his sword and cried, "A rat, a rat!" Then he killed the old man.*

Mad as the sea and wind, when both contend
Which is the mightier: in his lawless fit,
Behind the arras hearing something stir,
Whips out his rapier, cries, 'A rat, a rat!'
And, in this brainish apprehension, kills
The unseen good old man.

## KING CLAUDIUS

*Oh, what a terrible thing! It would have been me, if I had been there. His freedom is a threat to everyone. How are we going to answer this murder? It is our responsibility to restrain this young madman. We loved him so much we could not see clearly. Now, this has happened like a contagious disease. Where is he, now?*

O heavy deed!
It had been so with us, had we been there:
His liberty is full of threats to all;
To you yourself, to us, to every one.
Alas, how shall this bloody deed be answer'd?
It will be laid to us, whose providence
Should have kept short, restrain'd and out of haunt,
This mad young man: but so much was our love,
We would not understand what was most fit;
But, like the owner of a foul disease,
To keep it from divulging, let it feed
Even on the pith of Life. Where is he gone?


## QUEEN GERTRUDE

*He has gone to dispose of the body. He is sorry for what he has done.*

To draw apart the body he hath kill'd:
O'er whom his very madness, like some ore
Among a mineral of metals base,
Shows itself pure; he weeps for what is done.


## KING CLAUDIUS

*Oh Gertrude, be sensible. We must send him away as soon as the sun rises. We will have to find some way to excuse this murder. Hey, Guildenstern.*

O Gertrude, come away!
The sun no sooner shall the mountains touch,
But we will ship him hence: and this vile deed
We must, with all our majesty and skill,
Both countenance and excuse. Ho, Guildenstern!

Re-enter ROSENCRANTZ and GUILDENSTERN

*Gentlemen, both of you go find some people to help Hamlet. Out of his madness, he has killed Polonius. Now he is dragging the body out of his mother's bedroom. Go speak to him and bring the body to the church. Hurry, please.*

Friends both, go join you with some further aid:
Hamlet in madness hath Polonius slain,
And from his mother's closet hath he dragg'd him:
Go seek him out; speak fair, and bring the body
Into the chapel. I pray you, haste in this.

Exeunt ROSENCRANTZ and GUILDENSTERN

*Come on, Gertrude, we'll get our wisest friends to let them know what we are doing and what has been done. Let's go! My soul is heavy.*

Come, Gertrude, we'll call up our wisest friends;
And let them know, both what we mean to do,
And what's untimely done. O, come away!
My soul is full of discord and dismay.

Exeunt

# Scene II
### *Another room in the castle*

Enter HAMLET

**HAMLET**

*There, the body is safely stowed away.*

Safely stowed.

**ROSENCRANTZ: GUILDENSTERN:**

[Within]

*Hamlet! Lord Hamlet!*

Hamlet! Lord Hamlet!

**HAMLET**

*What is that noise? Who is calling me? Here they come.*

What noise? who calls on Hamlet?
O, here they come.

Enter ROSENCRANTZ and GUILDENSTERN

**ROSENCRANTZ**

*What have you done with the body, my lord?*

What have you done, my lord, with the dead body?

**HAMLET**

*Put it in the dirt.*

Compounded it with dust, whereto 'tis kin.

**ROSENCRANTZ**

*Tell us where it is so we can take it to the church.*

Tell us where 'tis, that we may take it thence
And bear it to the chapel.

**HAMLET**

*I don't believe it.*

Do not believe it.

**ROSENCRANTZ**

*Believe what?*

Believe what?

**HAMLET**

*That I can trust you and expose my secret. Besides, who are you, a mere sponge, to command the son of a king?*

That I can keep your counsel and not mine own.
Besides, to be demanded of a sponge! what
replication should be made by the son of a king?

**ROSENCRANTZ**

*You think I am a sponge, my lord?*

Take you me for a sponge, my lord?

**HAMLET**

*Yes sir, that soaks up whatever the king says and does. He is just using you and when he is done, you will be left high and dry.*

Ay, sir, that soaks up the king's countenance, his
rewards, his authorities. But such officers do the
king best service in the end: he keeps them, like
an ape, in the corner of his jaw; first mouthed, to
be last swallowed: when he needs what you have
gleaned, it is but squeezing you, and, sponge, you
shall be dry again.

**ROSENCRANTZ**

*I don't understand, my lord.*

I understand you not, my lord.


**HAMLET**

*I am glad. You are too foolish to understand.*

I am glad of it: a knavish speech sleeps in a
foolish ear.


**ROSENCRANTZ**

*My lord, you must tell us where the body is and go with us to the king.*

My lord, you must tell us where the body is, and go
with us to the king.


**HAMLET**

*The body is with the king, but he is not there. The king is just a thing…*

The body is with the king, but the king is not with
the body. The king is a thing--


**GUILDENSTERN**

*A thing, my lord!*

A thing, my lord!


**HAMLET**

*He is a thing of no importance. Take me to him and tell him to hide.*

Of nothing: bring me to him. Hide fox, and all after.

Exeunt

# Scene III
*Another room in the castle*

Enter KING CLAUDIUS, attended

**KING CLAUDIUS**

*I have sent someone to find him and bring back the body. He is dangerous on the loose. But, we can't put the law on him too strongly. He's very loved by the people, and they will not take too kindly to his punishment. The only way to handle this is to send him away. Desperate times call for desperate measures.*

I have sent to seek him, and to find the body.
How dangerous is it that this man goes loose!
Yet must not we put the strong law on him:
He's loved of the distracted multitude,
Who like not in their judgment, but their eyes;
And where tis so, the offender's scourge is weigh'd,
But never the offence. To bear all smooth and even,
This sudden sending him away must seem
Deliberate pause: diseases desperate grown
By desperate appliance are relieved,
Or not at all.

Enter ROSENCRANTZ

*What's going on?*

How now! what hath befall'n?

**ROSENCRANTZ**

*He won't tell us where the body is hidden.*

Where the dead body is bestow'd, my lord,
We cannot get from him.

**KING CLAUDIUS**

*Where is he?*

But where is he?

**ROSENCRANTZ**

*He is being guarded outside.*

Without, my lord; guarded, to know your pleasure.

**KING CLAUDIUS**

*Bring him here.*

Bring him before us.

**ROSENCRANTZ**

*Hey, Guildenstern! Bring in my lord.*

Ho, Guildenstern! bring in my lord.

Enter HAMLET and GUILDENSTERN

**KING CLAUDIUS**

*Now, Hamlet, where's Polonius?*

Now, Hamlet, where's Polonius?

**HAMLET**

*He is at supper.*

At supper.

**KING CLAUDIUS**

*Where at supper?*

At supper! where?

**HAMLET**

*He is not eating, but being eaten by worms. We all become worm food in the end.*

Not where he eats, but where he is eaten: a certain
convocation of politic worms are e'en at him. Your

worm is your only emperor for diet: we fat all
creatures else to fat us, and we fat ourselves for
maggots: your fat king and your lean beggar is but
variable service, two dishes, but to one table:
that's the end.

## KING CLAUDIUS

*Enough, enough!*

Alas, alas!

## HAMLET

*The same worm that eats a king may become food for a fish which serves as the dinner for a cat.*

A man may fish with the worm that hath eat of a
king, and eat of the fish that hath fed of that worm.

## KING CLAUDIUS

*What are you talking about?*

What dost you mean by this?

## HAMLET

*I just want to show you what happens to a king's body after he is gone.*

Nothing but to show you how a king may go a
progress through the guts of a beggar.

## KING CLAUDIUS

*Where is Polonius?*

Where is Polonius?

## HAMLET

*In heaven. Send someone to see and if your messenger does not find him there, go look for yourself in the other place. If you can't find him there, you'll be able to smell him in the next month as you go into the lobby.*

In heaven; send hither to see: if your messenger
find him not there, seek him i' the other place
yourself. But indeed, if you find him not within
this month, you shall nose him as you go up the
stairs into the lobby.

**KING CLAUDIUS**

*Go look there.*

Go seek him there.

To some Attendants

**HAMLET**

*He's not going anywhere.*

He will stay till ye come.

Exeunt Attendants

**KING CLAUDIUS**

*For this deed you have committed, you are going to have to leave for awhile. You must be ready quickly, so go prepare yourself. The boat is ready to take you and your associates to England.*

Hamlet, this deed, for thine especial safety,--
Which we do tender, as we dearly grieve
For that which thou hast done,--must send thee hence
With fiery quickness: therefore prepare thyself;
The bark is ready, and the wind at help,
The associates tend, and every thing is bent
For England.

**HAMLET**

*For England!*

For England!

**KING CLAUDIUS**

*Yes, Hamlet.*

Ay, Hamlet.

285

## HAMLET

*Good.*

Good.

## KING CLAUDIUS

*You act as if you knew what we were going to do.*

So is it, if thou knew'st our purposes.

## HAMLET

*A little angel told me. So, off to England. Farewell, dear mother.*

I see a cherub that sees them. But, come; for
England! Farewell, dear mother.

## KING CLAUDIUS

*I am your loving father, Hamlet.*

Thy loving father, Hamlet.

## HAMLET

*You're my mother. Like it says, when a man takes a wife, they become of one flesh. So, you are my mother. Come on, off to England!*

My mother: father and mother is man and wife; man
and wife is one flesh; and so, my mother. Come, for England!

Exit

## KING CLAUDIUS

*Follow him closely, and see he gets on board quickly. Don't delay. I want him gone tonight.*

Follow him at foot; tempt him with speed aboard;
Delay it not; I'll have him hence to-night:
Away! for every thing is seal'd and done
That else leans on the affair: pray you, make haste.

Exeunt ROSENCRANTZ and GUILDENSTERN

*And, while in England, if you love me, and you should considering what all the Danes have done in the past, you will not hesitate to kill Hamlet. Obey me, England, and cure me of my sickness. I will not be well until it is done.*

And, England, if my love thou hold'st at aught--
As my great power thereof may give thee sense,
Since yet thy cicatrice looks raw and red
After the Danish sword, and thy free awe
Pays homage to us--thou mayst not coldly set
Our sovereign process; which imports at full,
By letters congruing to that effect,
The present death of Hamlet. Do it, England;
For like the hectic in my blood he rages,
And thou must cure me: till I know 'tis done,
Howe'er my haps, my joys were ne'er begun.

Exit

# Scene IV
## *A plain in Denmark*

Enter FORTINBRAS, a Captain, and Soldiers, marching

**PRINCE FORTINBRAS**

*Go, Captain, and greet the Danish king. Tell him that I would like to march through his kingdom, with his permission. You know the place. Let him know we will grant him his favor.*

Go, captain, from me greet the Danish king;
Tell him that, by his licence, Fortinbras
Craves the conveyance of a promised march
Over his kingdom. You know the rendezvous.
If that his majesty would aught with us,
We shall express our duty in his eye;
And let him know so.

**Captain**

*I will do it, my lord.*

I will do't, my lord.

**PRINCE FORTINBRAS**

*Go quietly.*

Go softly on.

Exeunt FORTINBRAS and Soldiers

Enter HAMLET, ROSENCRANTZ, GUILDENSTERN, and others

**HAMLET**

*Hello sir. Whose army is this?*

Good sir, whose powers are these?

**Captain**

*They are from Norway, sir.*

They are of Norway, sir.

**HAMLET**

*What is their purpose, sir?*

How purposed, sir, I pray you?

**Captain**

*They are on their way to Poland.*

Against some part of Poland.

**HAMLET**

*Who is in command, sir?*

Who commands them, sir?

**Captain**

*The nephew to the old king of Norway, Fortinbras.*

The nephews to old Norway, Fortinbras.

**HAMLET**

*Is he attacking the heart of Poland or some part of it?*

Goes it against the main of Poland, sir,
Or for some frontier?

**Captain**

*We are going to gain a little land that I wouldn't pay five dollars to farm.*

Truly to speak, and with no addition,
We go to gain a little patch of ground
That hath in it no profit but the name.
To pay five ducats, five, I would not farm it;
Nor will it yield to Norway or the Pole

A ranker rate, should it be sold in fee.

## HAMLET

*Well, then the Poles will never defend it.*

Why, then the Polack never will defend it.

## Captain

*Yes they will. It is already guarded.*

Yes, it is already garrison'd.

## HAMLET

*Two thousand souls and twenty thousand dollars will not settle this dispute. This is the result of too much money and peace. It is quite pointless. Thank you for the information, sir.*

Two thousand souls and twenty thousand ducats
Will not debate the question of this straw:
This is the imposthume of much wealth and peace,
That inward breaks, and shows no cause without
Why the man dies. I humbly thank you, sir.

## Captain

*God be with you, sir.*

God be wi' you, sir.

Exit

## ROSENCRANTZ

*Are you ready to go, my lord?*

Wilt please you go, my lord?

## HAMLET

*Go ahead. I'll be there soon.*

    I'll be with you straight go a little before.

Exeunt all except HAMLET

*Everything is telling me to hurry up and get on with my plan. What is a man if he only eats and sleeps? He is no more than a beast. God did not create us to waste our minds and abilities. There is a reason for my existence. Let me not ignore this opportunity, a silly young prince led by selfish ambition is offering his life for the sake of honor. I will not have another idle thought. I will think of nothing but revenge.*

How all occasions do inform against me,
And spur my dull revenge! What is a man,
If his chief good and market of his time
Be but to sleep and feed? a beast, no more.
Sure, he that made us with such large discourse,
Looking before and after, gave us not
That capability and god-like reason
To fust in us unused. Now, whether it be
Bestial oblivion, or some craven scruple
Of thinking too precisely on the event,
A thought which, quarter'd, hath but one part wisdom
And ever three parts coward, I do not know
Why yet I live to say 'This thing's to do;'
Sith I have cause and will and strength and means
To do't. Examples gross as earth exhort me:
Witness this army of such mass and charge
Led by a delicate and tender prince,
Whose spirit with divine ambition puff'd
Makes mouths at the invisible event,
Exposing what is mortal and unsure
To all that fortune, death and danger dare,
Even for an egg-shell. Rightly to be great
Is not to stir without great argument,
But greatly to find quarrel in a straw
When honour's at the stake. How stand I then,
That have a father kill'd, a mother stain'd,
Excitements of my reason and my blood,
And let all sleep? while, to my shame, I see
The imminent death of twenty thousand men,
That, for a fantasy and trick of fame,
Go to their graves like beds, fight for a plot
Whereon the numbers cannot try the cause,
Which is not tomb enough and continent
To hide the slain? O, from this time forth,
My thoughts be bloody, or be nothing worth!

Exit

# Scene V
### *Elsinore. A room in the castle*

Enter QUEEN GERTRUDE, HORATIO, and a Gentleman

**QUEEN GERTRUDE**

*I will not speak with her.*

I will not speak with her.

**Gentleman**

*She won't go away. She needs to be pitied.*

She is importunate, indeed distract:
Her mood will needs be pitied.

**QUEEN GERTRUDE**

*What does she want?*

What would she have?

**Gentleman**

*She talks about her father. She says there are tricks in the world and cries and beats her heart. She is talking out of her head. People listen to her and hear what they want. It seems she is trying to tell something horrible.*

She speaks much of her father; says she hears
There's tricks i' the world; and hems, and beats her heart;
Spurns enviously at straws; speaks things in doubt,
That carry but half sense: her speech is nothing,
Yet the unshaped use of it doth move
The hearers to collection; they aim at it,
And botch the words up fit to their own thoughts;
Which, as her winks, and nods, and gestures
yield them,
Indeed would make one think there might be thought,
Though nothing sure, yet much unhappily.

**HORATIO**

*She needs to be spoken with because she is causing people to think the unthinkable.*

'Twere good she were spoken with; for she may strew
Dangerous conjectures in ill-breeding minds.

**QUEEN GERTRUDE**

*Bring her in.*

Let her come in.

Exit HORATIO

*Everything within me tells me something awful about to happen. Perhaps it is just my guilt eating away at me.*

To my sick soul, as sin's true nature is,
Each toy seems prologue to some great amiss:
So full of artless jealousy is guilt,
It spills itself in fearing to be spilt.

Re-enter HORATIO, with OPHELIA

**OPHELIA**

*Where is her majesty of Denmark?*

Where is the beauteous majesty of Denmark?

**QUEEN GERTRUDE**

*How are you, Ophelia?*

How now, Ophelia!

**OPHELIA**

[Sings]
*How can you tell your true love from another? By his hat and walking stick or his shoe?*

How should I your true love know
From another one?
By his cockle hat and staff,
And his sandal shoon.

**QUEEN GERTRUDE**

*What brings about this song?*

Alas, sweet lady, what imports this song?

**OPHELIA**

*Did you say something? No? Just listen.*

Say you? nay, pray you, mark.

Sings

*He is dead and gone, lady. Dead and gone. Grass grows over his head and a stone is placed at his foot.*

He is dead and gone, lady,
He is dead and gone;
At his head a grass-green turf,
At his heels a stone.

**QUEEN GERTRUDE**

*Stop, Ophelia…*

Nay, but, Ophelia,--

**OPHELIA**

*I beg you to listen.*

Pray you, mark.

Sings

*His shroud is as white as the mountain snow…*

White his shroud as the mountain snow,--

Enter KING CLAUDIUS

**QUEEN GERTRUDE**

*At last, look at this girl, my lord.*

Alas, look here, my lord.

**OPHELIA**

[Sings]
*Covered in sweet flowers which were tossed to the ground by true love showers.*

Larded with sweet flowers
Which bewept to the grave did go
With true-love showers.


**KING CLAUDIUS**

*How are you, pretty lady?*

How do you, pretty lady?


**OPHELIA**

*I'm well, and may God give you yours. They say the baker's daughter was an owl. My lord, we know what we are, but not what we are to become. May God be at your table.*

Well, God 'ild you! They say the owl was a baker's
daughter. Lord, we know what we are, but know not
what we may be. God be at your table!


**KING CLAUDIUS**

*She is thinking about her father.*

Conceit upon her father.


**OPHELIA**

*I beg you to not talk about that. But, when asked tell them the song means:*

Pray you, let's have no words of this; but when they
ask you what it means, say you this:

Sings

*Tomorrow is Saint Valentine's day, and in the early morning, I will be at your window to be your Valentine. Then he got up and dressed and opened the bedroom door. He let in a maid, but let out a woman.*

To-morrow is Saint Valentine's day,

All in the morning betime,
And I a maid at your window,
To be your Valentine.
Then up he rose, and donn'd his clothes,
And dupp'd the chamber-door;
Let in the maid, that out a maid
Never departed more.

**KING CLAUDIUS**

*Pretty Ophelia!*

Pretty Ophelia!

**OPHELIA**

*I promise, I will end it soon…*

Indeed, la, without an oath, I'll make an end on't:

Sings

*By Jesus and Saint Charity, shame young men who must do it. They are to blame. She said you promised to marry me before you brought me into your bed, but now you won't because I came to your bed.*

By Gis and by Saint Charity,
Alack, and fie for shame!
Young men will do't, if they come to't;
By cock, they are to blame.
Quoth she, before you tumbled me,
You promised me to wed.
So would I ha' done, by yonder sun,
An thou hadst not come to my bed.

**KING CLAUDIUS**

*How long has she been like this?*

How long hath she been thus?

**OPHELIA**

*I hope everything works out well. We must wait and see. But I can't help crying, thinking about his body in the cold ground. My brother will be told about this, so thank you. Thank you for your advice. Come on, Driver. Good night, sweet ladies. Good night.*

I hope all will be well. We must be patient: but I
cannot choose but weep, to think they should lay him
i' the cold ground. My brother shall know of it:
and so I thank you for your good counsel. Come, my
coach! Good night, ladies; good night, sweet ladies;
good night, good night.

Exit

**KING CLAUDIUS**

*Follow her closely and watch her.*

Follow her close; give her good watch,
I pray you.

Exit HORATIO

*This is the result of deep grief. It comes from the death of her father. Sadness comes in swells. First, her father is killed. Next, your son is sent away by his own doings. Poor Ophelia did not get to mourn her father properly; we buried him so quickly. Now, the people are spreading nasty rumors about his death. She is now crazy with grief, and her brother who has secretly returned from France hears the gossip. He is going to think I killed his father, which is killing me.*

O, this is the poison of deep grief; it springs
All from her father's death. O Gertrude, Gertrude,
When sorrows come, they come not single spies
But in battalions. First, her father slain:
Next, your son gone; and he most violent author
Of his own just remove: the people muddied,
Thick and unwholesome in their thoughts and whispers,
For good Polonius' death; and we have done but greenly,
In hugger-mugger to inter him: poor Ophelia
Divided from herself and her fair judgment,
Without the which we are pictures, or mere beasts:
Last, and as much containing as all these,
Her brother is in secret come from France;
Feeds on his wonder, keeps himself in clouds,
And wants not buzzers to infect his ear
With pestilent speeches of his father's death;
Wherein necessity, of matter beggar'd,
Will nothing stick our person to arraign
In ear and ear. O my dear Gertrude, this,
Like to a murdering-piece, in many places
Gives me superfluous death.

A noise within

**QUEEN GERTRUDE**

*What was that?*

Alack, what noise is this?


**KING CLAUDIUS**

*Where are my guards? Let them stand by the door.*

Where are my Switzers? Let them guard the door.

Enter another Gentleman

*What is going on?*

What is the matter?


**Gentleman**

*Save yourself, my lord. Young Laertes is leading a riotous group across the lowlands. The crowds call him lord and shout, "We want Laertes to be our king," like they have forgotten our customs. They are throwing their caps in the air and cheering, "King Laertes."*

Save yourself, my lord:
The ocean, overpeering of his list,
Eats not the flats with more impetuous haste
Than young Laertes, in a riotous head,
O'erbears your officers. The rabble call him lord;
And, as the world were now but to begin,
Antiquity forgot, custom not known,
The ratifiers and props of every word,
They cry 'Choose we: Laertes shall be king:'
Caps, hands, and tongues, applaud it to the clouds:
'Laertes shall be king, Laertes king!'


**QUEEN GERTRUDE**

*They sound so cheerful, but they are after the wrong dog!*

How cheerfully on the false trail they cry!
O, this is counter, you false Danish dogs!

**KING CLAUDIUS**

*The doors are breaking.*

The doors are broke.

Noise within

Enter LAERTES, armed; Danes following

**LAERTES**

*Where is the king? Sirs, surround the area.*

Where is this king? Sirs, stand you all without.

**Danes**

*No, let's go in.*

No, let's come in.

**LAERTES**

*I ask that you give me a moment.*

I pray you, give me leave.

**Danes**

*We will.*

We will, we will.

They retire without the door

**LAERTES**

*Thank you. Guard the door. Oh you vile king, give me my father!*

I thank you: keep the door. O thou vile king,
Give me my father!

**QUEEN GERTRUDE**

*Calm down, good Laertes.*

Calmly, good Laertes.

**LAERTES**

*I have one drop of blood that's calm and it calls me a bastard-child, my father a fool, and my mother a harlot.*

That drop of blood that's calm proclaims me bastard,
Cries cuckold to my father, brands the harlot
Even here, between the chaste unsmirched brow
Of my true mother.

**KING CLAUDIUS**

*What is wrong, Laertes? Why are you leading this giant rebellion? Let him go, Gertrude. We have no need to fear, because God will protect us against traitors. Tell me, Laertes, why are you so angry? Let him go, Gertrude. Speak, man.*

What is the cause, Laertes,
That thy rebellion looks so giant-like?
Let him go, Gertrude; do not fear our person:
There's such divinity doth hedge a king,
That treason can but peep to what it would,
Acts little of his will. Tell me, Laertes,
Why thou art thus incensed. Let him go, Gertrude.
Speak, man.

**LAERTES**

*Where is my father?*

Where is my father?

**KING CLAUDIUS**

*He is dead.*

Dead.

**QUEEN GERTRUDE**

*But the king didn't kill him.*

But not by him.

**KING CLAUDIUS**

*Let him make his demands.*

Let him demand his fill.

**LAERTES**

*How did he die? I will not be lied to or threatened with hell. I don't care what happens anymore. I just want revenge for my father.*

How came he dead? I'll not be juggled with:
To hell, allegiance! vows, to the blackest devil!
Conscience and grace, to the profoundest pit!
I dare damnation. To this point I stand,
That both the worlds I give to negligence,
Let come what comes; only I'll be revenged
Most thoroughly for my father.

**KING CLAUDIUS**

*Who's controlling you?*

Who shall stay you?

**LAERTES**

*I am acting by my will alone, and I will use whatever means I have against you.*

My will, not all the world:
And for my means, I'll husband them so well,
They shall go far with little.

**KING CLAUDIUS**

*Good Laertes, if you want to know the details of your father's death despite hurting his enemies and his friends?*

Good Laertes,
If you desire to know the certainty
Of your dear father's death, is't writ in your revenge,
That, swoopstake, you will draw both friend and foe,

Winner and loser?


**LAERTES**

*No, only his enemies.*

None but his enemies.


**KING CLAUDIUS**

*Do you know his enemies?*

Will you know them then?


**LAERTES**

*I will open my arms to his friends like a mother bird. I will die for them.*

To his good friends thus wide I'll ope my arms;
And like the kind life-rendering pelican,
Repast them with my blood.


**KING CLAUDIUS**

*Now, you're talking like a good child and gentleman. I am innocent of your father's death, and quite frankly I am still grieving.*

Why, now you speak
Like a good child and a true gentleman.
That I am guiltless of your father's death,
And am most sensible in grief for it,
It shall as level to your judgment pierce
As day does to your eye.


**Danes**

[Within]

*Let her in.*

Let her come in.

**LAERTES**

*What's going on?*

How now! what noise is that?

Re-enter OPHELIA

*Oh heat, dry up my brains and salty tears sting my eyes. I swear I will get revenge for my sweet sister's madness. Oh sweet rose! Dear sweet sister, Ophelia! My sister has lost her mind over our father's death.*

O heat, dry up my brains! tears seven times salt,
Burn out the sense and virtue of mine eye!
By heaven, thy madness shall be paid by weight,
Till our scale turn the beam. O rose of May!
Dear maid, kind sister, sweet Ophelia!
O heavens! is't possible, a young maid's wits
Should be as moral as an old man's life?
Nature is fine in love, and where 'tis fine,
It sends some precious instance of itself
After the thing it loves.


**OPHELIA**

[Sings]
*They carried him away in his coffin. Hey non nonny, hey nonny. And on his grave, cried many a tear. Good bye, my dove!*

They bore him barefaced on the bier;
Hey non nonny, nonny, hey nonny;
And in his grave rain'd many a tear:--
Fare you well, my dove!


**LAERTES**

*If you had your sanity and persuaded me to take revenge, I would not be as moved as I am now.*

Hadst thou thy wits, and didst persuade revenge,
It could not move thus.


**OPHELIA**

[Sings]
*You must sing a-down, a-down. And you call him a-down-a. Oh, how the wheels turn around, that stole his master's daughter.*

You must sing a-down a-down,
An you call him a-down-a.
O, how the wheel becomes it! It is the false
steward, that stole his master's daughter.


**LAERTES**

*This means more than sensible talk.*

This nothing's more than matter.


**OPHELIA**

*Rosemary is for remembrance. Remember. There are pansies for thoughts.*

There's rosemary, that's for remembrance; pray,
love, remember: and there is pansies. that's for thoughts.


**LAERTES**

*She is simply mad with memories.*

A document in madness, thoughts and remembrance fitted.


**OPHELIA**

*Here are fennel and columbines for you. And here is rue for you and me. There is a daisy and violets, but they withered up when my father died. He died well.*

There's fennel for you, and columbines: there's rue
for you; and here's some for me: we may call it
herb-grace o' Sundays: O you must wear your rue with
a difference. There's a daisy: I would give you
some violets, but they withered all when my father
died: they say he made a good end,--

Sings

*The sweet robin is my joy.*

For bonny sweet Robin is all my joy.


**LAERTES**

*Despite her affliction, she is focusing on what is pretty.*

Thought and affliction, passion, hell itself,
She turns to favour and to prettiness.


**OPHELIA**

[Sings]
*And will he come again? Will he come again? No, no he is dead, and in his death-bed. He will never come again. His beard is white as snow, and his hair was white, too. He is gone, gone, and we moan, "God have mercy on his soul!" And all the Christian souls, I pray God be with you.*

And will he not come again?
And will he not come again?
No, no, he is dead:
Go to thy death-bed:
He never will come again.
His beard was as white as snow,
All flaxen was his poll:
He is gone, he is gone,
And we cast away moan:
God ha' mercy on his soul!
And of all Christian souls, I pray God. God be wi' ye.

Exit

**LAERTES**

*Do you see this, God?*

Do you see this, O God?


**KING CLAUDIUS**

*Laertes, don't deny me my grief. Go and find your wisest friends to listen to both of us and judge between you and me. If they find me at fault for your father's death, then I will give you the kingdom. If they find me innocent, then I will work to satisfy your need to know about your father's death. But, you must be patient.*

Laertes, I must commune with your grief,
Or you deny me right. Go but apart,
Make choice of whom your wisest friends you will.
And they shall hear and judge 'twixt you and me:
If by direct or by collateral hand
They find us touch'd, we will our kingdom give,
Our crown, our life, and all that we can ours,
To you in satisfaction; but if not,

Be you content to lend your patience to us,
And we shall jointly labour with your soul
To give it due content.


**LAERTES**

*Fine, but I need to know how he died and why there wasn't a proper funeral. Why was it kept so quiet?*

Let this be so;
His means of death, his obscure funeral--
No trophy, sword, nor hatchment o'er his bones,
No noble rite nor formal ostentation--
Cry to be heard, as 'twere from heaven to earth,
That I must call't in question.


**KING CLAUDIUS**

*And, so you shall. May justice prevail. Go with me, now.*

So you shall;
And where the offence is let the great axe fall.
I pray you, go with me.

Exeunt

# Scene VI
*Another room in the castle*

Enter HORATIO and a Servant

**HORATIO**

*Who are the people who want to speak with me?*

What are they that would speak with me?

**Servant**

*Sailors, sir. They have letters for you.*

Sailors, sir: they say they have letters for you.

**HORATIO**

*Let them come in.*

Let them come in.

Exit Servant

*I do not know who else would be sending me a letter from abroad, except Hamlet.*

I do not know from what part of the world
I should be greeted, if not from Lord Hamlet.

Enter Sailors

**First Sailor**

*God bless you, sir.*

God bless you, sir.

**HORATIO**

*May he bless you, too.*

Let him bless thee too.

**First Sailor**

*He will, sir, if it pleases him. Here is a letter for you, sir. It comes from the ambassador, Lord Hamlet. If you are Horatio, let me know.*

He shall, sir, an't please him. There's a letter for
you, sir; it comes from the ambassador that was
bound for England; if your name be Horatio, as I am
let to know it is.


**HORATIO**

[Reads]

*"Dear Horatio, when you have looked at this letter send the message to the king. We were at sea only two days when a pirate ship overtook us. We tried to escape, but were too slow, so we fought. I am now the lone prisoner on board. They have treated me well, and want me to do them a favor. Please come to me as quickly as you can. I have much to tell you. These messengers will bring you to me. Rosencrantz and Guildenstern are still on their way to England. I have much to tell you about them. Yours truly, Hamlet."  Come men. I'll show you where to take these letters, so you can take me to Hamlet.*

'Horatio, when thou shalt have overlooked
this, give these fellows some means to the king:
they have letters for him. Ere we were two days old
at sea, a pirate of very warlike appointment gave us
chase. Finding ourselves too slow of sail, we put on
a compelled valour, and in the grapple I boarded
them: on the instant they got clear of our ship; so
I alone became their prisoner. They have dealt with
me like thieves of mercy: but they knew what they
did; I am to do a good turn for them. Let the king
have the letters I have sent; and repair thou to me
with as much speed as thou wouldst fly death. I
have words to speak in thine ear will make thee
dumb; yet are they much too light for the bore of
the matter. These good fellows will bring thee
where I am. Rosencrantz and Guildenstern hold their
course for England: of them I have much to tell
thee. Farewell.
'He that thou knowest thine, HAMLET.'
Come, I will make you way for these your letters;
And do't the speedier, that you may direct me
To him from whom you brought them.

Exeunt

# Scene VII
*Another room in the castle*

Enter KING CLAUDIUS and LAERTES

**KING CLAUDIUS**

*Now you must believe that I am your friend, since the man who killed your father was trying to kill me.*

Now must your conscience my acquaintance seal,
And you must put me in your heart for friend,
Sith you have heard, and with a knowing ear,
That he which hath your noble father slain
Pursued my life.

**LAERTES**

*It appears so, but tell me why didn't you do anything about it.*

It well appears: but tell me
Why you proceeded not against these feats,
So crimeful and so capital in nature,
As by your safety, wisdom, all things else,
You mainly were stirr'd up.

**KING CLAUDIUS**

*I have two reasons, but you may think they are weak. First the queen is his mother, and she is devoted to him. She is a great part of my life, and I don't think I could live without her. The other reason is the people of Denmark love him. I could not do anything to him without them revolting.*

O, for two special reasons;
Which may to you, perhaps, seem much unsinew'd,
But yet to me they are strong. The queen his mother
Lives almost by his looks; and for myself--
My virtue or my plague, be it either which--
She's so conjunctive to my life and soul,
That, as the star moves not but in his sphere,
I could not but by her. The other motive,
Why to a public count I might not go,
Is the great love the general gender bear him;
Who, dipping all his faults in their affection,
Would, like the spring that turneth wood to stone,

Convert his gyves to graces; so that my arrows,
Too slightly timber'd for so loud a wind,
Would have reverted to my bow again,
And not where I had aim'd them.


**LAERTES**

*So, I have lost a noble father, and my sister has been driven insane. I will get my revenge in the end.*

And so have I a noble father lost;
A sister driven into desperate terms,
Whose worth, if praises may go back again,
Stood challenger on mount of all the age
For her perfections: but my revenge will come.


**KING CLAUDIUS**

*Don't worry about that. You mustn't think that I am so old and dull that I can sit idly by while being threatened. You will soon hear more about my plans. I loved your father and I love myself enough to…*

Break not your sleeps for that: you must not think
That we are made of stuff so flat and dull
That we can let our beard be shook with danger
And think it pastime. You shortly shall hear more:
I loved your father, and we love ourself;
And that, I hope, will teach you to imagine--

Enter a Messenger

*What's going on? Do you have news for me?*

How now! what news?


**Messenger**

*Letters, my lord, from Hamlet. This is for the queen.*

Letters, my lord, from Hamlet:
This to your majesty; this to the queen.


**KING CLAUDIUS**

*Letters from Hamlet? Who brought them?*

From Hamlet! who brought them?

**Messenger**

*Sailors, my lord, although I didn't see them. The letters were brought by Claudio.*

Sailors, my lord, they say; I saw them not:
They were given me by Claudio; he received them
Of him that brought them.

**KING CLAUDIUS**

*Laertes, you can listen. Leave us.*

Laertes, you shall hear them. Leave us.

Exit Messenger

Reads

*"High and mighty, You will know that I am returning to Denmark and I ask that you will see me. I apologize for my actions. I will tell you how I came back to Denmark so suddenly. Hamlet." What does this mean? Is everyone back or is this some joke?*

'High and mighty, You shall know I am set naked on
your kingdom. To-morrow shall I beg leave to see
your kingly eyes: when I shall, first asking your
pardon thereunto, recount the occasion of my sudden
and more strange return. 'HAMLET.'
What should this mean? Are all the rest come back?
Or is it some abuse, and no such thing?

**LAERTES**

*Do you recognize the handwriting?*

Know you the hand?

**KING CLAUDIUS**

*It's Hamlet's. Here he states he wants to see me alone. What do you think?*

'Tis Hamlets character. 'Naked!
And in a postscript here, he says 'alone.'

Can you advise me?

**LAERTES**

*I don't understand it, my lord. But let him come. It warms my heart and sets my soul ablaze to know that I will live to tell him to his face what he has done.*

I'm lost in it, my lord. But let him come;
It warms the very sickness in my heart,
That I shall live and tell him to his teeth,
'Thus didest thou.'

**KING CLAUDIUS**

*If it is to be, Laertes, will you let me guide you? Of course you will.*

If it be so, Laertes--
As how should it be so? how otherwise?--
Will you be ruled by me?

**LAERTES**

*Yes, my lord. Just don't think I will be persuaded to act peacefully.*

Ay, my lord;
So you will not o'errule me to a peace.

**KING CLAUDIUS**

*No, just to give you some inner peace. If he is back without any means to continue on his trip, then I am going to put in place a plan that will surely kill him. Even his mother will think it was an accident.*

To thine own peace. If he be now return'd,
As checking at his voyage, and that he means
No more to undertake it, I will work him
To an exploit, now ripe in my device,
Under the which he shall not choose but fall:
And for his death no wind of blame shall breathe,
But even his mother shall uncharge the practise
And call it accident.

**LAERTES**

*My lord, I will follow your lead, but I would like to be the instrument of Hamlet's death, if possible.*

My lord, I will be ruled;
The rather, if you could devise it so
That I might be the organ.


### KING CLAUDIUS

*That should work. You are very popular in some aspects, and Hamlet may be envious of your special talent.*

It falls right.
You have been talk'd of since your travel much,
And that in Hamlet's hearing, for a quality
Wherein, they say, you shine: your sum of parts
Did not together pluck such envy from him
As did that one, and that, in my regard,
Of the unworthiest siege.


### LAERTES

*What talent is that, my lord?*

What part is that, my lord?


### KING CLAUDIUS

*It's nothing really. But just two months ago, I met a Norman who was a very skillful man on a horse. Even now, I cannot fathom how he did his tricks.*

A very riband in the cap of youth,
Yet needful too; for youth no less becomes
The light and careless livery that it wears
Than settled age his sables and his weeds,
Importing health and graveness. Two months since,
Here was a gentleman of Normandy:--
I've seen myself, and served against, the French,
And they can well on horseback: but this gallant
Had witchcraft in't; he grew unto his seat;
And to such wondrous doing brought his horse,
As he had been incorpsed and demi-natured
With the brave beast: so far he topp'd my thought,
That I, in forgery of shapes and tricks,
Come short of what he did.

**LAERTES**

*You say he was a Norman?*

A Norman was't?

**KING CLAUDIUS**

*Yes, a Norman.*

A Norman.

**LAERTES**

*I bet it was Lamond.*

Upon my life, Lamond.

**KING CLAUDIUS**

*Yes, it was.*

The very same.

**LAERTES**

*I know him well. He is much loved in his nation.*

I know him well: he is the brooch indeed
And gem of all the nation.

**KING CLAUDIUS**

*He said that you were the best swordsman in all of the world. This made Hamlet very envious.*

He made confession of you,
And gave you such a masterly report
For art and exercise in your defence
And for your rapier most especially,
That he cried out, 'twould be a sight indeed,
If one could match you: the scrimers of their nation,
He swore, had had neither motion, guard, nor eye,
If you opposed them. Sir, this report of his

Did Hamlet so envenom with his envy
That he could nothing do but wish and beg
Your sudden coming o'er, to play with him.
Now, out of this,--


## LAERTES

*What's the poing, my lord?*

What out of this, my lord?


## KING CLAUDIUS

*Laertes, was your father important to you? Or are you just putting on a show?*

Laertes, was your father dear to you?
Or are you like the painting of a sorrow,
A face without a heart?


## LAERTES

*Why do you ask this?*

Why ask you this?


## KING CLAUDIUS

*It's not that I think you didn't love your father, but I've seen how time changes the love you feel for someone. As the days go by, the fire of love weakens and dies out. We should act when we feel motivated and not wait. My point is Hamlet is coming back. What do you want to do to prove your love for your father.*

Not that I think you did not love your father;
But that I know love is begun by time;
And that I see, in passages of proof,
Time qualifies the spark and fire of it.
There lives within the very flame of love
A kind of wick or snuff that will abate it;
And nothing is at a like goodness still;
For goodness, growing to a plurisy,
Dies in his own too much: that we would do
We should do when we would; for this 'would' changes
And hath abatements and delays as many
As there are tongues, are hands, are accidents;
And then this 'should' is like a spendthrift sigh,

That hurts by easing. But, to the quick o' the ulcer:--
Hamlet comes back: what would you undertake,
To show yourself your father's son in deed
More than in words?


**LAERTES**

*I would cut his throat in the church.*

To cut his throat i' the church.


**KING CLAUDIUS**

*No one should commit murder in a church. Although revenge has no bounds, I'd like for you to use some restraint. Stay in your room and when Hamlet comes back, we will let him know you are home. We will make much over your abilities the Frenchman mentioned. Then we will bet him he cannot beat you. You will have your chance to take his life and revenge your father.*

No place, indeed, should murder sanctuarize;
Revenge should have no bounds. But, good Laertes,
Will you do this, keep close within your chamber.
Hamlet return'd shall know you are come home:
We'll put on those shall praise your excellence
And set a double varnish on the fame
The Frenchman gave you, bring you in fine together
And wager on your heads: he, being remiss,
Most generous and free from all contriving,
Will not peruse the foils; so that, with ease,
Or with a little shuffling, you may choose
A sword unbated, and in a pass of practise
Requite him for your father.


**LAERTES**

*I will do it. I will prepare my sword, and I'll poison the tip so if it slightly touches him, he will surely die.*

I will do't:
And, for that purpose, I'll anoint my sword.
I bought an unction of a mountebank,
So mortal that, but dip a knife in it,
Where it draws blood no cataplasm so rare,
Collected from all simples that have virtue
Under the moon, can save the thing from death
That is but scratch'd withal: I'll touch my point

With this contagion, that, if I gall him slightly,
It may be death.


**KING CLAUDIUS**

*Let's think about this a little more. We need to think about the time and place. We mustn't fail. If our first plan doesn't work, we need another plan in place. Let me see. You must keep him jumping, so he gets hot and sweaty. Then, when he asks for something to drink, we will have a cup filled with poison prepared for him.*

Let's further think of this;
Weigh what convenience both of time and means
May fit us to our shape: if this should fail,
And that our drift look through our bad performance,
'Twere better not assay'd: therefore this project
Should have a back or second, that might hold,
If this should blast in proof. Soft! let me see:
We'll make a solemn wager on your cunnings: I ha't.
When in your motion you are hot and dry--
As make your bouts more violent to that end--
And that he calls for drink, I'll have prepared him
A chalice for the nonce, whereon but sipping,
If he by chance escape your venom'd stuck,
Our purpose may hold there.

Enter QUEEN GERTRUDE

*What is it, sweet queen?*

How now, sweet queen!


**QUEEN GERTRUDE**

*Another tragedy has struck. Your sister has drowned, Laertes.*

One woe doth tread upon another's heel,
So fast they follow; your sister's drown'd, Laertes.


**LAERTES**

*Drowned! Where?*

Drown'd! O, where?

## QUEEN GERTRUDE

*There is a willow tree growing by the brook with limbs stretching over the water. She was there with her flowers when she slipped into the brook. She looked like a mermaid in the water singing her hymns, unaware of the danger she was in. Finally, her drenched clothes, weighed her down.*

There is a willow grows aslant a brook,
That shows his hoar leaves in the glassy stream;
There with fantastic garlands did she come
Of crow-flowers, nettles, daisies, and long purples
That liberal shepherds give a grosser name,
But our cold maids do dead men's fingers call them:
There, on the pendent boughs her coronet weeds
Clambering to hang, an envious sliver broke;
When down her weedy trophies and herself
Fell in the weeping brook. Her clothes spread wide;
And, mermaid-like, awhile they bore her up:
Which time she chanted snatches of old tunes;
As one incapable of her own distress,
Or like a creature native and indued
Unto that element: but long it could not be
Till that her garments, heavy with their drink,
Pull'd the poor wretch from her melodious lay
To muddy death.


## LAERTES

*So, she is dead?*

Alas, then, she is drown'd?


## QUEEN GERTRUDE

*Drowned.*

Drown'd, drown'd.


## LAERTES

*Ophelia had enough water, so I will not cry anymore. Nature is too strong and makes me cry anyway. When I am finished, I will not act like a woman. Goodbye, my lord. I have more fiery words to say, but my tears won't let me.*

Too much of water hast thou, poor Ophelia,
And therefore I forbid my tears: but yet
It is our trick; nature her custom holds,

Let shame say what it will: when these are gone,
The woman will be out. Adieu, my lord:
I have a speech of fire, that fain would blaze,
But that this folly douts it.

Exit

**KING CLAUDIUS**

*Let's follow him, Gertrude. I have worked so hard to calm him down and I'm afraid this might start him up again. So, let's follow him.*

Let's follow, Gertrude:
How much I had to do to calm his rage!
Now fear I this will give it start again;
Therefore let's follow.

Exeunt

# Act V

# Scene I
*A churchyard*

Enter two Clowns, with spades, & c

**First Clown**

*Are they going to give her a Christian burial to try and save her after she did the unforgivable.*

Is she to be buried in Christian burial that
wilfully seeks her own salvation?

**Second Clown**

*I'm telling you they are; therefore, maker her grave straight. The coroner has said it was an accident.*

I tell thee she is: and therefore make her grave
straight: the crowner hath sat on her, and finds it
Christian burial.

**First Clown**

*How can that be? Did she drown herself in self-defense?*

How can that be, unless she drowned herself in her
own defence?

**Second Clown**

*I guess so.*

Why, 'tis found so.

**First Clown**

*I think she knew what she was doing. She acted on her own wits.*

It must be 'se offendendo;' it cannot be else. For
here lies the point: if I drown myself wittingly,
it argues an act: and an act hath three branches: it
is, to act, to do, to perform: argal, she drowned

herself wittingly.

## Second Clown

*No, listen to me, gravedigger.*

Nay, but hear you, goodman delver,--

## First Clown

*Just let me finish. Here is the water, right? Here is the man. If the man goes into the water and drowns himself it is his will. If the water comes to him, then it is an accident. If you don't mean to kill yourself, then you can receive salvation.*

Give me leave. Here lies the water; good: here
stands the man; good; if the man go to this water,
and drown himself, it is, will he, nill he, he
goes,--mark you that; but if the water come to him
and drown him, he drowns not himself: argal, he
that is not guilty of his own death shortens not his own life.

## Second Clown

*Is that the law?*

But is this law?

## First Clown

*Yes, it is the law of the coroner.*

Ay, marry, is't; crowner's quest law.

## Second Clown

*I think if she hadn't been wealthy, she would not have received a Christian burial.*

Will you ha' the truth on't? If this had not been
a gentlewoman, she should have been buried out o'
Christian burial.

**First Clown**

*Isn't that a shame. Great people are poor, like gardeners, ditch-diggers, and gravediggers. Yet, they have the same profession as Adam.*

Why, there thou say'st: and the more pity that
great folk should have countenance in this world to
drown or hang themselves, more than their even
Christian. Come, my spade. There is no ancient
gentleman but gardeners, ditchers, and grave-makers:
they hold up Adam's profession.


**Second Clown**

*Was he a great man.*

Was he a gentleman?


**First Clown**

*He was the first man with arms.*

He was the first that ever bore arms.


**Second Clown**

*Didn't he have any?*

Why, he had none.


**First Clown**

*Are you a heathen. Don't you read the scripture? It says, "Adam dug." He could not do this without arms. Let me ask you something.*

What, art a heathen? How dost thou understand the
Scripture? The Scripture says 'Adam digged:'
could he dig without arms? I'll put another
question to thee: if thou answerest me not to the
purpose, confess thyself--


**Second Clown**

*Go ahead.*

Go to.


**First Clown**

*Who can build stronger than a mason, a ship builder, or a carpenter?*

What is he that builds stronger than either the
mason, the shipwright, or the carpenter?


**Second Clown**

*The man who builds gallows. His work outlives many who use it.*

The gallows-maker; for that frame outlives a
thousand tenants.


**First Clown**

*That's rather smart. You think the gallows are stronger than the church.*

I like thy wit well, in good faith: the gallows
does well; but how does it well? it does well to
those that do in: now thou dost ill to say the
gallows is built stronger than the church: argal,
the gallows may do well to thee. To't again, come.


**Second Clown**

*Who builds stronger than a mason, a ship builder, or a carpenter.*

'Who builds stronger than a mason, a shipwright, or
a carpenter?'


**First Clown**

*Yes. Tell me what you think.*

Ay, tell me that, and unyoke.


**Second Clown**

*I've got it.*

Marry, now I can tell.

**First Clown**

*Go ahead.*

To't.

**Second Clown**

*I swear. I can't think.*

Mass, I cannot tell.

Enter HAMLET and HORATIO, at a distance

**First Clown**

*Don't overthink it. You are dumb to get it. The gravedigger is the greatest builder, because what he builds lasts until the end of time. Now, go and get me some liquor.*

Cudgel thy brains no more about it, for your dull
ass will not mend his pace with beating; and, when
you are asked this question next, say 'a
grave-maker: 'the houses that he makes last till
doomsday. Go, get thee to Yaughan: fetch me a
stoup of liquor.

Exit Second Clown

He digs and sings

*When I was younger, I did love, did love. I thought it was very sweet. To set the day and time for us to meet.*

In youth, when I did love, did love,
Methought it was very sweet,
To contract, O, the time, for, ah, my behove,
O, methought, there was nothing meet.

**HAMLET**

*Does this guy have no respect for the dead; he is singing while digging a grave.*

Has this fellow no feeling of his business, that he

sings at grave-making?

## HORATIO

*He is just numb to his work after doing it for so long.*

Custom hath made it in him a property of easiness.

## HAMLET

*I agree. He has so much to do, he can't afford to be sensitive.*

'Tis e'en so: the hand of little employment hath
the daintier sense.

**First Clown**

[Sings]
*Old age has snuck up on me, and got me in his clutches. He slipped into the land, as if I never existed.*

But age, with his stealing steps,
Hath claw'd me in his clutch,
And hath shipped me intil the land,
As if I had never been such.

Throws up a skull

## HAMLET

*That skull once had a tongue in it and could sing. Now that fool tosses it to the ground as if it belonged to a murderer! It might have belonged to a silver-tongued politician, and now this guy is overthrowing him. Right?*

That skull had a tongue in it, and could sing once:
how the knave jowls it to the ground, as if it were
Cain's jaw-bone, that did the first murder! It
might be the pate of a politician, which this ass
now o'er-reaches; one that would circumvent God,
might it not?

## HORATIO

*It might have been.*

It might, my lord.

## HAMLET

*Or it could have been a courtier who said, "Good morning, sweet lord! How are you?" Couldn't it?*

Or of a courtier; which could say 'Good morrow,
sweet lord! How dost thou, good lord?' This might
be my lord such-a-one, that praised my lord
such-a-one's horse, when he meant to beg it; might it not?

## HORATIO

*Yes, my lord.*

Ay, my lord.

## HAMLET

*Even if that's true, it now belongs to Lady Worm. He has been knocked around with a shovel. It is worthless now. It makes me ache to think about it.*

Why, e'en so: and now my Lady Worm's; chapless, and
knocked about the mazzard with a sexton's spade:
here's fine revolution, an we had the trick to
see't. Did these bones cost no more the breeding,
but to play at loggats with 'em? mine ache to think on't.

## First Clown

[Sings]
*A pick-ax and a shovel for a dead man's burial clothes with a bed of clay.*

A pick-axe, and a spade, a spade,
For and a shrouding sheet:
O, a pit of clay for to be made
For such a guest is meet.

Throws up another skull

## HAMLET

*There goes another one. Maybe that one is a lawyer. Where are his tricks and fees, now? Why does he let this guy treat him like this? Or, it could be a great land owner with his lumps of money and renter's fees. Is this the fine for him, having his skull filled with dirt? The only thing he has to his name is his coffin.*

There's another: why may not that be the skull of a
lawyer? Where be his quiddities now, his quillets,
his cases, his tenures, and his tricks? why does he
suffer this rude knave now to knock him about the
sconce with a dirty shovel, and will not tell him of
his action of battery? Hum! This fellow might be
in's time a great buyer of land, with his statutes,
his recognizances, his fines, his double vouchers,
his recoveries: is this the fine of his fines, and
the recovery of his recoveries, to have his fine
pate full of fine dirt? will his vouchers vouch him
no more of his purchases, and double ones too, than
the length and breadth of a pair of indentures? The
very conveyances of his lands will hardly lie in
this box; and must the inheritor himself have no more, ha?


### HORATIO

*Not much more, my lord.*

Not a jot more, my lord.


### HAMLET

*Isn't paper made of sheepskins?*

Is not parchment made of sheepskins?


### HORATIO

*Yes, my lord, and calf-skins, too.*

Ay, my lord, and of calf-skins too.


### HAMLET

*Only sheep and calves have assurance of their purpose after death. I am going to speak to this guy. Whose grave is this, sir?*

They are sheep and calves which seek out assurance
in that. I will speak to this fellow. Whose
grave's this, sirrah?

**First Clown**

*Mine, sir.*

Mine, sir.

Sings

*Oh, a pit of clay to be made for the dead to meet.*

O, a pit of clay for to be made
For such a guest is meet.


**HAMLET**

*You'll think it's yours when you're lying in it.*

I think it be thine, indeed; for thou liest in't.


**First Clown**

*You may lay in it, sir, but it would not be yours; however, I don't lay in it and it is mine.*

You lie out on't, sir, and therefore it is not
yours: for my part, I do not lie in't, and yet it is mine.


**HAMLET**

*One must lay in it for it to be theirs. It is for the dead, not the living, you liar.*

'Thou dost lie in't, to be in't and say it is thine:
'tis for the dead, not for the quick; therefore thou liest.


**First Clown**

*It's just a little lie, sir.*

'Tis a quick lie, sir; 'twill away gain, from me to
you.


**HAMLET**

*What man do you dig it for?*

What man dost thou dig it for?

**First Clown**

*It is not for a man.*

For no man, sir.

**HAMLET**

*What women, then?*

What woman, then?

**First Clown**

*None.*

For none, neither.

**HAMLET**

*Who is to be buried in it?*

Who is to be buried in't?

**First Clown**

*Well, she was a woman, but now she is dead.*

One that was a woman, sir; but, rest her soul, she's dead.

**HAMLET**

*How simple-minded this fool is! We must be so specific or he doesn't get it. I swear, Horatio, there is a fine line between the peasants and the educated. How long have you been a gravedigger?*

How absolute the knave is! we must speak by the card, or equivocation will undo us. By the Lord, Horatio, these three years I have taken a note of it; the age is grown so picked that the toe of the peasant comes so near the heel of the courtier, he

gaffs his kibe. How long hast thou been a
grave-maker?

### First Clown

*I became a gravedigger the day the late King Hamlet defeated Fortinbras.*

Of all the days i' the year, I came to't that day
that our last king Hamlet overcame Fortinbras.

### HAMLET

*How long has that been?*

How long is that since?

### First Clown

*Don't you know that? Every fool knows that day; the day young Hamlet, the one who went mad and was sent to England, was born.*

Cannot you tell that? every fool can tell that: it
was the very day that young Hamlet was born; he that
is mad, and sent into England.

### HAMLET

*Oh yes, and why was he sent to England?*

Ay, marry, why was he sent into England?

### First Clown

*I think it was because he was mad, and needed some time to regain his senses. If he doesn't it does not matter.*

Why, because he was mad: he shall recover his wits
there; or, if he do not, it's no great matter there.

### HAMLET

*Why?*

Why?

**First Clown**

*Because there, no one will notice.*

'Twill, a not be seen in him there; there the men are as mad as he.

**HAMLET**

*Why did he go crazy?*

How came he mad?

**First Clown**

*People say it was very strange?*

Very strangely, they say.

**HAMLET**

*How so?*

How strangely?

**First Clown**

*He lost his mind.*

Faith, e'en with losing his wits.

**HAMLET**

*On what grounds?*

Upon what ground?

**First Clown**

*Here in Denmark. I have lived here the past thirty years.*

Why, here in Denmark: I have been sexton here, man
and boy, thirty years.

## HAMLET

*How long does it take a man to rot once he is buried?*

How long will a man lie i' the earth ere he rot?

## First Clown

*If he is not rotten before he dies, and we see that a lot these days, he will last eight or nine years. A leather-maker will last at least nine years.*

I' faith, if he be not rotten before he die--as we
have many pocky corses now-a-days, that will scarce
hold the laying in--he will last you some eight year
or nine year: a tanner will last you nine year.

## HAMLET

*Why does he last longer?*

Why he more than another?

## First Clown

*Because his skin is so tough from his line of work, it keeps the water out. Water is what decays the body. This skull here has been in the earth twenty-three years.*

Why, sir, his hide is so tanned with his trade, that
he will keep out water a great while; and your water
is a sore decayer of your whoreson dead body.
Here's a skull now; this skull has lain in the earth
three and twenty years.

## HAMLET

*Whose was it?*

Whose was it?

**First Clown**

*Some crazy guy. Who do you think it was?*

A whoreson mad fellow's it was: whose do you think it was?

**HAMLET**

*I don't know.*

Nay, I know not.

**First Clown**

*This guy was a crazy pest! He poured a whole bottle of wine on my head once. This, sir, was Yorick, the kin's jester.*

A pestilence on him for a mad rogue! a' poured a
flagon of Rhenish on my head once. This same skull,
sir, was Yorick's skull, the king's jester.

**HAMLET**

*This?*

This?

**First Clown**

*Yes, that.*

E'en that.

**HAMLET**

*Let me see.*

Let me see.

Takes the skull

*Oh, poor Yorick! I knew him, Horatio. He was a funny fellow. He rode me on his back a thousand times. This is terrible and makes me sick. Here is where his lips, I kissed, used to be. Where are your jokes, now? Your songs? Your humor that used to make everyone laugh? Now, go to my lady's room and tell her she is going to end up like you someday. That'll make her laugh. Tell me one thing, Horatio.*

Alas, poor Yorick! I knew him, Horatio: a fellow of infinite jest, of most excellent fancy: he hath borne me on his back a thousand times; and now, how abhorred in my imagination it is! my gorge rims at it. Here hung those lips that I have kissed I know not how oft. Where be your gibes now? your gambols? your songs? your flashes of merriment, that were wont to set the table on a roar? Not one now, to mock your own grinning? quite chap-fallen? Now get you to my lady's chamber, and tell her, let her paint an inch thick, to this favour she must come; make her laugh at that. Prithee, Horatio, tell me one thing.

## HORATIO

*What's that, my lord?*

What's that, my lord?

## HAMLET

*Do you think Alexander the Great looked like this when he was buried?*

Dost thou think Alexander looked o' this fashion i' the earth?

## HORATIO

*Probably so.*

E'en so.

## HAMLET

*And smelled this bad? Whew!*

And smelt so? pah!

    Puts down the skull

## HORATIO

*Yes, my lord.*

E'en so, my lord.

## HAMLET

*It's horrible what happens to us in the end, Horatio! Can you believe the noble dust of Alexander the Great could end up as a plug?*

To what base uses we may return, Horatio! Why may
not imagination trace the noble dust of Alexander,
till he find it stopping a bung-hole?

## HORATIO

*It's hard to imagine.*

'Twere to consider too curiously, to consider so.

## HAMLET

*No, not really. Follow me: First he died and was buried. Then he returns to the dust which is basically the earth. The earth creates loam and the loam is used to plug a beer barrel. Ceasar, died and was turned into clay. He might stop a hole to keep out the wind. Oh, to think the once great man now plugs up a wall. But, wait! Be quiet! Here comes the king.*

No, faith, not a jot; but to follow him thither with
modesty enough, and likelihood to lead it: as
thus: Alexander died, Alexander was buried,
Alexander returneth into dust; the dust is earth; of
earth we make loam; and why of that loam, whereto he
was converted, might they not stop a beer-barrel?
Imperious Caesar, dead and turn'd to clay,
Might stop a hole to keep the wind away:
O, that that earth, which kept the world in awe,
Should patch a wall to expel the winter flaw!
But soft! but soft! aside: here comes the king.

Enter Priest, & c. in procession; the Corpse of OPHELIA, LAERTES and Mourners following; KING CLAUDIUS, QUEEN GERTRUDE, their trains, & c

*Who are the queen and her courtiers following? And with such somber ceremony. This means the corpse took its own life. Must be from a wealthy fellow. Let's stay and watch a while.*

The queen, the courtiers: who is this they follow?
And with such maimed rites? This doth betoken
The corse they follow did with desperate hand
Fordo its own life: 'twas of some estate.
Couch we awhile, and mark.

Retiring with HORATIO

**LAERTES**

*What ceremony are you going to preach?*

What ceremony else?

**HAMLET**

*Look. That is Laertes, a very noble young man.*

That is Laertes,
A very noble youth: mark.

**LAERTES**

*What ceremony are you going to preach?*

What ceremony else?

**First Priest**

*I've said as much as I can, since her death was suspicious. She should be buried outside the church graveyard, and have stones thrown onto her grave. Instead, she is here, buried in sacred ground, dressed like a virgin with flowers all around and the tolling of the bells.*

Her obsequies have been as far enlarged
As we have warrantise: her death was doubtful;
And, but that great command o'ersways the order,
She should in ground unsanctified have lodged
Till the last trumpet: for charitable prayers,
Shards, flints and pebbles should be thrown on her;
Yet here she is allow'd her virgin crants,
Her maiden strewments and the bringing home
Of bell and burial.

**LAERTES**

*Isn't there anything else that can be done?*

Must there no more be done?


**First Priest**

*No more can be done. It would be disrespectful to the other dead if we gave her any more rites.*

No more be done:
We should profane the service of the dead
To sing a requiem and such rest to her
As to peace-parted souls.


**LAERTES**

*Go ahead then, and lay her in the ground. May violets grow from her grave. I tell you priest, my sister will be an angel in heaven while you're howling in hell.*

Lay her i' the earth:
And from her fair and unpolluted flesh
May violets spring! I tell thee, churlish priest,
A ministering angel shall my sister be,
When thou liest howling.


**HAMLET**

*What? The beautiful Ophelia!*

What, the fair Ophelia!


**QUEEN GERTRUDE**

*Flowers for the sweet. Goodbye!*

Sweets to the sweet: farewell!

Scattering flowers

*I had hoped you would be my daughter-in-law. I rather be decorating your bridal bed than your grave, sweet girl.*

I hoped thou shouldst have been my Hamlet's wife;
I thought thy bride-bed to have deck'd, sweet maid,
And not have strew'd thy grave.

**LAERTES**

*Oh, my troubles. May curses fall ten times on the head who cause this. Wait! Let me hold her once more!*

O, treble woe
Fall ten times treble on that cursed head,
Whose wicked deed thy most ingenious sense
Deprived thee of! Hold off the earth awhile,
Till I have caught her once more in mine arms:

Leaps into the grave

*Now throw the dirt on both of us until you have made a mountain.*

Now pile your dust upon the quick and dead,
Till of this flat a mountain you have made,
To o'ertop old Pelion, or the skyish head
Of blue Olympus.


**HAMLET**

[Advancing]

*Who is the one whose grief is so loud and whose words are so sad the stars stand still. It is me, Hamlet the Dane.*

What is he whose grief
Bears such an emphasis? whose phrase of sorrow
Conjures the wandering stars, and makes them stand
Like wonder-wounded hearers? This is I,
Hamlet the Dane.

Leaps into the grave

**LAERTES**

*May the devil take your soul!*

The devil take thy soul!

Grappling with him

**HAMLET**

*You don't know how to pray. Take your fingers from my throat. Be smart, and do not make me angry. Take your hands off of me.*

Thou pray'st not well.
I prithee, take thy fingers from my throat;
For, though I am not splenitive and rash,

Yet have I something in me dangerous,
Which let thy wiseness fear: hold off thy hand.

## KING CLAUDIUS

*Pull them out.*

Pluck them asunder.

## QUEEN GERTRUDE

*Hamlet, Hamlet!*

Hamlet, Hamlet!

## All

*Gentlemen...*

Gentlemen,--

## HORATIO

*Good my lord, be quiet.*

Good my lord, be quiet.

The Attendants part them, and they come out of the grave

## HAMLET

*I will fight him over this until my eyes are permanently closed.*

Why I will fight with him upon this theme
Until my eyelids will no longer wag.

## QUEEN GERTRUDE

*Oh my son, what are fighting for?*

O my son, what theme?

## HAMLET

*I loved Ophelia. Forty thousand brothers could not have loved her more. What are you going to do for her?*

I loved Ophelia: forty thousand brothers
Could not, with all their quantity of love,
Make up my sum. What wilt thou do for her?


## KING CLAUDIUS

*Oh, he is crazy, Laertes.*

O, he is mad, Laertes.


## QUEEN GERTRUDE

*For the love of God don't listen to him.*

For love of God, forbear him.


## HAMLET

*Show me what you are going to do. Will you cry? Will you fight? Will you fast? Will you tear at your skin? Will you drink bile? Eat a crocodile? I'll do all of that. Did you come here to cry and whine? To outdo me by jumping in her grave. To be buried with her? So, will I. You want them to over us with dirt. Let them make mountains over us. See, I can talk as well as you.*

'Swounds, show me what thou'lt do:
Woo't weep? woo't fight? woo't fast? woo't tear thyself?
Woo't drink up eisel? eat a crocodile?
I'll do't. Dost thou come here to whine?
To outface me with leaping in her grave?
Be buried quick with her, and so will I:
And, if thou prate of mountains, let them throw
Millions of acres on us, till our ground,
Singeing his pate against the burning zone,
Make Ossa like a wart! Nay, an thou'lt mouth,
I'll rant as well as thou.


## QUEEN GERTRUDE

*This is crazy. He will be like this for a while. It will pass and he will be as peaceful as a dove.*

This is mere madness:

And thus awhile the fit will work on him;
Anon, as patient as the female dove,
When that her golden couplets are disclosed,
His silence will sit drooping.

**HAMLET**

*Listen to me, sir. Why are you acting towards me like this? I've always loved you. But, it doesn't matter. Even Hercules can't make change the way a cat or dog acts.*

Hear you, sir;
What is the reason that you use me thus?
I loved you ever: but it is no matter;
Let Hercules himself do what he may,
The cat will mew and dog will have his day.

Exit

**KING CLAUDIUS**

*Please, Horatio, get him out of here.*

I pray you, good Horatio, wait upon him.

Exit HORATIO

To LAERTES

*Remember what we talked about last night and be patient. We'll put this matter to rest soon. Gertrude, get someone to watch over your son. We will build a monument to put on this grave. Now, we have the quiet we need, so please proceed.*

Strengthen your patience in our last night's speech;
We'll put the matter to the present push.
Good Gertrude, set some watch over your son.
This grave shall have a living monument:
An hour of quiet shortly shall we see;
Till then, in patience our proceeding be.

Exeunt

# Scene II
### *A hall in the castle*

Enter HAMLET and HORATIO

**HAMLET**

*That's enough about that, sir. Let me tell you about what happened. You remember what was going on you.*

So much for this, sir: now shall you see the other;
You do remember all the circumstance?

**HORATIO**

*Remember, my lord?*

Remember it, my lord?

**HAMLET**

*Sir, I was in constant turmoil, and I couldn't sleep. It was worse than being a prisoner. I acted crazily and hastily, but my plans were stalled. God's will always prevails, no matter how far we stray.*

Sir, in my heart there was a kind of fighting,
That would not let me sleep: methought I lay
Worse than the mutines in the bilboes. Rashly,
And praised be rashness for it, let us know,
Our indiscretion sometimes serves us well,
When our deep plots do pall: and that should teach us
There's a divinity that shapes our ends,
Rough-hew them how we will,--

**HORATIO**

*That's for sure.*

That is most certain.

**HAMLET**

*When I was out to sea, I came up from my cabin and looked around in the dark. I found papers, which I took back to my own room, and discovered the King had ordered my death.*

Up from my cabin,
My sea-gown scarf'd about me, in the dark
Groped I to find out them; had my desire.
Finger'd their packet, and in fine withdrew
To mine own room again; making so bold,
My fears forgetting manners, to unseal
Their grand commission; where I found, Horatio,--
O royal knavery!--an exact command,
Larded with many several sorts of reasons
Importing Denmark's health and England's too,
With, ho! such bugs and goblins in my life,
That, on the supervise, no leisure bated,
No, not to stay the grinding of the axe,
My head should be struck off.


## HORATIO

*Are you serious?*

Is't possible?


## HAMLET

*Here's the letter. Read it for yourself. But, let me tell you the rest.*

Here's the commission: read it at more leisure.
But wilt thou hear me how I did proceed?


## HORATIO

*Please.*

I beseech you.


## HAMLET

*There I was trapped. So, I wrote a new commission. My education came in handy for I wrote like a diplomat. Do you want to know what I wrote?*

Being thus be-netted round with villanies,--
Ere I could make a prologue to my brains,
They had begun the play--I sat me down,

Devised a new commission, wrote it fair:
I once did hold it, as our statists do,
A baseness to write fair and labour'd much
How to forget that learning, but, sir, now
It did me yeoman's service: wilt thou know
The effect of what I wrote?

**HORATIO**

*Yes, of course, my lord.*

Ay, good my lord.

**HAMLET**

*I wrote an earnest plea from the King, with a lot of crap about the relationship between England and Denmark. I asked that the men delivering the letter be put to death without confession to a priest.*

An earnest conjuration from the king,
As England was his faithful tributary,
As love between them like the palm might flourish,
As peace should stiff her wheaten garland wear
And stand a comma 'tween their amities,
And many such-like 'As'es of great charge,
That, on the view and knowing of these contents,
Without debatement further, more or less,
He should the bearers put to sudden death,
Not shriving-time allow'd.

**HORATIO**

*How did you seal the letter?*

How was this seal'd?

**HAMLET**

*Even God's hand was in that as well. I had my father's signet ring with me, so I used it to seal the letter. Then, I exchanged the letters. The next day our ship was attacked, and you know the rest.*

Why, even in that was heaven ordinant.
I had my father's signet in my purse,
Which was the model of that Danish seal;
Folded the writ up in form of the other,

Subscribed it, gave't the impression, placed it safely,
The changeling never known. Now, the next day
Was our sea-fight; and what to this was sequent
Thou know'st already.

## HORATIO

*So Guildenstern and Rosencrantz are in big trouble.*

So Guildenstern and Rosencrantz go to't.

## HAMLET

*Yes, they are and it's their own fault. They were just commoners caught in a fight between two powerful men.*

Why, man, they did make love to this employment;
They are not near my conscience; their defeat
Does by their own insinuation grow:
'Tis dangerous when the baser nature comes
Between the pass and fell incensed points
Of mighty opposites.

## HORATIO

*What a king Claudius is!*

Why, what a king is this!

## HAMLET

*Don't you think it is time for me to kill the king, who killed my father and made my mother a whore? Isn't it time to put an end to him with my sword, and without damage to my conscience. And, wouldn't I be at fault if I let this devil continue to bring evil to our country?*

Does it not, think'st thee, stand me now upon--
He that hath kill'd my king and whored my mother,
Popp'd in between the election and my hopes,
Thrown out his angle for my proper life,
And with such cozenage--is't not perfect conscience,
To quit him with this arm? and is't not to be damn'd,
To let this canker of our nature come
In further evil?

**HORATIO**

*He's going to find out soon what happened in England.*

It must be shortly known to him from England
What is the issue of the business there.


**HAMLET**

*It will be soon, but I have some time. I am very sorry, Horatio, for what I did to Laertes. I lost control when I saw his overplayed grief. His situation is very much like mine, and I am going to be nice to him.*

It will be short: the interim is mine;
And a man's life's no more than to say 'One.'
But I am very sorry, good Horatio,
That to Laertes I forgot myself;
For, by the image of my cause, I see
The portraiture of his: I'll court his favours.
But, sure, the bravery of his grief did put me
Into a towering passion.


**HORATIO**

*Wait! Who's there?*

Peace! who comes here?

Enter OSRIC

**OSRIC**

*Welcome back to Denmark, my lord.*

Your lordship is right welcome back to Denmark.


**HAMLET**

*Thank you, sir. Do you know this fellow?*

I humbly thank you, sir. Dost know this water-fly?


**HORATIO**

*No, my lord.*

No, my good lord.

## HAMLET

*You're lucky. He's a great land owner, but he is a beast. He is treated well because he is wealthy.*

Thy state is the more gracious; for 'tis a vice to
know him. He hath much land, and fertile: let a
beast be lord of beasts, and his crib shall stand at
the king's mess: 'tis a chough; but, as I say,
spacious in the possession of dirt.

## OSRIC

*My lord, if you have a minute, I have a message from the king.*

Sweet lord, if your lordship were at leisure, I
should impart a thing to you from his majesty.

## HAMLET

*Go ahead, sir. I will listen in rapture, but put your hat back on.*

I will receive it, sir, with all diligence of
spirit. Put your bonnet to his right use; 'tis for the head.

## OSRIC

*Thank you, lord, it is very hot.*

I thank your lordship, it is very hot.

## HAMLET

*No, believe me, it's very cold. The wind is blowing from the north.*

No, believe me, 'tis very cold; the wind is
northerly.

## OSRIC

*Yes, I think it is cold.*

It is indifferent cold, my lord, indeed.

**HAMLET**

*Yet, I think the air is hot and humid, which is bad for my skin.*

But yet methinks it is very sultry and hot for my complexion.

**OSRIC**

*Right, my lord, it is humid. But, my lord, the king wants you to know he has placed a large wager on you. This is the deal…*

Exceedingly, my lord; it is very sultry,--as 'twere,--I cannot tell how. But, my lord, his majesty bade me signify to you that he has laid a great wager on your head: sir, this is the matter,--

**HAMLET**

*Please, go on…*

I beseech you, remember--

HAMLET moves him to put on his hat

**OSRIC**

*No, my lord, I'm fine, I swear. Laertes has come back. He is a great gentleman and very popular in society. If I may speak freely, I think he is the object of what a gentleman should be.*

Nay, good my lord; for mine ease, in good faith. Sir, here is newly come to court Laertes; believe me, an absolute gentleman, full of most excellent differences, of very soft society and great showing: indeed, to speak feelingly of him, he is the card or calendar of gentry, for you shall find in him the continent of what part a gentleman would see.

**HAMLET**

*Sir, I see you think very highly of him; you don't have to list his finer qualities. I don't even think you could break them all down. I doubt you can find a man as good as he.*

Sir, his definement suffers no perdition in you; though, I know, to divide him inventorially would dizzy the arithmetic of memory, and yet but yaw neither, in respect of his quick sail. But, in the verity of extolment, I take him to be a soul of great article; and his infusion of such dearth and rareness, as, to make true diction of him, his semblable is his mirror; and who else would trace him, his umbrage, nothing more.


**OSRIC**

*You are right, my lord.*

Your lordship speaks most infallibly of him.


**HAMLET**

Anyway, why are we talking about him?

The concernancy, sir? why do we wrap the gentleman in our more rawer breath?


**OSRIC**

*What, sir?*

Sir?


**HORATIO**

*Try it again.*

Is't not possible to understand in another tongue?
You will do't, sir, really.


**HAMLET**

*What is the significance of us talking about him?*

What imports the nomination of this gentleman?

**OSRIC**

*You mean Laertes?*

Of Laertes?

**HORATIO**

*His ability to comprehend has vanished.*

His purse is empty already; all's golden words are spent.

**HAMLET**

*Yes, sir. Laertes.*

Of him, sir.

**OSRIC**

*I know you know Laertes…*

I know you are not ignorant--

**HAMLET**

*I know him well enough. So…*

I would you did, sir; yet, in faith, if you did, it would not much approve me. Well, sir?

**OSRIC**

*Then you must know how excellent Laertes is…*

You are not ignorant of what excellence Laertes is--

**HAMLET**

*I wouldn't say I know what you are getting at.*

I dare not confess that, lest I should compare with him in excellence; but, to know a man well, were to know himself.

**OSRIC**

*I mean his known for his ability in fencing. No one is as good as he.*

I mean, sir, for his weapon; but in the imputation
laid on him by them, in his meed he's unfellowed.

**HAMLET**

*What is his weapon?*

What's his weapon?

**OSRIC**

*The rapier and the dagger.*

Rapier and dagger.

**HAMLET**

*Okay, that's two; go on.*

That's two of his weapons: but, well.

**OSRIC**

*The king, sir, has bet him six of his finest horses and six rapiers and dagger with their carriages.*

The king, sir, hath wagered with him six Barbary
horses: against the which he has imponed, as I take
it, six French rapiers and poniards, with their
assigns, as girdle, hangers, and so: three of the
carriages, in faith, are very dear to fancy, very
responsive to the hilts, most delicate carriages,
and of very liberal conceit.

**HAMLET**

*What are carriages?*

What call you the carriages?

## HORATIO

*I knew you were going to be stumped before we were done.*

I knew you must be edified by the margent ere you had done.

## OSRIC

*The carriages are the sheaths to put the swords in.*

The carriages, sir, are the hangers.

## HAMLET

*I would not use the word carriage. It sounds like you are carrying a canon on your side. I'll call it a hanger. However, that is a mighty steep bet. What is the bet upon?*

The phrase would be more german to the matter, if we
could carry cannon by our sides: I would it might
be hangers till then. But, on: six Barbary horses
against six French swords, their assigns, and three
liberal-conceited carriages; that's the French bet
against the Danish. Why is this 'imponed,' as you call it?

## OSRIC

*The king, sir, has bet that Laertes cannot beat you by three hits in a dozen rounds. If you'll accept, we can start right away.*

The king, sir, hath laid, that in a dozen passes
between yourself and him, he shall not exceed you
three hits: he hath laid on twelve for nine; and it
would come to immediate trial, if your lordship
would vouchsafe the answer.

## HAMLET

*What if I say no?*

How if I answer 'no'?

**OSRIC**

*You should tell them yourself.*

I mean, my lord, the opposition of your person in trial.

**HAMLET**

*Sir, I will walk here in the hall, and if it pleases the king, he can bring on the gentleman. I will do what I can to win the bet. If I don't, then I will only be slightly embarrassed.*

Sir, I will walk here in the hall: if it please his
majesty, 'tis the breathing time of day with me; let
the foils be brought, the gentleman willing, and the
king hold his purpose, I will win for him an I can;
if not, I will gain nothing but my shame and the odd hits.

**OSRIC**

*Shall I go tell them what you said?*

Shall I re-deliver you e'en so?

**HAMLET**

*Certainly, tell them whatever you want.*

To this effect, sir; after what flourish your nature will.

**OSRIC**

*I am at your service.*

I commend my duty to your lordship.

**HAMLET**

*And I am at yours.*

Yours, yours.

Exit OSRIC

*He must commend his service, himself, because no one else will.*

He does well to commend it himself; there are no
tongues else for's turn.

**HORATIO**

*He is kind of nutty.*

This lapwing runs away with the shell on his head.

**HAMLET**

*Yes, but he has gathered enough around here to get him by. But, he still is what he is.*

He did comply with his dug, before he sucked it.
Thus has he--and many more of the same bevy that I
know the dressy age dotes on--only got the tune of
the time and outward habit of encounter; a kind of
yesty collection, which carries them through and
through the most fond and winnowed opinions; and do
but blow them to their trial, the bubbles are out.

Enter a Lord

**Lord**

*My lord, the king has talked with Osric and wants to know if you are ready or if you need more time.*

My lord, his majesty commended him to you by young
Osric, who brings back to him that you attend him in
the hall: he sends to know if your pleasure hold to
play with Laertes, or that you will take longer time.

**HAMLET**

*Whenever.*

I am constant to my purpose; they follow the king's
pleasure: if his fitness speaks, mine is ready; now
or whensoever, provided I be so able as now.

**Lord**

*The king and queen are coming.*

The king and queen and all are coming down.

**HAMLET**

*In their own sweet time.*

In happy time.

**Lord**

*The queen wants you to speak with Laertes before you begin.*

The queen desires you to use some gentle
entertainment to Laertes before you fall to play.

**HAMLET**

*She always has some instructions for me.*

She well instructs me.

Exit Lord

**HORATIO**

*You will lose this wager, my lord.*

You will lose this wager, my lord.

**HAMLET**

*I don't think so. I've been practicing since he went to France. The odds are in my favor, but I still feel something is not quite right. Oh, well.*

I do not think so: since he went into France, I
have been in continual practise: I shall win at the
odds. But thou wouldst not think how ill all's here
about my heart: but it is no matter.

**HORATIO**

*This is not a good idea...*

Nay, good my lord,--

**HAMLET**

*I know it's foolish.*

It is but foolery; but it is such a kind of
gain-giving, as would perhaps trouble a woman.

**HORATIO**

*If you feel like something is not right, just say the word, and I'll stop the match.*

If your mind dislike any thing, obey it: I will
forestall their repair hither, and say you are not
fit.

**HAMLET**

*No way! I don't put a lot of faith in superstitions. If it's God's will, then so be it.*

Not a whit, we defy augury: there's a special
providence in the fall of a sparrow. If it be now,
'tis not to come; if it be not to come, it will be
now; if it be not now, yet it will come: the
readiness is all: since no man has aught of what he
leaves, what is't to leave betimes?

Enter KING CLAUDIUS, QUEEN GERTRUDE, LAERTES, Lords, OSRIC, and Attendants with foils, & c

**KING CLAUDIUS**

*Come Hamlet and shake hands.*

Come, Hamlet, come, and take this hand from me.

KING CLAUDIUS puts LAERTES' hand into HAMLET's

**HAMLET**

*Forgive me, sir. I've done you wrong. I'm afraid I was crazy. If I were in my right mind, I would have never committed such a heinous act. My madness is my true enemy. Please, know that I would never harm you intentionally.*

Give me your pardon, sir: I've done you wrong;

But pardon't, as you are a gentleman.
This presence knows,
And you must needs have heard, how I am punish'd
With sore distraction. What I have done,
That might your nature, honour and exception
Roughly awake, I here proclaim was madness.
Was't Hamlet wrong'd Laertes? Never Hamlet:
If Hamlet from himself be ta'en away,
And when he's not himself does wrong Laertes,
Then Hamlet does it not, Hamlet denies it.
Who does it, then? His madness: if't be so,
Hamlet is of the faction that is wrong'd;
His madness is poor Hamlet's enemy.
Sir, in this audience,
Let my disclaiming from a purposed evil
Free me so far in your most generous thoughts,
That I have shot mine arrow o'er the house,
And hurt my brother.


### LAERTES

*I am somewhat satisfied. The death of my father and sister is motivation for revenge, but I am an honorable man. I accept your apologies and love for what they are.*

I am satisfied in nature,
Whose motive, in this case, should stir me most
To my revenge: but in my terms of honour
I stand aloof; and will no reconcilement,
Till by some elder masters, of known honour,
I have a voice and precedent of peace,
To keep my name ungored. But till that time,
I do receive your offer'd love like love,
And will not wrong it.


### HAMLET

*Thank you. Let's play a friendly game. Give us the weapons.*

I embrace it freely;
And will this brother's wager frankly play.
Give us the foils. Come on.


### LAERTES

*Give me one, too.*

Come, one for me.

## HAMLET

*I'm going to go easy, Laertes, and make you look like a shining star in the darkest night.*

I'll be your foil, Laertes: in mine ignorance
Your skill shall, like a star i' the darkest night,
Stick fiery off indeed.

## LAERTES

*Don't mock me, sir.*

You mock me, sir.

## HAMLET

*I'm not.*

No, by this hand.

## KING CLAUDIUS

*Give them the weapons, young Osric. Hamlet, you know what's at stake?*

Give them the foils, young Osric. Cousin Hamlet,
You know the wager?

## HAMLET

*Yes, my lord. You have bet against the odds.*

Very well, my lord
Your grace hath laid the odds o' the weaker side.

## KING CLAUDIUS

*I'm not afraid. I have seen you both, but since he's better we've given him a handicap.*

I do not fear it; I have seen you both:
But since he is better'd, we have therefore odds.


## LAERTES

*This sword is too heavy. Let me see another.*

This is too heavy, let me see another.


## HAMLET

*This one fits me well. Are they all the same length?*

This likes me well. These foils have all a length?

They prepare to play

## OSRIC

*Yes, my lord.*

Ay, my good lord.


## KING CLAUDIUS

*Put the wine on that table. If Hamlet begins to win, I'll drink to his health. Then, I will put a poison in the cup stronger than the last four kings of Denmark combined. Give me the cups. Let the drum and trumpeters begin. Let's begin. Watch, judges.*

Set me the stoops of wine upon that table.
If Hamlet give the first or second hit,
Or quit in answer of the third exchange,
Let all the battlements their ordnance fire:
The king shall drink to Hamlet's better breath;
And in the cup an union shall he throw,
Richer than that which four successive kings
In Denmark's crown have worn. Give me the cups;
And let the kettle to the trumpet speak,
The trumpet to the cannoneer without,
The cannons to the heavens, the heavens to earth,
'Now the king dunks to Hamlet.' Come, begin:
And you, the judges, bear a wary eye.


## HAMLET

*Come on, sir.*

Come on, sir.

**LAERTES**

*Come, my lord.*

Come, my lord.

They play

**HAMLET**

*One.*

One.

**LAERTES**

*No.*

No.

**HAMLET**

*Judges?*

Judgment.

**OSRIC**

*It was a hit.*

A hit, a very palpable hit.

**LAERTES**

*Well, try that again.*

Well; again.

**KING CLAUDIUS**

*Someone give me a drink. Hamlet, this pearl is for you, and here's to your health.*

Stay; give me drink. Hamlet, this pearl is thine;
Here's to thy health.

Trumpets sound, and cannon shot off within

*Give him the cup.*

Give him the cup.


**HAMLET**

*I don't want it right now. Just, set it down. Come on.*

I'll play this bout first; set it by awhile. Come.

They play

*I think that was another hit. And, you?*

Another hit; what say you?


**LAERTES**

*You did touch me, I confess.*

A touch, a touch, I do confess.


**KING CLAUDIUS**

*Our son is going to win.*

Our son shall win.


**QUEEN GERTRUDE**

*He's fat and out of breath. Here, Hamlet, take my napkin and rub the sweat out of your eyes. I drink to your future, Hamlet.*

He's fat, and scant of breath.
Here, Hamlet, take my napkin, rub thy brows;
The queen carouses to thy fortune, Hamlet.

## HAMLET

*Thank you, madam!*

Good madam!

## KING CLAUDIUS

*Gertrude, do not drink from that cup.*

Gertrude, do not drink.

## QUEEN GERTRUDE

*I will, my lord. Now, if you'll excuse me.*

I will, my lord; I pray you, pardon me.

## KING CLAUDIUS

[Aside]

*It's the poisoned cup. It's too late.*

It is the poison'd cup: it is too late.

## HAMLET

*I don't want anything to drink, yet. Maybe, later.*

I dare not drink yet, madam; by and by.

## QUEEN GERTRUDE

*Come, let my wipe your face.*

Come, let me wipe thy face.

## LAERTES

*My lord, I'll hit him now.*

My lord, I'll hit him now.

## KING CLAUDIUS

*I don't think so.*

I do not think't.

## LAERTES

[Aside]

*I almost feel wrong about this.*

And yet 'tis almost 'gainst my conscience.

## HAMLET

*Have you come for the third, Laertes. You are too late. Take your best shot. I'm not a child; I'm ready.*

Come, for the third, Laertes: you but dally;
I pray you, pass with your best violence;
I am afeard you make a wanton of me.

## LAERTES

*Oh yea? Come on.*

Say you so? come on.

They play

## OSRIC

*They are so close.*

Nothing, neither way.

## LAERTES

*Here's one for you.*

Have at you now!

LAERTES wounds HAMLET; then in scuffling, they change rapiers, and HAMLET wounds LAERTES

**KING CLAUDIUS**

*Pull them apart. They aren't playing.*

Part them; they are incensed.

**HAMLET**

*No, let us go again.*

Nay, come, again.

QUEEN GERTRUDE falls

**OSRIC**

*Someone look after the queen!*

Look to the queen there, ho!

**HORATIO**

*They are both bleeding. How are you, my lord?*

They bleed on both sides. How is it, my lord?

**OSRIC**

*How are you, Laertes?*

How is't, Laertes?

**LAERTES**

*Like a trapped animal, Osric. I am killed by my own evil desires.*

Why, as a woodcock to mine own springe, Osric;
I am justly kill'd with mine own treachery.

**HAMLET**

*How's the queen?*

How does the queen?

**KING CLAUDIUS**

*She just fainted at the sight of the blood.*

She swounds to see them bleed.


**QUEEN GERTRUDE**

*No, no, it's the drink. Oh, my dear Hamlet, the drink is poisoned. I am dying.*

No, no, the drink, the drink,--O my dear Hamlet,--
The drink, the drink! I am poison'd.

Dies

**HAMLET**

*Oh, what villains! Lock the door. Find out who did this.*

O villany! Ho! let the door be lock'd:
Treachery! Seek it out.


**LAERTES**

*Here, Hamlet. You are as good as dead. Nothing can save you now. You have less than an hour. The sword's tip was poisoned. Your mother is poisoned, and it's the king's fault.*

It is here, Hamlet: Hamlet, thou art slain;
No medicine in the world can do thee good;
In thee there is not half an hour of life;
The treacherous instrument is in thy hand,
Unbated and envenom'd: the foul practise
Hath turn'd itself on me lo, here I lie,
Never to rise again: thy mother's poison'd:
I can no more: the king, the king's to blame.


**HAMLET**

*The sword is poisoned. Then, let the venom do its work!*

The point!--envenom'd too!
Then, venom, to thy work.

Stabs KING CLAUDIUS

**All**

Treason! Treason!

Treason! treason!


**KING CLAUDIUS**

*I am only hurt. Defend me, friends.*

O, yet defend me, friends; I am but hurt.


**HAMLET**

*Here you incestuous, murderous, Dane. Damn you to hell. Drink the rest of this, and go with my mother.*

Here, thou incestuous, murderous, damned Dane,
Drink off this potion. Is thy union here?
Follow my mother.

KING CLAUDIUS dies

**LAERTES**

*He got what he deserved. He poisoned himself. Please forgive me, Hamlet, and I will forgive you. My father's death or mine are not your fault, just like your death is not my fault.*

He is justly served;
It is a poison temper'd by himself.
Exchange forgiveness with me, noble Hamlet:
Mine and my father's death come not upon thee,
Nor thine on me.

Dies

**HAMLET**

*God will free you in heaven. I am on my way. I am dying, Horatio! Goodbye, wretched queen. If I had time, I could tell you all a thing or two, but death waits for no man. Horatio, tell them everything and set this story straight.*

Heaven make thee free of it! I follow thee.
I am dead, Horatio. Wretched queen, adieu!
You that look pale and tremble at this chance,
That are but mutes or audience to this act,
Had I but time--as this fell sergeant, death,
Is strict in his arrest--O, I could tell you--

But let it be. Horatio, I am dead;
Thou livest; report me and my cause aright
To the unsatisfied.


## HORATIO

*No one will believe it. I am more like an ancient Roman, than a corrupt Dane. Here's some poisonous drink.*

Never believe it:
I am more an antique Roman than a Dane:
Here's yet some liquor left.


## HAMLET

*Give me that cup. Let go. I swear, I'll take it from you, Horatio. If you ever cared about me, then don't do this. Stay and tell my story.*

As thou'rt a man,
Give me the cup: let go; by heaven, I'll have't.
O good Horatio, what a wounded name,
Things standing thus unknown, shall live behind me!
If thou didst ever hold me in thy heart
Absent thee from felicity awhile,
And in this harsh world draw thy breath in pain,
To tell my story.

March afar off, and shot within

*What is that noise?*

What warlike noise is this?


## OSRIC

*Young Fortinbras is returning from his triumph in Poland to greet the English ambassadors.*

Young Fortinbras, with conquest come from Poland,
To the ambassadors of England gives
This warlike volley.


## HAMLET

*Oh, I'm dying, Horatio. The poison is strong. I will not live to hear the news from England, but do tell Fortinbras he has my support.*

O, I die, Horatio;
The potent poison quite o'er-crows my spirit:
I cannot live to hear the news from England;
But I do prophesy the election lights
On Fortinbras: he has my dying voice;
So tell him, with the occurrents, more and less,
Which have solicited. The rest is silence.

Dies

**HORATIO**

*Here lies a noble heart. Good night, sweet prince. May angels sing you to sleep! Why are those drums approaching?*

Now cracks a noble heart. Good night sweet prince:
And flights of angels sing thee to thy rest!
Why does the drum come hither?

March within

Enter FORTINBRAS, the English Ambassadors, and others

**PRINCE FORTINBRAS**

*What is going on?*

Where is this sight?

**HORATIO**

*What do you think you see? If you've come to see a tragedy, you've found it.*

What is it ye would see?
If aught of woe or wonder, cease your search.

**PRINCE FORTINBRAS**

*This looks like a massacre. Oh proud Death, what are you planning with so many royals dead at one time?*

This quarry cries on havoc. O proud death,
What feast is toward in thine eternal cell,
That thou so many princes at a shot
So bloodily hast struck?

**First Ambassador**

*This is a horrible sight. We are too late from England to tell the news of his wishes being fulfilled. Rosencrantz and Guildenstern are dead. Who is here to thank us?*

The sight is dismal;
And our affairs from England come too late:
The ears are senseless that should give us hearing,
To tell him his commandment is fulfill'd,
That Rosencrantz and Guildenstern are dead:
Where should we have our thanks?


**HORATIO**

*If he had the ability to thank you, Hamlet would. The king never gave the order. He did. But, since you are here to witness this scene, tell your men to put these bodies on display, and I will tell you what happened.*

Not from his mouth,
Had it the ability of life to thank you:
He never gave commandment for their death.
But since, so jump upon this bloody question,
You from the Polack wars, and you from England,
Are here arrived give order that these bodies
High on a stage be placed to the view;
And let me speak to the yet unknowing world
How these things came about: so shall you hear
Of carnal, bloody, and unnatural acts,
Of accidental judgments, casual slaughters,
Of deaths put on by cunning and forced cause,
And, in this upshot, purposes mistook
Fall'n on the inventors' reads: all this can I
Truly deliver.


**PRINCE FORTINBRAS**

*Hurry. Let us hear it. Get all of the noblemen to hear it. It is with great sadness that I accept my good fortune, since I can now claim the throne.*

Let us haste to hear it,
And call the noblest to the audience.
For me, with sorrow I embrace my fortune:
I have some rights of memory in this kingdom,
Which now to claim my vantage doth invite me.

**HORATIO**

*I also have something to say about that from Hamlet, himself. Let's go ahead and start before any more madness begins.*

Of that I shall have also cause to speak,
And from his mouth whose voice will draw on more;
But let this same be presently perform'd,
Even while men's minds are wild; lest more mischance
On plots and errors, happen.


**PRINCE FORTINBRAS**

*Let four captains carry Hamlet, like a soldier, to the stage. He is the rightful heir to the throne. Let there be military honors to portray his heroism. Pick up the rest of the bodies. This looks like a battlefield. Fire your guns in honor of Hamlet.*

Let four captains
Bear Hamlet, like a soldier, to the stage;
For he was likely, had he been put on,
To have proved most royally: and, for his passage,
The soldiers' music and the rites of war
Speak loudly for him.
Take up the bodies: such a sight as this
Becomes the field, but here shows much amiss.
Go, bid the soldiers shoot.

*A dead march. Exeunt, bearing off the dead bodies; after which a peal of ordnance is shot off.*

## About BookCaps

We all need refreshers every now and then. Whether you are a student trying to cram for that big final, or someone just trying to understand a book more, BookCaps can help. We are a small, but growing company, and are adding titles every month.

Visit www.bookcaps.com to see more of our books, or contact us with any questions.

Made in the USA
Las Vegas, NV
27 January 2024

84969641R00208